Asian Spirituality, Ta

Blue Dragon
White Tiger

TAOIST RITES OF PASSAGE

Michael Saso

The Taoist Center · Washington, D.C.

ISBN 0-8248-1361-8

Camera-ready copy was prepared by the author

The paper used in this publication meets the minimum requirements
of American National Standard for Information
Sciences/-permanence of Paper for Printed Library Materials
ANSI Z39.48-1984

Distributed by
University of Hawaii Press
2840 Kolowalu Street
Honolulu, Hawaii 96822

TABLE OF CONTENTS

ACKNOWLEDGEMENTS

The author wishes to thank
Chuang Chao-hsin, Taoist of
Hsinchu, N. Taiwan, the Taoists
of Mao Shan and Lung-hu Shan,
Prof. Kubo Noritada of the
Toyo Bunka, Tokyo University,
Paul O'Brien S.J., the late
Al Klaeser S.J., my students
in Rel. 203 at the University
of Hawaii, Theresa and Maria,
Mr. Chao Chen-tung and the staff
of the Yüan-hsüan Hsüeh Yüan,
Dr. Wu Jing-nuan of the Taoist
Center, Wash. D.C. and staff,
and all the others who helped
gather the texts and put these
pages in print. All errors and
ommissions are solely mine.

INTRODUCTION

Blue Dragon White Tiger is a study of Chinese religion from the viewpoint of the religious Taoist, i.e., the man or woman called upon by
farmers, merchants, artisans, and all walks of life to perform village festival. Taoism is one of the three teaching systems that inform Chinese
religion. Buddhism and Confucianism, together with Taoism, make up
a unified ritual system, sometimes referred to as (*san-chiao kuei-i*),
in traditional Chinese religious practice.[1] That is to say, Confucian
ethics and morality, Buddhist notions of compassion and the afterlife,
and Taoist attitudes towards the cyclical changes of nature, inform the
typical Chinese attitude toward culture and religion. Whether or not an
individual ascribes to a certain religious belief system, these three sets
of religio-cultural values lie deep within the Chinese psyche.

   Though Confucianism provides practical norms for human behavior, and Buddhism offers burial ritual and memorial services for the
deceased, neither of these two systems are complete without the practical attitudes of Taoism to nature and its cyclical changes. That Taoism
is the root and source of the Chinese outlook on man's role in nature is
cognately affirmed in poetry, novels, drama, and festivals. The role of
Taoism is often difficult to understand apart from the symbol or image,
since it is by self definition a way that does not cling to words or com-
parisons. Taoism does not make itself known in the world of the rich,
famous, or powerful. Its ways are not approved by the Confucian
literatus or the Buddhist savant. It is, however, one of the necessary
keys to unlock and understand the popular festivals and rites of passage
which define religion in China.

   The Taoist tradition honors all forms of Chinese religious belief,
including the ethical norms of the Confucian system, the ideas of the afterlife from Buddhism, and the more recently arrived religions of Islam
and Christianity. Because of the underlying tendency of Taoism to
develop the intuitive or direct mode of apprehending reality, rather
than the indirect, deductive, theoretical mode of understanding, Taoism
never developed a dogmatic belief system such as in western religions
or Buddhism. Instead, it wholeheartedly adopted the philosophy of the
yin-yang five element system, as a structural norm for meditation and
its expression through ritual. It also accepted the common tenets and
beliefs of China's folk religion, with its multi-layered world of spirits

who were thought to reside over the annual changes in nature, and the human life cycle.

To this world of spirits the Taoists brought a sense of order and hierarchy, modeled after the Confucian bureaucracy in the visible world that surrounds ordinary mortals. Spirits that control the heavens, earth, and underworld are addressed by memorials, messages, and documents composed by Taoist literati, in a manner quite similar to the documents sent to the visible earthly emperor by the Confucian mandarins and literati. The spirits respond to the prayers of the people in lengthy rescripts that are also composed by the village Taoist. When a baby is born, a bride to be married, a deceased loved one to be buried, the local Taoist is called upon to help. The Taoist priest (whether man or woman) is by trade an expert in the rites of passage and the annual festivals. He or she can be asked to provide ritual, or a theoretical explanation, or simply give advice about how to handle life's passages, in the manner described in *Blue Dragon White Tiger*.

If called upon to provide ritual, the Taoist is able to respond with a broad range of liturgies created for almost any situation.[2] When asked to explain the reason why a ritual is celebrated, the Taoist invariably replies in the words of the Yin-yang Five Element system, as explained in Chapter One below. When asked to instruct disciples in the ascesis of internal alchemy (nei-tan) the Taoist master teaches the emptying meditations based on Lao-tzu and Chuang-tzu, such as found in Chapter Two. When asked to give advice on how to perform the rites of passage or the annual festivals, the Taoist master refers to the classical Confucian manuals such as used in chapters four through seven, of *Blue Dragon White Tiger*.

There are also times when the Taoist is not called upon for an answer, as may happen at burial. At such times the people of the farming villages and marketing cities of China invoke the Buddhist system for ritual and "meaning of existence" answers. Chapter three therefore looks at the Buddhist tradition in China from the viewpoint of practice rather than theory. The Buddhists who speak to the needs of the people do not always use the same terms as do scholars who write for fellow scholars in learned journals. Though Buddha may never have spoken of an afterlife, a soul, or a Divine Being, the devout believers in Buddhism throughout much of Asia invoke Amida Buddha to free souls from afterlife punishments into a heavenly Pure Land.

There are many other philosophical aspects to Buddhism that are treated in a very pragmatic, matter-of-fact way in China, that would alarm or dismay the textbook scholar. The famous "Middle Way" theory (Madhyamika, *San-lun*) has provided centuries of scholastic discussion for Buddhist scholars. The Buddha twice chose a middle way. The first was the mean between extreme luxury and extreme penitence, the subject of Buddha's first enlightenment. The second was the middle way between materialism that denied all spiritual reality, and idealism that denied matter to be self caused, an insight that brought about the first of the eightfold path to enlightenment, i.e., co-dependent origination. In practice, East Asian Buddhism often interprets this middle way to be simply a method of no judgment, i.e., neither affirming or denying the extremes of philosophic or any other form of reasoned attachment. Though Buddha did not speak of philosophy or an afterlife, the success of Buddhism in China depended on both of these topics as a practical means for acceptance in China.

In describing the coming of Buddhism to China and it success in winning the hearts of the people to its doctrines, such as the Four Noble Truths, Eightfold Path, the Middle Way, and so forth, we have limited our discussion to a brief third chapter. More than a dozen volumes would be insufficient to cover these topics, for which the reader is referred to the works of such eminent Buddhologists as E. Lamotte, *The History of Buddhism in India* (Louvain:1988), E. Zürcher, *The Buddhist Conquest of China*, (Leiden:1959), the prolific works of David Kalupahana on the Pali and Sanskrit traditions of Buddhism, and the standard works of E. Conze, D.T. Suzuki, and Kenneth Ch'en. The exhaustive bibliography of Laurence G. Thompson, *Chinese Religion in Western Languages* contains 88 pages on Chinese Buddhism alone, out of 268 pages on various aspects of Chinese religion. The forthcoming work of Jan Nattier, *The Candragharbha-sutra in Central and East Asia* (Harvard: Ph.D. Thesis, 1988) provides an invaluable study of variations wrought in Buddhism across the silk route from India to China. These works are recommended to the reader for expert treatises on Buddhism in China.

There are also many excellent works about religion in China that complete and supplement the facts and ideas found in these pages. The works of Laurence Thompson, *Chinese Religion: An Introduction*, and *The Chinese Way in Religion*, the many studies of of Wolfram Eberhard, Henri Dore, J.J.M. De Groot, Edward Schaefer, Derk Bodde, among many others, are required reading for students and scholars of China. Modern works on religious Taoism, Taoist meditation, healing, and ritual fill shopping mall book shops. Over 200 translations of the *Lao-tzu Tao-te Ching* and its meaning are found in western languages. Taoist scholars such as Kristopher Schipper, Anna Seidel, Nathan Sivin, Michel Strickmann, Judith Boltz, Isabelle Robinet, John Lagerwey, Stephan Bokenkamp, Livia Knaul, Norman Girardot, among many others, have made religious Taoism a lively and timely topic.

Blue Dragon White Tiger relies on the above and many other works for its inspiration. It does not attempt to be comprehensive, or to re-examine materials studied with greater authority and scholarly perfection by others. Rather, it hopes to test the simple hypothesis that Yin-yang five element theory provides the underlying structure of a given set of Chinese rituals. The inspiration for this theory is found in the ritual manuals used by Taoists, and popular prompt books sold in temple bookshops, not in the theories of scholars who interpret the meaning of festive ritual. In both of these purely Chinese sources yin-yang and the five elements are seen to be underlying principles of organization and explanation. From studying these sources the reader can piece together for him or herself the manner in which religious ritual is performed, the place to stand during the rite, the kinds of food to place on the altar, the basic spatial and temporal principles on which the festival is structured.

In choosing the word structure, I do not feel competent to defend or enter into the theories of the French structural anthropologists, or its opponents in the modern American schools of pragmatic or scientific measurement of field data. I do not argue for or against any theory on which field research is based, other than the need to examine and report on the ritual or festival on its own terms. Though my own feelings are for the stimulating writings of the French structuralists and post-structuralists, the detailed description of how and why ritual is performed precludes any departure from the meaning assigned by the Chinese expert or lay person to the liturgical text. To indulge in foreign words and discourses that go beyond the manner in which the Taoist expert or the villager use the ritual text would destroy the authenticity of this experience. My presentation of Taoist texts and their meaning is therefore taken directly from oral and written sources.

These sources may sometimes differ from the interpretation of Taoist materials culled from the field work of other scholars of Taoism. To enter into the debate over the meaning of Taoist texts in the liturgical and meditative tradition is also beyond the scope of the task we have set before us. The goal of *Blue Dragon White Tiger* is to present one aspect of a multi-faceted diamond, that is, the viewpoint of a selected group of experts, rather than all interpretations and all expert schools of thought that might be brought to bear on the significance of Chinese religious ritual in practice. My sources in chapters one and two, for instance, are limited to the Taoist ritual and meditation books used during observed ritual. These sources are found in the footnotes, and the bibliography.

The interpretation of the ritual manuals used by the lay people in chapters four through seven is also derived from the authors who wrote them, rather than my own theories of what they should or should not mean. Once this gathering task has been done, i.e., when the rituals have been described as a semiotic system with coherent inner meaning derived from pre-existing symbolic actions, rites, and dramatic climax on their own, then we may get to the task of interpreting their meaning. Questions about the meaning of the Rites of Passage and annual festivals can only be asked when seen in their entirety, i.e., in precise and unfiltered detail. Unlike the college classroom where the question is sometimes more important than the answer, in ritual and festival the sign and action are more important than the question of meaning.

Furthermore, as we shall see again and again in the text, the meaning itself is deliberately left open, or deferred to the creative interpretation of the wayside expert. It would be wrong to conclude that there is no universal order in Chinese ritual because each informant who was asked the same question gave a different answer. A different answer is expected of each informant, just as each story teller may create or make up is own ending to a romantic tale. The order is found in the semiotic system, not in the word, in the spatial and temporal structure, not in the details of material culture.

To explain this basic assumption further, the very notion of a semiotic sign, pointed out so well in Julia Kristeva's *Desire in Language*, is like a container open to multiple content and meaning.[3] (The concrete masculine form *le sémiotique* in French refers to the concrete, bodily disposition or drives, while the feminine form *la sémiotique* means the science of signs). In this way, the meaning (feminine form) is derived from the disposition; i.e., the meaning of the ritual is assigned after the spatial-temporal disposition is determined. Chinese rituals are by their very nature semiotic signs, structurally built on the predisposed order of nature. The yin-yang five element system, cognate in the in-out, male-female symbology of the *I-ching* Book of Changes, existed as a semiotic system before its verbal formulation in the 5th and 4th century BCE China. The system is cognate, according to the hypothesis of *Blue Dragon White Tiger* in the celebration of the rites and the annual festivals. Were it to be formulated by peasant informant to foreign anthropologist in a consistent, unchanging way, so that the text was no longer open to interpretation, at that moment, in the best dialectic sense, Chinese religion would begin to die.

The purpose of *Blue Dragon White Tiger* is to explain the Yin-yang Five Element System, and show how it structures the festive, meditative, and ritual aspects of Chinese religious practice. The Taoist way, which is at the core of this system, as well as Buddhism, Confucianism, Capitalism, and Socialism, all accept the Yin-yang Five Element structured rites and festivals as essential to Chinese social life and culture.

NOTES

1. The term *San-chiao Kuei-i* sometimes refers to a popular syncretic cult popular in southeast China. Here it simply means the function of all three systems in providing ritual for the needs of the folk religion.
2. See Saso, M., *Chuang-lin Hsü Tao-tsang* (Taipei: 1975), 25 volumes, for examples of Taoist rituals provided for the rituals and festivals of Chinese religion.
3. Kristeva, Julia, *Desire in language*, New York: 1980, p. 18, the introduction of Leon Roudiez.

1. THE TAO OF RITUAL
The Theory and Practice of Chinese Religion

Chinese Religion can be defined as a cultural system that governs the rites of passage and the annual festivals celebrated by the people of China. It is to be distinguished from Confucianism, folk Buddhism and Taoism, which give ritual norms and ethical values to the religious system, and from the Buddhist, Christian, and Islamic religious belief systems which entered China from abroad. Unlike these latter faiths, Chinese religion is not a belief system. It has no creeds, dogmas, or a revealed scripture to which the Chinese peasant must give allegiance in order to belong. It is compatible with Buddhist, Islamic, Christian, and Marxist belief systems, and has survived all attempts to usurp its pre-eminent, fundamental position at the roots of Chinese cultural and social life.

The rites of passage and annual festivals are internally structured and programmed by a proto-scientific system called the Yin-yang five element philosophy. Even though foreign field researchers and hard-working Chinese peasants may not recognize the all pervasive presence of the system, ancient and modern manuals which explain how to perform rites of passage base their instructions on this ancient cosmology. Rites celebrating change in nature, the life-cycle of humans, as well as the physical layout of a temple or altar, are all structured by the semiotics of Yin-yang and the five elements.[1]

Though not yet formulated in clear terms, the Yin-yang system is already cognate in the oldest of all Chinese books, the *I-ching* Book of Changes.[2] In the symbolic mathematics of this ancient manual, the yang, male, moving forces of the universe are represented as an unbroken line ___ , while the female, yin, life-bearing powers are represented by a broken line -- . The six unbroken lines of the hexagram ch'ien 乾 , the yang symbol of cosmic change, represents the completion of a cycle: *yüan* 元 for primordial insemination; *heng* 亨 for nesting and offering sacrificial prayer for maturation; *li* 利 for harvest or birthing; and *chen* 真 for contemplation, rest, and divining the future. The six broken lines of the hexagram k'un 坤 symbolize the birthing and nourishing rest of a mare (female horse) after insemina-

1

tion and maturation. The southwest earth direction brings friendly nourishing rains, while the northeast demon brings unfriendly, deadly-cold winds that harm.[3]

The mathematical configuration of the *I-ching* is similar to the "0" "1" (off-on, in-out) bytes of the modern computer, classifying all natural data in terms of 8, 16, 32, 64, 128, 256, 512, 1024 etc., numerical divisions. The numbers are important symbolic elements in alchemy, meditation, art, and architecture, as will be seen in later discussions. The eight trigrams, the sixteen yin-yang positions around the meditating Taoist (represented as a lion and a heron in the Taoist *fa-lu* meditation for creating a sacred meditation space), thirty-two constellations, and the sixty-four hexagrams of the *I-ching* are frequently used numbers of the semiotic system, and are symbolic forerunners of Yin-yang philosophy.

This proto-scientific way of harmonizing human and natural changes was developed into a metaphysics of kenosis in the *Lao-tzu Tao-te Ching* (The Classic for Attaining the Tao), and into a consistent cosmology of change by the philosopher Tsou Yen, sometime between the sixth and fourth centuries BCE, roughly equivalent to the development of the Platonic and Aristotelian systems of classical Greek philosophy. The theory of the five elemental forces or movers, originally developed separately from the yin-yang system, became joined as a single philosophy of symbols by the third century BCE. It was the dominant intellectual force in reshaping the so called "New Text" (Chin-wen) school, which rewrote Confucian ritual in accord with yin-yang thought during the second and first centuries BCE[4]

During the Han dynasty (200 BCE to 200 CE) the Yin-yang five element theory became the basis for Han dynasty court ritual, the Rites of Passage, and the formation of liturgical and meditative Taoism. The reason for Lao-tzu's rejection of Confucian formalities *Li*, and later Taoists' creation and development of a massive, complex liturgical system, will be examined in Chapter Two of *Blue Dragon White Tiger*. Two of the reasons why Taoists accepted *Li* ritual, we shall see, are the conversion of New Text (i.e., Han Dynasty Yin-yang five element) Confucianists to the new Taoist religion, and the political forces of early Imperial China, which first favored the theory, then rejected its

2

proponents. Politics was, however, only a partial reason for the success of the yin-yang philosophy, which in fact lay, in its more primitive form, at the very heart of Chinese culture.

It is the goal of the first chapter of *Blue Dragon White Tiger* to explore the depths of the Yin-yang five element theory, and see how it is applied to the daily practice of Chinese religion. We shall begin by examining the various paradigmatic relations of these structural symbols, realizing that they are first and foremost a structural system, in which polarity (yin-yang) and cyclical change (five elements) are expressed by any given number of related symbols or concepts. I.e., any related series of words may fit the paradigmatic slots.

yang = male, motion, action, sun, spring-summer, seed planting

yin = female, rest, passion, moon, autumn-winter, birth-harvest

The cosmic symbol of yang is the sun, the source of daylight, while the cosmic sign of yang is moon and night. In religious iconography yang is blue dragon, and yin is white tiger whose eternal play in sea and sky bring about spring rains, summer heat, fall harvest, and winter rest.[5] Man and woman are in the center of macro and microcosmic changes in the inner and outer world. They are constant observers and meditators of Tao's eternal working in the cosmos:[6]

element	organ	season	body	space	spirit	planet
1. wood	liver	spring	left	east	Fu Hsi	Jupiter
2. fire	heart	summer	front	south	Shen-nung	Mars
3. metal	lungs	autumn	right	west	Shao-hao	Venus
4. water	kidneys	winter	back	north	Chüan-hsü	Mercury
5. earth	spleen	man - in - the center			Huang-ti	Saturn

As in the yin-yang system, so with the five elements, the image, concept, or symbol are limited only by the ability of the mind to assign a word within the limits of the Chinese language to signify the orderly or structured changes of nature. Thus, the five colors blue-green for east, bright red for south, bright white for west, purple-black for north, and yellow gold for center, as well as five fragrances for the sense of smell, five sounds for the sense of hearing (the Lydian scale), five art symbols and so forth, can be added ad infinitum (limited only by the cultural boundaries of language) to the system:

element	symbol	sound	taste	smell	month	sense
wood	dragon	chiao	sour	goatish	1-2	eye
fire	phoenix	chih	bitter	burning	4-5	tongue
earth	caldron	kung	sweet	fragr.	3,6,9,12	mouth
metal	tiger	shang	acrid	rank	7-8	nose
water	tortoise	yü	salty	rotten	10-1	ear

The above relationships are pure "structures," that is, the conceptual image is arbitrary, or less important than the fact that there are five divisions or slots to fill with related words. The system can accommodate a wider division, for instance a six-fold or eightfold structure (the six hexagrams, a "hex" system, or the eight trigrams *Pa-kua* of the *I-ching* system), and fill these slots too with a series of symbolic or conceptual relationships. The point to be stressed here is the genius of the ancient Chinese mind to discern the similarity between cyclical change in the body and the rhythms of the greater universe. Religion expresses in ritual and festival that very process of cyclical change that occurs in the macro and microcosm. The musical note (sound), color, and fragrance relate to inner bodily organs. These relationships are seen in Figure One, The Yin-yang five element cosmos:

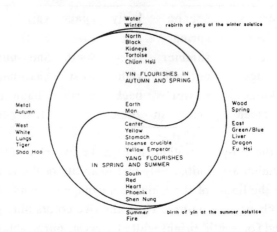

Fig. 1. The Yin-yang five element chart of the micro and macrocosmos.

In the Chinese system, north appears at the bottom of the chart and south at the top, when signifying the world of change. The chart is reversed when the world of the "prior heavens" i.e., when the Tao of

4

transcendent or non-act is present in center. This latter form, (north at top) is also called a Ho-t'u or River Chart, the term for the regalia of a King in ancient China. Confucius, when asked why he wasn't a King (Lun-yü, Ch. 9) replied that he did not have a Ho-t'u. The Han dynasty Apocryphal texts (Ku Wei Shu) taught that the Ho-t'u, usually described as a jade tablet bearing inscriptions of the stars, was related to the Prior Heavens configuration of the trigrams, i.e., when the trigram ch'ien (pure yang) was in the south, and the trigram k'un (pure yin) in the north. When the trigrams are used to symbolize change, ch'ien moves to the northwest, "Gate of heaven," and k'un to the southwest, Gate of Earth. This configuration is called a Lo-shu, i.e., writings from the Lo river. The King is a person who has the Ho-t'u, i.e., Tao is always in the center of his or her life.

A number of late Warring States and early Ch'in-Han dynasty texts (400 BCE to 180 BCE) use the above lists of yin-yang five element relationships to define court ritual. One of the most influential of these texts , the Yüeh-ling 月令 "Monthly Commands" chapter of the Book of Rites, determines explicit days for court ritual to the five directions, elements, spirits, and their subordinates. The color of ritual vestments must conform to the season, direction, the constellations, the patron spirit of the heavens and the earth, and the internal organs of the body:[7]

time	space	color	emperor	spirit	stars	organ
Spring	East	Green	T'ai-hau	Chü-mang	....	hsien-p'i
Summer	South	Red	Yen-ti	Chü-jung	....	hsien-fei
Center	Earth	Yellow	Huang-ti	Hou-t'u	....	hsien-hsin
Autumn	West	White	Shao-hao	Jung-shou	....	hsien-kan
Winter	North	Black	Chüan-hsü	Hsüan-ming	....	hsien-shen

The names in the slots are again not as important as the structural elements of the system. The Heavenly Emperors are recognized in Taoist meditation and ritual. The stars, represented as dots, stand for the constellations recognized as moving through the heavens according to seasonal changes. This early Han dynasty document established a clear relationship between the microcosm and the macrocosm for seasonal ritual. From it, we can recognize the importance of relating the interior of the human body (the microcosm) to the external world of nature, (the macrocosm) in the celebration of Chinese ritual and festival. For ancient and modern China, ritual symbolizes man's integral role in the natural environment. Every act within the interior of the human body has eternal consequences in the yin-yang structured cosmos.

The five elements can be arranged in any number of combinations, according to the season, use (ritual, meditative, secular function) and viewer's perspective. These variations are noted by Joseph Needham, *Science and Civilization in China*, Vol. II, pp. 232-65, summarizing Wolfram Eberhard, *Beitrage zur kosmoligischen Spekulation Chinas in der Han Zeit.*[8] The sequence in which the elements come into being, the so-called "cosmogonic order," is found in the *Tso Chuan*, a classic commentary on the Confucian Spring-Autumn Annals, the chapter entitled *Duke Chao, Ninth Year*. In this list, water is considered of primary importance, then fire, wood, metal, and earth. The primacy of water as a basic principle of Taoist philosophy is first noted in the Lao-tzu *Tao-te Ching*, and systematically developed in the T'ang dynasty Taoist work of Wang Shih-yüan, *K'ang Ts'ang-tzu*. In this latter work (see Needham, II, p. 255) Wang ascribes the causal antecedents of water to *ch'i* primordial breath, ch'i to emptiness (hsü) and emptiness to Tao (water < ch'i < emptiness < Tao). A similar progression is found in the Taoist meditation (see Chapter Two, Section III).

Religious Taoism and folk religion make special use of the complementary "mutual producing and destroying" order of the elements. The *hsiang-sheng* 相生 or order of mutual reproduction shows the five elements as giving birth to each other. The late archaic *Kuan-tzu* and the early Han text *Huai-nan-tzu* describe the birthing of the elements in terms of the seasonal changes of nature: spring-wood gives birth to summer-fire, fire to the 3-6-9-12 months' of earth, earth to autumn's metal, and metal to winter's water. It's opposite, the order of mutual conquest, *hsiang-sheng* 相勝 brings about successive destruction of one element by another. In this reversal sequence, each element is thought to conquer its predecessor. Thus, wood conquers earth by "growing" from it. Metal conquers wood by chopping it. Fire conquers metal by melting it. Water conquers fire by extinguishing it. Finally, earth conquers water by filling estuaries and rivers with silt and mud.

The mutual conquest order is perhaps the oldest expression of the five element theory, since it appears as a fragment from one of the missing works of the original yin-yang philosopher Tsou Yen.[9] The theory is historically important because it is used to explain the rise and fall of successive dynasties. Ssu-ma Ch'ien, China's first historian, quotes a passage from the work of Tsou Yen, to explain how the ancient Hsia kingdom, influenced by the element wood, was overcome by the Shang dynasty's metal. The Shang yielded to the Chou dynasty's fire. The Chou was succeeded by the Ch'in dynasty, and the element water. Last of all, the Han dynasty took the element earth and the imperial color yellow, as successors to the Ch'in.

The Han dynasty author of the *Li-chi* (ca. 180-160 BCE) used the theory to advocate (or as the case may be, create) the Monthly Commands chapter, where the Emperor is advised to offer ritual to all five directions, seasons, and their spiritual rulers, in succession. The ritual is to be offered in the *Ming-t'ang* Bright Temple, described in a subsequent chapter of the *Li-chi*. The structure of this rite is borrowed by the creators of religious Taoism at the end of the Han period, and is even today one of the basic liturgies of Taoist monks and village priests, the so called *An Ling-pao Chen-wen* rite.[10] The Taoists interpreted the Ling-pao Five True Writs to be a Ho-t'u, a sign of Tao's presence in the village temple, center of the village and the macrocosm, and in the "Yellow Court" center of the human body. The ritual for planting the Five True Writs in the macro-microcosm is called Su-ch'i, and is still used as a basic element in Taoist renewal liturgy.

So expert did Taoists become at ritual that later emperors often appointed Taoist masters to the Board of Rites. Taoists were sometimes commanded to perform the spring Feng and Shan sacrifices on the sacred mountain of the east, Mt. T'ai, or in temples dedicated to the Eastern Peak throughout China, as well as the Ming-t'ang rite (Su'ch'i) in the emperor's stead.[11] From these historical and literary records, it is easy to see the importance of the Yin-yang five element theory in court as well as in Taoist and popular ritual, an influence which lasts in the case of Taoism and village festival, until the present day. The theory is best summed-up in the words of the *Lü-shih Ch'un-ch'iu, Mr. Lü's Commentary on the Spring-Autumn Annals*, as follows:[12]

> Heaven and earth and all things are like the body of one
> man; this is what is called the Great Unity. The multiplicity
> of ears, eyes, nose, and mouths, five grains, cold and heat,
> are called the myriad differences. Thus, all things are made
> one whole. Heaven makes all things flourish. The sage notes

7

them, so as to see... how yin and yang form the essence of
things, and how people, birds, and beasts are at peace.

There are many early Han dynasty classics from which passages
can be cited in support of the theory that the macro and microcosm are
part of a single, unified system, dependent on the Tao (the first,
transcendent, unmoved mover) to maintain this unity. Of these, the
early Han dynasty *Huai-nan-tzu* is the most eloquent and consistent.
The team efforts of Professor D.C. Lau and Roger Ames to translate
the ancient text preserve the poetic and literary quality of the original
Chinese:[13]

> As for the Tao,
> It shelters the heavens and supports the earth,
> Extends beyond the four (directions)(of the compass)
> And enfolds to the eight points of the (compass).
> It is high beyond bounds, and deep beyond reckoning;
> It envelops the cosmos, and gives to the yet formless....
> By virtue of it, mountains are high, abysses are deep;
> Animals run, birds fly; the sun and moon are bright;
> Stars and celestial bodies turn;
> The unicorn rambles about; the phoenix soars.

The ancient cosmology that first expressed this system is summarized in the Forty-second chapter of the *Lao-tzu Tao-te Ching* (The
Classic for Attaining the Tao) as follows:

> The Tao gave birth to the One; The One gave birth to
> the Two; The Two gave birth to the Three;
> The Three gave birth to the myriad things.

Early Taoist school texts interpret the cryptic passage of the
Lao-tzu text in two ways.[14] The "One" of the Lao-tzu text is always
taken to mean *yüan-ch'i* "primordial breath"[15] In the interpretation of
the religious Taoist system. Tao, Wu-wei (transcendent act), gives birth
to Te, Yu-wei (immanent act) or ch'i. Ch'i is seen as a cosmic egg, the
white and yolk interior (white and yellow of the egg) of which are en-
cased in a bright purple (hsüan 玄) shell.

The first interpretation of the text defines the "One" as T'ai-chi
the Great Ultimate First mover, or *Yüan-ch'i* 元炁 Primordial Breath; the
"two" as yang, and the "three" as yin. Thus, Tao (0) gives birth to Ch'i
(1), Ch'i gives birth to Yang (2), and yin (3). These three principles,
Ch'i, yang, and yin, gestate the myriad things of nature. A second, later

interpretation defines "One" as primordial breath, "Two" as yin and yang, and "Three" as heaven, earth, and underworld in the macrocosm, and head, chest, and belly in man. [16] These relationships are seen in the following illustrations:

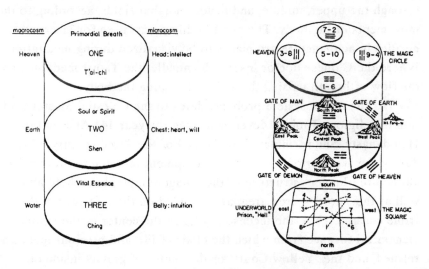

Fig. 2. The Tao gives birth to the Myriad creatures.

The Taoists use of ch'i, yang, and yin is as follows:

No.	Symbol	microcosm	macrocosm	color-aura	Tao
1.	ch'i	head, mind	heaven	purple	gestating
2.	yang	heart, will	earth	yellow	mediating
3.	yin	belly, intuit	water	white	indwelling

The above structure can be again expanded in terms of Taoist meditation (internal alchemy, nei-tan 內丹) as follows:

No.	Symbol	microcosm	macrocosm	color-aura	Tao
1.	ch'i	upper cinna-bar field	Primordial Heav-enly Worthy	Yüan-shih T'ien-tsun	hsüan
2.	yang	middle cinna-bar field	Ling-pao Heav-enly Worthy	Ling-pao T'ien-tsun	yüan
3.	yin	lower cinna-bar field	Tao-te Heav-enly Worthy	Tao-te T'ien-tsun	shih

9

It should be noted that for the meditating Taoist, the ch'i 炁, breath is equivalent to *t'ai-chi* 太極, which in turn is *hun-tun* 混沌 or *yu-wei chih Tao,* 有為之道 the moving Tao. Thus when performing the graceful T'ai-chi exercises, the Taoist meditates on the flow of breath through the upper, middle, and lower cinnabar fields, according to the movements of the body. The same bodily points used for inserting needles in acupuncture are places to be visualized during meditation. Where the Chinese doctor inserts the needle, the Taoist meditates on the flow of breath pulsing through and healing the body.

The above system probably dates to the Celestial Master tradition of religious Taoism, developed since the year 144 ACE in the late Han dynasty, and formulated by the end of the Third century ACE during the Wei period.[17] In the development of Chinese liturgical architecture, the very structure of the village temple, household altar, as well as the Taoist sacred area, are modeled on the structure of the triple cosmos. Thus, the incense burner in the center of the temple, the alchemical furnace from which the elixir of life and precious metals are refined, and the "Yellow Court" or the center of gravity inside the human body, are centers from which the meditator comes in contact with the Transcendent Wu-wei chih Tao. On the ceiling above the spot where the incense burner is placed is inscribed the eight trigrams, symbolizing the Tao's presence.

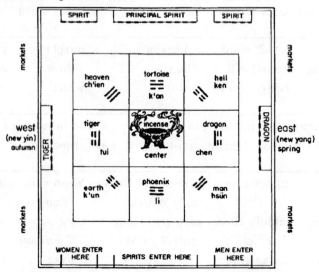

Fig. 3. The Village temple, the body, and an alchemical furnace, modeled on the Yin-yang five element cosmos.

The theory of the three divisions of the cosmos, and the five elemental movers of nature were not originally developed as a single consistent system. It is to the genius of religious Taoism, after the mid Han period and the founding of the Celestial Master and subsequently the Shang-ch'ing (Highest Pure) Taoism during the Wei (220-265 ACE) and the later Chin and north-south period (265-588 ACE) that the "three-fives" and the "three enfold the one" meditations of internal alchemy became a meditative-ritual system. The five elements were given a double meditative relationship, the "raw" and the "cooked," i.e., the elements as directly gestated from the Tao, Ch'i, yin and yang, (the elements of the "prior" heavens), and the same elements as subject to change in the posterior heavens, the elements of the *I-ching* Book of Changes. The raw numbers 1, 2, 3, 4, and 5 were assigned the role of leading the meditator back to the origin, to plumb the depths of the Tao as *wu* 無 as expressed in the Lao-tzu, Chapter I, line 5, *Ku ch'ang* 故常無 *wu, yü yi kuan ch'i miao*: 欲以觀其妙 "therefore stay with the *wu* [raw being, uncooked, sheng] to see the Tao's mysteries."[18]

The numbers 6, 7, 8, 9, and 10, for reading the *I-ching*, and plumbing the Tao's workings in nature, were *shu* 熟 , cooked, referring to the next line of the Lao-tzu (Chapter I, line 6): *Ch'ang yu, yü yi kuan ch'i chiao,* remain with the *yu* [being held on to, cooked, shu] to touch the Tao's outermost limits." The five "raw" elements were said to *ch'ao yüan* have audience with the Tao of the origin, as seen in the following woodblock print:

Fig. 4. Wu-hsing ch'ao yüan, the Five elements have audience with the Tao of origin. From *Hsing-ming Kuei-chih*, Ch'ing woodblock.

Applied to the spatial order, the Chinese city, the household altar, and the village temple are physically structured according to these principles. The following three illustrations visually demonstrate the use of yin-yang five element theory in design and architecture. The first shows a typical Chinese city, with temples at each of the four gates, pointing to the four directions. The illustration does not show the use of a Buddhist temple to guard the "Gate of Demon" (kuei-men 鬼門), that is, the trigram ken 艮 of the "cooked" or moving arrangement of the I-ching. Note that the Enryaku-ji temple northeast of Kyoto, in Japan, was built with the thought in mind of fulfilling the function of protecting the city from evil. The Taoists perform the chin-t'an 禁壇 purification in the village temple to close the "Gate of Demon" before festive ritual. The use of the Eight Trigrams and yin-yang structure is a basic element in religious art and architecture.

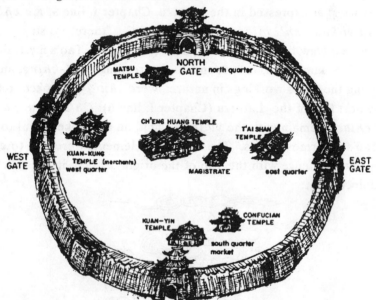

Fig. 5. Hsinchu city, north Taiwan, during the nineteenth century.

In figure five we can see the clear application of yin-yang theory to the building of a Chinese city. The Eastgate district is dedicated to T'ai Shan, the sacred peak of the east in Shantung, where the emperor traditionally offered the feng and shan sacrifices for fertility in spring.[19] The Southgate district holds a Kuanyin temple, and a large farmer's market. Westgate has the merchant's temple to the red faced general

12

Kuan-kung, patron of business and the martial arts. Northgate's temple to Matsu, the patron of fishermen, holds the city's largest fish market. The very center of the city houses the Ch'eng-huang temple, 城隍 the equivalent in the spiritual order to the Yamen city magistrate's offices. The Ch'eng-huang spirit governs the city's spiritual affairs, and metes out punishments to the deceased in a nine-squared hell directly below the city.[20]

The Chinese family altar is structured in accordance to the yin-yang five element theory, with the ancestor tablet usually placed on the left (yin) side. The patron spirit of the family, a symbol of the religious belief (Buddhist, Taoist, Islamic, or Christian) or of the professional trade of the family head is placed in the center of tha altar. Thus, Christians might have a crucifix, Muslims an Arabic inscription, Buddhists a ststaue of Kuanyin, and merchants a statue of Kuan Kung the Warrior in the center. Implements for prognosticating the future such as numbered yarrow stalks and an almanac on the right or east side of the altar. The temple altar and the ancestral shrine with its separate altar are variations of the basic altar model. A typical family altar is seen in the following illustration:

Fig. 6. The family altar.

The center in the Chinese temple and altar system is the place where the incense burner is located, and from which Tao's presence is realized. Ritual north, the wall against which the altar is placed, is

13

reserved for the deity, the emperor, and the patron spirit or protector of the family. East represents the future, the place for keeping the almanac or the *I-ching*, and performing rites of prognostication. The left side is the ritual west, for commemorating the afterlife, and keeping the ancestor tablets. The place from which the family prays is in the south, facing north, the position from which ritual petitions are offered and audience with the emperor is conducted. These rules are true for the imperial as well as the peasant household, and are found with various modifications throughout China.

The Chinese temple is even more obviously structured in accord with the Yin-yang five element theory. No matter in what direction the temple actually faces in reality, the back wall against which the statue or figure of the major spirit or deity is placed is considered to be ritual north, and the temple icons and symbols are similar to the pattern of the Chinese altar.

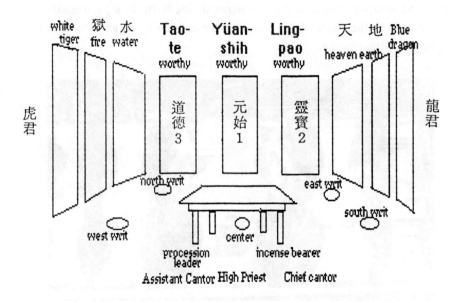

Fig. 7. The Chinese temple, a Taoist model.

In figure seven we see a Chinese temple designed and set up in the Taoist fashion. The major deities, in this case the *San-ch'ing* 三清 Three Pure Ones, (Tao as Gestating, Mediating, and Indwelling) are

14

seen as scrolls suspended from the north wall. The spirits of heaven, earth, and Blue Dragon (yang) are represented on the east wall. The spirits of the mountains, water, and White Tiger (yin) are pictured on the right wall. The people of the village enter from the south of the temple, women through the left or yin entrance, men through the right or yang gate. Outside the temple on the west side is a furnace for burning paper money, a sign or semiotic symbol of human merit for good deeds that free the souls of loved ones from hell's sufferings. Any symbol, Buddhist Taoist, or popular, may fit any of the slots in the temple. The position, not the word or image is important in the Chinese temple and its structural relations.

In some temples, a pool is found on the west side (water stands for yin) and the furnace on the right side (fire for yang) thus reversing the position of the furnace for receiving paper money.[21] In Buddhist temples the four heavenly guardians (Szu t'ien wang; Jpn: Shitenno) are found at the gates of the temple. East's Keeper of the Kingdom (Ch'ih-kuo) and south's Increaser of Wealth (Tseng-chang) are to the right-yang side of the gateway, while west's "Wide Eyes" (Kuang-mu) and north's "All Hearer" or "tuned-in" (Vaisravana) are on the left-yin. The Great General guardian of the Myriad Souls, a fierce image of the Bodhisattva of compassion (Kuanyin) is found at the entrance of Buddhist and Taoist shrines throughout China. What seems eclectic to the casual observer or "illiterate" foreign anthropologist is in fact strictly governed by the structural rules of yin-yang semiotics.

In summary, the Yin-yang five element theory acts as a "deep" (subconscious) structure, which determines how a city, temple, and altar are built and decorated, how ritual is initiated, and the cosmos is conceived in its macro (nature) and micro (body) environments. Whether recognized by the casual informant, or hidden in the memory banks of the expert Taoist priest, the structure of Chinese religious architecture, festival, and meditation is operative everywhere in China.

As stated above, the theory of Chinese religion was developed during the early Han period, between 220-180 BCE The "New text" scholars re-wrote the Confucian classics and created a whole new ritual system, based on the Yin-yang five element theory. The Ssu-ma Ch'ien, China's first historian, writes of the influence of Tung Chung-shu (179-104 BCE) at the court of Emperors Ching (154-141) and Wu (140-87 BCE). The earlier Confucian writings were embellished by a series of new text scholars, including Tung's *Ch'un-ch'iu Fan-lu*, the *Li-chi*, other Books of Ritual, and the *Lü shih ch'un-ch'iu* (Mr. Lu's commentary on the Ch'un-ch'iu, written by 240 BCE, before the Han period.[22] In the legal system developed by the New Text scholars, proper ritual as well as ethical conduct preserved the right of the Emperor to rule, and won blessings from nature.

Parallel to the Confucian New text movement, a school of Yin-yang Taoism grew during the early and later Han period which had a deep and lasting influence on the practice of Chinese religion, at the popular village level. The appendages to the *I-ching* Book of Changes, the *Huai-nan-tzu* (quoted above), the later *Ts'an-t'ung Ch'i* (The Triple Union Contract), and the *Ku wei-shu* (The Ancient Apocryphal Texts) were influential in the formation of Han Taoism.[23] The development of religious Taoism as a ritual system is treated more fully in Chapter Two. In the remainder of chapter one we shall examine the practice of Chinese religion from the influence of these two complementary systems. The result, we shall see, is that of a generative syntax of religious i.e., ritual Taoism, which expresses the values of the Yin-yang five element and the Confucian ethical system.

Confucianism is called the warp, and Taoism the woof of Chinese religion. It is precisely in the Taoist woof that creativity, color, and variable meaning are woven. The golden threads of Buddhism are blended into this grand tapestry after the initial weaving of the Han dynasty cultural fabric. The Confucian threads, which run in a perpendicular manner from the top to the bottom of Chinese society, define the ethical norms of Chinese behavior. The Taoist woof, which runs on a horizontal axis from the beginning to the end of life, defines the changing relations of the human condition with nature (tzu-jan 自然,). Chinese religion cannot be understood without knowing the relationship between these two interwoven threads, hidden beneath the external form of religious practice.

The New Text school of Confucianism taught that offering of ritual, the punishment for crime, as well as the observance of social virtue by rulers and public officials, must be "timely," i.e., in line with the movement of yin-yang and the five elemental forces of nature. This teaching was a modification of Confucius' original summation of sixth and fifth century BCE ethical norms, before the formulation of the yin-yang theory.[24] In the original Confucian teaching, the observance of

16

basic social norms by the *chun-tzu* 君子 ruler who possessed princely
virtue brought nature's blessing for the kingdom, and proved that the
king had heaven's mandate to rule. The "little" man had no such talent
or propensity for princely virtue.

It was the genius of Han dynasty Taoism to generate from the
best of yin-yang ritual, ethical values, and the theory that human actions
influenced the entire cosmos, a semiotic, generative, eidetic expression
of Chinese religion.[25] The virtues which Confucius thought proper for
the chun-tzu man of princely virtue, who ruled from the city's ad-
ministrative center, became generative virtues for every man and
women in the four quarters (fang 方) of the outer city. The priesthood
and administrators of this new religious-cultural movement, which included healing, medicine, meditation, ritual, and hermetic asceticism,
were called *fang-shih* 方士 , masters of the four city and village
quarters, as opposed to the Confucian administrator's in the empty circular center.[26] Their successors, Taoist masters at the end of the Han
taught that all men and women of the village must practice timely
virtue, to win nature's blessing.[27]

From this large and diverse storehouse of ideas and movements
that influenced Han dynasty religion we shall focus on three elements
of practical importance for understanding modern Chinese religion.
These are 1) the Confucian value system as reinterpreted by Taoist syntax, i.e., as it informs human relationships at the personal, family, and
village level; 2) the notion of the tripartite soul, and immortality in the
Chuang-tzu; and 3) the care for the spirit-soul in the afterlife, a duty
relegated to Buddhist and Taoist liturgy. The first of these themes, i.e.,
the ethical value system defined by Confucius, remains deeply embedded in the hearts of the men and women of China, even in modern
socialist China.[28]

The following lovely poem of the eighth century BCE *Shih
Ching* Book of Odes has been used by many modern scholars to explain
the basic Chinese social relationships.[29]

> (1) I beg you, Chung-tzu, do not climb into our home,
> Do not break the willows we have planted.
> Not that I mind the willows,
> But I respect my father and mother.
> Chung-tzu I do love, but I fear father and mother.
> (2) I beg you, Chung-tzu, don't climb the wall.

Don't break the mulberry trees we have planted.
Not that I mind the mulberry trees, but I respect
My brothers. Chung-tzu I dearly love;
But I fear what my brothers will say.
(3) I beg you, Chung-tzu, do not enter the garden,
Do not break the (willows) we have planted.
Not that I mind the willows, but I respect what the
People (villagers) will say. Chung-tzu I truly love;
But I fear what the villagers will say.

Confucian scholars claim that courtship and romance poetry of the *Shih Ching* Book of Odes illustrate the ethical value system of the Chinese religious world view. The judgments of the girl, reflected in the lyrics of the song meant to be sung to a zither or lute, repeat again and again the need to respect parents, brothers-friends, and the entire village. The Confucian virtues of *li* 禮 for respect, *hsiao* 孝 for parental-child love (sometimes translated as "filiality'), *yi* 義 for the reciprocal relationship of friendship, and *jen* 仁 for benevolence towards villagers and strangers, symbolized in the ancient folk song, remain at the core of family and village relationships today.

jen 仁
yi 義
hsiao 孝
li 禮

ego
respect
parent-child love
reciprocal friendship
benevolence to stranger

Later Taoist manuals use these and other Confucius virtues as structural elements in yin-yang five element charts describing ascetical and meditation practice.[30] The virtues reserved for kingly and gentry practice become the basis for nature's blessing in the villages and countryside of late Han dynasty China, and remain at the core of Chinese social relationships until the present.[31] The rites enunciated by Confucian New Text school also generated the formation of a new village oriented Taoist ritual. When the "Old Text" Confucian movement became dominant in the later Han dynasty, (23-220 CE) the yin-yang "New Text" ritualists were exiled to the villages and towns of countryside China. Taoist liturgy, owes much to converted New Text Confucian exiles.[32]

The second theme of Han religious texts, the tripartite nature of the soul, became the syntax for generating the Taoist system of internal alchemy, meditation, and kenotic emptying of mind, heart, and emotions for the "encounter with the Tao" described in the *Chuang-tzu Nei-p'ien*.[33] In this system, based on the forty-second chapter of the Lao-tzu, the tripartite division of the cosmos is reflected within the microcosm by a triple function of the soul-spirit. The head houses the powers of *ch'i* 炁 for intellect and imagination, i.e., image projection; the heart is the seat of the *shen* 神 power of will, rule, and love; and the solar plexus below the navel is the seat of *ching* 精 intuition, and emotion. The emotions are further analyzed into seven forms of response to external stimuli, namely: joy, anger; sorrow, merriment; likes, dislikes; desire.[34] These relationships are represented as ten images, in the following popular woodblock print:

Fig. 8. The three *hun* 魂 souls, eidetic symbols for intellect, will, and intuition, and the seven *p'o* 魄 spirits, symbol of the emotions. *Hsing-ming Kuei-chih*, Ch'ing dynasty woodblock.

The three powers of the soul-spirit are given the semiotic term hun 魂 in popular religious iconography, as symbols of intellect, will, and intuition. These spirits are housed in the head, (the upper cinnabar field, pineal gland, or *ni-wan* 泥丸 dark purple palace), the heart (the middle cinnabar field, will, ruler of the body), and the belly (the lower cinnabar field, where ch'i breath can be joined with ching-intuition, and centered by meditative concentration on the Tao). Three colors are visualized in Taoist meditation, as associated with these energy centers. *Ch'i*, housed in the brain, is purple. *Shen*, or soul-spirit in the heart, is bright yellow. *Ching* intuition in the belly is white. When selfishness, argument, fame, name, or glory occupy the heart-mind, the three spirits become three worms that eat away the interior and cause death. When the heart-mind is *hsü* 虛 emptied of formal image, word, or symbol, the Tao (as purple-gestating, yellow-mediating, and white-indwelling) is present.[35] The semiotics of Taoist eidetic (creative) alchemy meditation free the mind from the paradigms imposed by the Confucian and popular systems.

In the third aspect, i.e., the popular ritual order, Chinese religious imagery pictures the soul-spirit *shen* to be immortal, i.e., the soul-spirit continues to exist after death. It must be escorted through the punishments of a hell like underworld by the merits of the living, and can cause illness to the living if left unattended in hell's prison. Both Taoist and Buddhist ritual was created to assist the soul in this process. Notions of an afterlife are found in the *Chuang-tzu Nei-p'ien*,[36] and in the ancient oracle bones.[37] The care of the soul in the afterlife remains one of the most important functions of Chinese religion. Taoist burial ritual and Buddhist memorial services for the deceased were among the first religious practices to be restored in China after the promulgation of the freedom of religion act in 1979, and the end of the Great Cultural Revolution in China (see Chapter 8).

Death in the natural order occurs, according to the syntax of popular yin-yang cosmology, when ch'i breath and ching intuitive feelings are exhausted. The *hun* soul separates from the body and the seven *p'o* emotional spirits, when the natural life cycle is completed. The *hun* soul-spirit (shen) continues to exist as a separate entity in the invisible world of yin (underworld, yin-chieh 陰界) or the invisible heavenly world of yang (heaven, yang-chieh 陽界), while the *p'o* are buried in the grave, with the body. Burial ritual, post funerary Buddhist memorial services, and Ancestor ritual reflect this belief in the continuing relationship between living family members and the soul of a deceased loved one. These practices are discussed in Chapter 6, and in Chapter 3 with a description of the ten stages of Buddhist and Taoist hell. A further corollary of the separated soul spirit determines the enfeoffment of heroic shen soul-spirits who die tragic deaths before the cosmic charge of ch'i breath and ching essence are used up. Chapter 7 shows how the saints and spirits of popular folk religion are always heroic men and women who died before their time in the service of the people.[38] All of these convictions are based on the yin-yang five element philosophy, which acts as a subconscious language of symbols structuring the rites of passage and annual festivals.

Even though Taoism has had a profound influence on Chinese popular religion, and in spite of the fact that Taoists, along with Buddhist and Confucian, continue to act as teachers and ritual masters for the practice of Chinese rites of passage and festivals, still there is a great gulf that separates the Three Teachings from popular Chinese religion. This gulf lies precisely between the semiotic belief in spirits and ancestors of the popular religion, and the attitude of the three teachings toward voiding the heart-mind of imagery, imagination, and the reality of the spirit world portrayed in Chinese temples and on family altars. By symbolically sending away the spirits, i.e., by protecting the people from their fears, rendering the fears "benevolent," the kataphatic (mind-heart filling) religion of the masses approximates the apophatic (emptying) spirituality of the Taoist recluse. The Taoist is the mandarin of the spirits, and of nature. More immediate than the Confucian official, the Taoist meditator penetrated to the very core of the Tao's working in the cosmos.

For Confucius, and the two-and-a-half millennia of Confucian scholarship, the spirits of Chinese popular religion are not considered a part of accepted state ritual worship, or proper objects for literary study. The phrase *Ching kuei-shen er yüan chih* (respect disembodied demons and spirits from a distance) exemplifies Confucius' attitude to all spirits other than immediate ancestors. The Confucian teachings promote ancestor rites at the household level. Officially approved state and imperial sacrifices may only be conducted by experts appointed by the Board of Rites. Reports from mandarin officials in the provincial and county offices are filled with disapproving or at least disinterested memorials to the throne about "lewd" or quaint local cults, a safe thing

21

to tell the emperor and ministers in the capital. Local and provincial
Gazetteers provide a descriptive source for studying local practice,
without a deep analysis of origins or content. [39]

Buddhist monks and nuns, perhaps the most iconoclastic of the
three ritual teachers, disapproved entirely the practices of popular
religion and Taoism. The use of statues, scrolls, rituals, or meat offerings from the popular religion are forbidden in Buddhist temples. Yet
the Buddhist temples of China allow the reading of fortunes, the chanting of prayers to the Patron Spirit of the Soil on the first and fifteenth
days of the lunar month, and other acquiescences to popular fervor.
Further, an elaborate set of rituals for the deceased, a complete
capitulation to the Chinese belief in a soul and the afterlife, developed
at a very early date in China and Japan. Whatever the teachings of
Buddhologists, philosophers, and scholars, the Buddhist care for the
soul in the afterlife became the main upaya (fang-pien) convenient and
skillful means for winning Chinese converts to the foreign religion from
India. Buddhist philosophy for the intellectual, and popular burial services for the people, endeared Buddhism in the hearts of the people.

Of the three teaching systems, Taoism was always the closest to
Chinese popular religion, providing rituals for all occasions, and adapting in every possible way to local cults and practice. But at its roots and
source, Taoism too teaches that the spirits of popular religion, and even
the secret registers of Taoist meditation practice, are all to be emptied
from the microcosm in order to be aware of the transcendent Tao.
When the Taoists are called upon to perform popular village ritual of
renewal called Chiao, all of the statues of the popular religion are
taken outside of the temple to a table, (ritual south), or covered and
hidden from view if left inside during ritual.[40] The paradigm of
Chinese temple structure is thus syntactically used as a basis for emptying out all spirits, for an encounter with the Tao. The cleansing of a
void center, the filling of the micro and macrocosm with the generating
power of the Tao, become a visible drama in Taoist ritual.

Taoist's construct a sacred area called a *t'an*壇, in order to have
audience with the Tao. The sacred area is filled with scrolls depicting
the Heavenly Worthies and sacred spirits proper to the Taoist tradition.
This list of spirits that create a pure void space is called a *lu* 籙 or
register. Only the Taoist knows how to envision and summon these
purifying images. Their scrolls, semiotic signs for eidetic-creative vision,

22

are displayed in the interior of the temple (see Fig. 7), during Taoist ritual. The members of the community and scholars chosen to join the Taoists may ask the names of the spirits. But what the people, and frequently the scholar are not told, is that these Taoist spirits too are to be exorcised, sent forth, and totally eradicated from the Taoist eidetic (generative) imagination. Taoist prayer, following the tradition of the Chuang-tzu and the Lao-tzu, is basically a prayer of kenosis or image emptying.[41] We may therefore say that the spirits of Taoism and the goal of true Taoist prayer is an emptying process. Even though the prayer of the people of China is a filling, asking, and petitionary process, Taoist ritual makes prayer into a form of giving kenosis.

Taoists respond to the needs of the people by acting out rites of renewal, healing, burial, and blessing, in the manner of the people, by asking for material things. Memorials and petitions are read in public, and sent off to the heavens, earth, and underworld. The names of the men and women of the community and their needs are read publicly. The spirits of the folk religion, removed from the void center of the temple, are addressed in a public courtyard in front of the temple. The petitions are sent off to heaven by burning, to the earth by burial, and to the watery underworld by floating on a river. But in fact the goal of the Taoist of emptying and giving away, and the goal of the people to gain material wealth and blessing are made one in this process. Imitate heaven in giving, not earth in grasping, the Taoist sings. The act of parental-child love of the Confucian system, and the father-mother role of Tao and nature in the Taoist system, are equally a kenotic-giving process.[42] Taoist public ritual is a drama visually acting out the syntax of kenotic giving.

Thus the goals of Chinese religion, and the three teachers of Chinese religion, differ only in external word and appearance. All three promote a sense of emptying, compassion, and concern for human feeling. Though Confucius spoke frequently of the "rectification of names," (a single connotative meaning) and Buddhism saw name and reality as empty, in fact the Taoist emptying of name and image, Confucius concern for parent-child bond, and Buddhist compassion are analogies of the syntaxis of giving by emptying. The act of winning blessing by giving generously is close to the popular Chinese religious spirit. Just as parent empties self for child, and child gives self for parent, so too, the Lao-tzu points out, the Tao eternally empties self, ie, spins breath, gestates and forms the entire cosmos. The Tao gives equally to friend and foe, loved and unloved. These values lie at a deep level of the living Chinese religious spirit.

NOTES

1. See *Li Chi*, The Book of Rites; Monthly Command Chapter; also, *Ta-T'ang K'ai-yüan Li*, cited below in Ch. 3, note 1. 禮記月令. 大唐開元禮
2. The *I-ching* basic text dates from the early Chou period; the wings and commentaries are much later Han dynasty additions.
3. See Kao Heng, *Chou-i ku-ching chin-chu*, Hongkong: Chunghua Press, 1963, pp. 1-12 for the text and interpretation.
4. See Li Han-san, *Hsien-ch'in Liang-Han chih Yin-yang Wu-hsing Shuo* (Taipei:1967).
5. See Chapter 2. Yüan, heng, li, and chen of the *I-ching* are related symbolically to spring, summer, autumn, and winter in the macrocosm of nature. Also to birth, puberty, marriage, and old age-death in the microcosmic rites of passage, Chs. 4-6.
6. See Joseph Needham, *Science and Civilization in China*, Vol. II , pg. 262-263, Table 12; pp. 232-261. See also, *Ku-shih P'ien*, Vol. 5, the discussions of Ku Chieh-kang and Liang Ch'i-ch'ao.
7. The terms in the last column name the bodily organ by the one preceding it, i.e.,(liver) before spleen, (heart) before lungs, (spleen) before heart, (lungs) before liver, (kidney 1) before kidney(2), see Needham, Vol. II, pp. 253-61. The dots in the row labeled "star" represent the twenty-eight constellations of the Chinese zodiac.
8. Needham, op. cit. Vol. II, Cambridge University Press, 1956.
9. See Needham, Vol.II, p. 238; Fung, Vol.I, p. 162.
10. Cf.Ch. 2, under Taoism, the Ling-pao Wu Chen-wen, i.e., and *The Teachings of Taoist Master Chuang*, New Haven: 1978, chapter 5.
11. Liu Ts'un-yan, *Selected Papers from the Hall of Harmonious Wind*, Leiden, 1976; and "The Penetration of Taoism into the Ming Neo-confucianist Elite," *T'oung-pao* #57, 1971.
12. Lü-shih Ch'un-ch'iu, Ch. 13, p. Chu-tzu Hui-yao edition, Taipei reprint, 1965.
13. Lao, D.C., and Ames, Roger T., *Huai Nan Tzu, Treatise I; Yuan Tao: Tracing the Origins of the Tao*, manuscript soon to be published; section one quoted with permission of Roger Ames.

14. See the clear exposition of the Huai-nan-tzu text in Charles Le Blanc, *Huai-nan Tzu*, Hong Kong University Press, 1985, pp. 199 ff.

15. Le Blanc, op. cit., pg. 203, note 32.

16. Lao-tzu, Ho-shang Kung Commentary, Ch. 42; *Tao-tsang Ching-hua*, #16.1, p. 316, (Taipei reprint, of a Ming woodblock, 1979).

17. The *Tung-shen Pu* section of the Taoist Canon, *Cheng-i Fa-wen T'ien-shih Chiao chieh-k'o ching*, shows the three-fold aspects of the Tao, hsüan, yüan, and shih. See Lagerwey, John, *Taoist Ritual in Chinese Society and History*, 1988, p. 37-8, for the T'an altar.

18. The "raw" numbers, based on the meditative chart called Ho-t'u are used in Taoist meditation; the "cooked" numbers refer to cycling aspects of the *I-ching*, symbolized by the Lo-shu. See Saso, Michael *Taoism and the Rite of Cosmic Renewal*, (Pullman: 1990) Ch. 3.

19. See Liu Ts'un-yan, *Selected Papers from the Hall of Harmonious Wind*, Leiden: E.J.Brill, 1976.

20. See Ch. 3 for the nine sections of Buddhist-Taoist hell.

21. The Wan-fu Kung temple atop Greater Mao Shan, Chianghsi province, Chü-jung district uses this arrangement.

22. See Hsü Dau-lin, Crime and Cosmic Order, in *Harvard Journal of Asian Studies*, Vol. 30, 1970: pp. 111-125.

23. Anna Seidel suggest that the Wei Apocrypha influenced the upper political more than the lower level popular religion; see Taoist Sacraments, in *Tantric and Taoist Studies in honor of R. Stein*, Vol. II, Bruxelles: Melanges Chinois et Bouddhiques, Vol. XXI, 1983, pp. 292-371, 287 notes.

24. See Hsü, Dau-lin, op. cit., pp. 115-116.

25. Cf. *Chuang-tzu Nei-p'ien*, Ch. 2, Chai-wu Lun.

26. The Taoist notion of the void center, derived from the *Chuang-tzu Nei-p'ien*, and the *Yellow Court Canon* of the Highest Pure Mao Shan tradition, is treated more fully in Ch. 2.

27. see Kenneth J. DeWoskin, *Doctors, Diviners, and Magicians of Ancient China: Biographies of Fang-shih*, New York: Columbia University Press, 1983, pp. 1-42. See also Maspero, Henri, *Taoism and Chinese Religion*, Amherst: University of Massachusetts, 1981.

28. See Saso, Michael, "Religion in Modern China," China News Analysis, Dec. 15, 1987.

29. Modeled after the Translation of Arthur Waley, *The Book of Songs*, New York: Grove Press edition, 1960, #24, p. 35.

30. See Liu I-ming, *I-tao Hsin-fa*, pg. 1, charts.

31. See Stein, Rolf, Religious Taoism and Popular Religion from the second to the seventh centuries, in Welch & Seidel, *Facets of Taoism*, New Haven: Yale University Press, 1979, p. 69 ff.

32. See Stein, Rolf, "Remarques sur les mouvements du Taoisme politico-religieux au IIe siécle AP. T.-C.," in *T'oung Pao*, Leiden: E.J.Brill, 1963, Vol. L., pp. 1-78.

33. See Saso, Michael, The Chuang-tzu Nei-p'ien, in V. Mair, ed., *Experimental Essays on the Chuang-tzu*, Honolulu: University of Hawaii Press, 1983, pp. 140-157.

34. see Saso, M., *Taoism and the Rite of Cosmic Renewal*, Pullman: Washington State University Press, 1990 p. 13.

35. See chapter two, the section on Taoist ritual meditation for a further development of this theme.

36. *Chuang-tzu Nei-p'ien*, Ch. VI, sec. 14, t'ung yü Ta-t'ung.

37. The character *t'a* 走 for possession or illness caused by a deceased relative, represented a foot being bit by a yin-serpent from under the earth, in ancient oracle bone symbols.

38. The term *pai jih sheng t'ien* means that the Taoist adept "ascends to heaven in broad daylight," by-passing hell's alchemical purification by Taoist prayer and ascesis. See Ch. 2.

39. See M. Saso, *Index to the Beijing Gazetteer*, State Paper Room, British Museum, for memorials on popular religious practices.

40. See Ch. 2. below for the two kinds of reformed Taoist practice: the popular spirit oriented and the classical meditations of kenosis.

41. kenosis (kevóσis), a Greek word meaning to empty, is used in the initial Greek sense here, as a way of explaining the Taoist *hsin-chai* fasting in the heart-mind, and *tsuo-wang*, sitting in forgetfulness.

42. Lao-tzu, Ch. 4, line 1, "The Tao is empty, yet use does not drain it," and Ch. 5, line 15, describing the void.

2. THE TAO OF EMPTYING
From Theory to Practice of Chinese Religion

In the first chapter we examined the roots of Chinese religion in the yin-yang five element theory. From ancient times the Chinese held the view that the human body and nature's changes were intimately related. That theory grew into a religious system called Taoism by the end of the Han dynasty, ca. 200 CE. In the second chapter we shall sketch the way in which the theory developed *diachronically* through history, and *synchronically* within the practices of Taoist ritual and meditation in China. The historical period covered in this chapter extends from the end of the Han period, ca. 200 CE, to the end of the Sung period, 1280 CE, during which time China experienced profound spiritual changes. Among these changes were 1) the development of a Taoist liturgical and monastic meditation system; 2) the entrance of Buddhism into China and its profound influence on Chinese thinking (see chapter three); and 3) a religious reformation more positive and popular than the 400 year later Protestant reformation in Europe.

This period, from the traditional Chinese historian's viewpoint, includes the political division between north and south China, when Buddhism and Taoism developed during a time of strife and disunity, 220-580 CE; the Sui-t'ang period when China reached new heights of poetic and artistic expression, 581-906 CE; and the Five Kingdoms-Sung period when popular culture, reforms in Buddhism and Taoism, and the rise of Mongol supremacy became dominant, from 906-1280 CE. Since the traditional historians of China tended to see history through the biases of the official reigning dynasty, Buddhism, Taoism, and other religious movements received little if any notice in official Confucian records. The biographies of Buddhists, Taoists, women, and non-Chinese were always placed at the end of official dynastic histories, in very abbreviated form.

I. An Outline of Religious Taoism in China
For ease of understanding, we shall divide the history of Chinese religion into four great periods, after the manner of the *I-ching* described in chapter one; 1)*yüan* 元 the primordial spring of Chinese religion before the influence of Yin-yang five element theory on the theory and structure of ritual; 2) *heng* 亨 the summer of religious

27

growth and maturity, when Buddhism and Taoism first grow and flourish; 3) *li* 利 the autumn of religion in China, from the religious reformation until the end of the traditional Chinese empire; and 4) *chen* 貞 the modern dormant period, including the founding of the socialist state until the present. During this last period Chinese religion, which lay hidden under the devastation of the Cultural Revolution, rises again like a phoenix from the ashes of socialist and capitalist materialism in mainland and maritime (Taiwan and overseas) China.

1. Spring: from oracle bones to the First Emperor, 1770-207 BCE. 春
2. Summer: from the Ch'in-Han to the end of T'ang dynasty, and the Five Kingdoms, 207 BCE - 960 CE. 夏
3. Autumn: from the Sung to the last emperor, 960-1912 CE. 秋
4. Winter: from 1912 to the rebirth of religion in China today. 冬

Since all divisions of history into periods are at best heuristic (teaching devices), at worst manifestations of intellectual bias (in as much as the historian arbitrarily decides which event is of historical importance, and which is to be left out), the above division must be taken only as a useful guide to the reader in following the history of religion in China. Unlike the historian, the archaeologist digs up and examines all artifacts found on a given site. The following list of events that occurred during the long development of religion in China should be treated as archeology, rather than history. Artifacts left by Buddhist and Confucian creators can be found in other lists and sources. The combined works of the Japanese scholars Yoshioka and Kubo, among others, provided a basis for the following list.[1]

1. Yüan 元 *The spring of Chinese Religion, 1770-221 BCE*
1200-1181 BCE. Reign of Wu Ting. Oracle divination used in the form of positive-negative modes, precursor of the yang-yin philosophy and the I-ching ___, __ __ cosmology.[2]

The oracle bones show a definite structure presaging the later *I-ching* Book of Changes, and the dichotomy of yin-yang, night-day, heaven-earth-underworld, and the hierarchical nature of the Chinese spiritual cosmos. A highest heavenly emperor *Ti* rules over the realms of heaven, earth, and a post-life underworld. Oracle inscriptions cover every aspect of Chinese life in Shang dynasty China, showing a clear predilection for ancestor memorial, sacrifice to the spirits of the heavens, earth, and underworld, and belief in the existence of a soul in the afterlife which can influence the living. The structure of modern Chinese religion is already cognate in the Shang oracle bones.

1000 BCE. The formation of the earliest *I-ching* text, the first sixty-four lines, before the Confucian commentary on the on the six hexagrams, and the later ten wings.

The *I-ching* is the structural norm for later religious Taoism, the rituals generated by Taoists for village performance, and the rites of prognostication in popular Chinese temples. Ritual meditation for the Taoist is begun by aligning the self with the cosmos, based on the theory that the hexagrams of the I-ching give access to the timeless presence of the Tao in the cosmos. The trigrams structure the sacred T'an area used for performing Taoist ritual.[3] The modern *T'ung-shu* almanac supersedes the *I-ching* as a manual for prognostication, but not as a source of Taoist meditation. Taoists continue to use the two configurations of the I-ching, the *Lo-shu* and *Ho-t'u* (Posterior and Prior Heavenly arrangements of the *I-ching*) as ritual diagrams.

6th-5th Cent BCE. The period of Lao-tzu, and other thinkers. (Kuan-tzu, Yang Chu, later Tao-chia schools).

4th-3rd Cent. BCE. Chuang-tzu, Tsou Yen, Yin-yang Five Element works such as the Lü Shih Ch'un-ch'iu, and early proto Taoists who were known as fang-shih.[4]

The *Lao-tzu Tao-te Ching* Classic, the *Chuang-tzu Nei-p'ien* and the Yin-yang five element cosmology inspire the creation of religious Taoism between 200 BCE to 400 CE. Taoists of the Celestial Master tradition meditate on the Lao-tzu, while the Mao Shan Shang-ch'ing tradition and the Sung dynasty reformed Ch'uan-chen Taoists meditate on the Chuang-tzu. Religious Taoism is a semiotic system that teaches Taoist philosophy by mime, music, and dance. Contrary to the opinion of many Confucian-western scholars, religious and philosophical Taoism are a way that never parted. Many streams feed the massive river of Taoism in China.

219 BCE. Ch'in Shih Huang-ti, the First Emperor, offers the *Feng* sacrifices on Mt. T'ai, and seeks immortality in the east ocean. *Fang-shih* 方士 , proto-Taoists, are popular at court. The First Emperor burns the Confucian books, dies from eating quicksilver for "immortality." The Yin-yang Five Element system becomes the basic cosmology for Chinese religious practice.

210 BCE. The legendary Chang Liang, Eighth generation ascendant of the founder of religious Taoism Chang Tao-ling, assists Liu Pang found the Han dynasty, with a martial art manual given by Huang Shih Kung (apparition of Lao-tzu).

2. *Heng* 亨 *. The summer of Chinese Religion,* 206 BCE - 960 CE

170 BCE. Record of the worship of Huang-Lao, i.e., the Yellow Emperor and Lao-tzu, by Empress Tou.[5]

150-141 BCE. The legendary Mao brothers practice Taoist ascetics and healing atop Mt. Chü-jung (Mao Shan).[6]

Mao Shan Taoism is named after the Mao brothers who founded a meditation and healing center for Taoist practice on Mao Shan, sixty kilometers to the southeast of the southern capital of Nanching (Chinling) in the early Han dynasty. From that time to the present Mao Shan has been a center for the healing arts, meditation, and Taoist legend. Meditation focusing on the circulation of breath, and the Tao's presence in the center of the microcosm, are typical of Mao Shan Taoism.

140 BCE. Han Wu-ti ascends the thrones; patronizes fang-shih, alchemists, and sacrifices atop Mt. T'ai to *T'ai-i* 太乙 The Ming-t'ang ritual to the five directions, spirit emperors, elements, and tones, model for the later Taoist Su-ch'i ritual to renew the five elements, is performed at court. 漢武帝在泰山行封禪事, 建禮記明堂儀

110 BCE. Han Wu-ti performs the *Feng* 封 sacrifices atop Mt. T'ai, and asks for the "Great Peace" (T'ai-p'ing) from the spirit emperor Huang-ti, Taoist patron of central imperial rule. 漢武帝在泰行封禪事,祭祈平安

10 CE. Wang Mang, usurper of the Han throne, takes the title *Shen-hsien Wang* 神仙王 (King of Spirit-immortals), indicating a new importance shown to religio-Taoist belief. 王莽稱神仙王

23 CE. Wang Mang dies, facing the direction in which the tail of *Ursa Major* points, an element in Taoist burial. 王莽向北斗罡位死.

60 CE. Ying, King of Ch'u, offers sacrifice to Huang-Lao and to Fu-t'uo, an early notice of Taoist-Buddhist belief. 英楚王記黃老浮圖

126-144 CE. The *Shun-ti* reign years. 順帝時,琅玡宮崧上獻太平清領書

Kung Ch'ung of Lang-yeh offers the 174 chapter *T'ai-p'ing Ching-ling Shu* to the emperor. Revealed in vision to the legendary Yü Chi, the book is the first religious Taoist manual, combining yin-yang five element cosmology with the rituals and other techniques of the *Fang-shih* religious experts of the four city quarters. 正一盟威天師道

Chang Ling (later Chang Tao-ling) leaves his home in the Kingdom of P'ei, northeast corner of Chianghsi province, central China, and travels to Ku-ming Shan in Szechuan. He founds Celestial Master Taoism, (called *Cheng-i Meng-wei Taoism*). His son and grandson establish a theocratic kingdom of 24 sees or bishoprics. Ts'ao Ts'ao legitimized the movement in 215 CE. The headquarters of this first religious Taoist sect eventually is established in Lung-hu Shan, Chianghsi province, southeast China.

147-168 CE. The *Huan-ti* reign years. Hsiang Kai brings notice of the *T'ai-p'ing ching* to the emperor, warning that the book will bring about great political, social, and religious changes. the Emperor offers official ritual to Lao-tzu at Ku Hsien. 襄楷上獻極高太平經。桓帝在苦縣祀老子.

168-189 CE. The *Ling-ti* reign years. The *T'ai-p'ing Tao* "Way of the Great Peace," a Politico-religious movement, sweeps the central provinces and is wiped out between 184-85 CE. The *T'ai-p'ing Ching* however, continued to have a profound influence on all forms of Taoism, including the Celestial master movement in west and later southeast China. During this time the religious Taoist book *Lao-tzu pien-hua Ching* (The eighty-one transformations of Lao-tzu) appears.

215-224 CE. The Celestial master *Cheng-i Meng-wei* sect is legalized in west China by Ts'ao Ts'ao, who founds the Wei dynasty in 220 CE.

Chang Lu, the third master of Cheng-i Taoism dies in 216 CE. The earliest Taoist catechetical work *Lao-tzu Hsiang-erh Chu* is in circulation by this period. Celestial Master Taoism is the basic source of all later religious Taoist movements. Its use of the *fa-lu* meditation for exteriorizing or voiding the body of all spirits in order to have audience with the Transcendent Tao is a basic ritual and meditative practice of religious Taoism. The Celestial Master Taoists also used the the Ling-pao Five True Writs to renew the five elements in the cosmos. The rite was modeled on the *Ming-t'ang* liturgy of the Han dynasty court to keep the kingdom in harmony with change in nature.

The legendary Ko Hsüan records the earliest *Ling-pao* Taoist scriptures, which he received from Hsü Lai-luo of Mt. Hui-chi. The scriptures were transmitted to master Cheng Szu-yüan, who gave them to Ko Hung before retiring as a recluse (see 302 CE, below). Popular Ling-pao liturgies for village festival were soon amalgamated with the Cheng-i rites of renewal, to create the grand *Chiao* 醮 festival celebrated throughout the length and breadth of China by emperors and peasants alike.[7] 葛玄. 徐來勒. 鄭思遠. 葛洪.

288 CE. Wei Hua-ts'un, a Cheng-i Meng-wei lady Taoist receives the *Yellow Court Canon*, the *Shang-ch'ing* scriptures, and other meditation manuals in a series of visions, in the Jinling (Nanjing), Chü-jung, and the Mao Shan spiritual environment. 魏華存收上清黃庭經

The Shang-ch'ing Highest Pure sect is founded by Wei Hua-ts'un, a woman, China's Theresa of Avila, in the early fourth century. based on the cryptic Inner Chapters of the *Yellow Court Canon*, the new meditative tradition demands that all spirits be emptied from the microcosm before the prayer of union with the Tao is possible. The use of the *Yellow Court Canon* as a meditation manual is proper to the orthodox Taoist tradition. The text is chanted during the Taoist Chiao festivals of Taiwan, Fukien, and other parts of southeast China.[8]

292 CE. Pao Ch'ing edits the *San-huang Wen*, the Writs of the Three Emperors. With the Cheng-i, Ling-pao, and Shang Ch'ing scriptures, the basic writings of religious Taoism are in the process of formulation. By the end of the Third Century three religious movements are transmitted by Taoist masters:

Cheng-i Meng-wei 正一盟威	Ling-pao, San-huang 靈寶三皇	Shang-ch'ing 上清
Lao-tzu Tao-te Ching	Ho-t'u, Lo-shu charts	Yellow Court
24 spirit registers;	Ling-pao Five Writs	Meditations of
Fa-lu rite for exter-	Three Emperors Writs	Emptying
iorizing spirits 老子道德經	Apocryphal texts 河圖洛書靈寶五符	*Chuang-tzu* 黃庭內經

300 CE. The *Hua Hu Ching* (Lao-tzu becomes Buddha in India, converts the Barbarians) is popular. First propagated by the Buddhist missionaries from India, then condemned by Buddhists, the book is forbidden by Buddhist favoring emperors. Buddhist canons are translated during this period by borrowing heavily from Taoist terminology. Hsüan-hsüeh or eccentric Taoist learning becomes popular with the intellectual class. Wang Pi and Kuo Hsiang write learned commentaries on Lao-tzu and Chuang-tzu. 化胡經

302 CE. Cheng Szu-yüan leaves his Taoist library with Ko Hung, and retires to the life of a recluse. Though Lady Wei Hua-ts'un had brought Cheng-i meng-wei Taoism and the *fa-lu* rite to south China, Ko Hung does not seem to understand the Cheng-i tradition, nor the meditations of kenosis-emptying in the later Shang-ch'ing Chuang-tzu tradition. 鄭思遠

317 CE. Ko Hung (D. 343 CE) completes the *Pao P'u Tzu* (The Master who Embraces Simplicity), with a list of Taoist books received from Cheng Szu-yüan. The *Shen-hsien Chuan* (Biography of Spirits and Immortals) is probably completed by this time. 葛洪. 抱朴子

334 CE. The death of Lady Wei Hua-ts'un, whose books are passed down by her sons to Yang Hsi and the two Hsü's, father and son, at the court of Nanjing. These courtiers later take over the works of Lady Wei and "receive them in vision" atop Mao Shan. 魏華存化仙

365 CE. Lady Wei appears in vision to Yang Hsi atop Mao Shan. Yang Hsi and the two Hsü's, whether in vision, under the influence of hemp-laced incense, or psychic vision, re-write the Shang-ch'ing scriptures and are given credit for founding the Mao Shan Shang-ch'ing sect. Whatever the creative or transmittal role of these gentry class courtiers, Mao Shan Taoism brings with it much more than the legacy of these three inspired calligraphers. The grottoes of Mao Shan were a fertile source of Taoism throughout history. 魏華存降傳上清法於楊羲

371 - 386 CE. 371: the death of Hsü Hui; 376: the passing of Hsü Mi; 386: the demise of Yang Hsi. The Shang-ch'ing scriptures are dispersed, to be collated again by T'ao Hung-ching who resides at Mao Shan from 492 CE. (See below). 許翽. 許謐 化仙

402 CE. The death of Sun En, leader of a Taoist rebellion. 孫恩過去

415-425 CE. K'ou Ch'ien-chih establishes the "new" Cheng-i sect. 寇謙之

429 CE. Death of Hsü Huang-min, who leaves the Shang-ch'ing scriptures with two devout laymen, Ma Lang, and Ma Han. 許黃民伍上請經給馮朗馬罕

454 CE. The uprising of Li Hung, a Taoist inspired rebellion.[9] 李弘妖亂起

471 CE. Lu Hsiu-ching's catalogue of the first Taoist Canon, and list of Taoist books. 陸修靜作三洞經書目錄．

Seventh master of Mao Shan, and the liturgical Ling-pao Tradition, Lu divides the Taoist Canon into Three Arcana: 1) The *Tung-chen*, (Cave of the Tao-realized) named after the Shang-ch'ing kenotic tradition; 2) the *Tung-hsüan* (Cave of the Mysterious) named after the Ling-pao ritual tradition; 3) and the *Tung-shen* (Cave of the Spirit), named after the San-huang tradition. Taoist sects are as yet unknown. Cheng-i Meng-wei scriptures seem to have been included under the third *Tung-shen* section. Lu Hsiu-ching dies in 477 CE.

472 CE. Taoists at Wu-tang Shan, home of the Pole Star and Martial Arts Taoism, make "immortal medicine;" (Sun Tao-yin). Liu Liang drinks it, and becomes immortal (dies). 洞真(上清), 洞玄(靈寶), 洞神(三皇)正一道藏．

492-536 CE. The scholar T'ao Hung-ching builds a study on Mao Shan, and with imperial patronage, collates and catalogues the Mao Shan Shang-ch'ing scriptures. 陶弘景隱居茅山．

A scholarly rather than a liturgical Taoist, T'ao is credited with saving and critically editing the Shang-ch'ing texts, a process described in the *Chen-kao* (TT. 637-640). One of the most respected men of his times, his funeral was attended by courtiers and Buddhists alike. T'ao Hung-ching's role was that of conserving the sacred Shang-ch'ing scriptures, rather than fulfilling the duties of a liturgical Taoist. Mao Shan Taoists were and continue to be experts in the prayer of internal alchemy, liturgy, and healing, rather than collators and editors of manuscripts.

528 CE. The birth of Wang Yüan-chih, tenth master of Mao Shan. 王遠智生

Wang succeeds T'ao, as a liturgical master of Mao Shan, rather than a collator of books. Wang lives through the end of the North-south period, the Sui dynasty, well into the T'ang (d. 653 CE., 125 years old). Wang and his successors added the ritual element to Shang-ch'ing Mao Shan Taoism, making it, with Ling-pao and Cheng-i, a part of what was later to become a "Three Mountain Alliance" during the Sung dynasty.

568 CE. Chen Luan, a Buddhist monk, completes the *Hsiao Tao Lun*, a treatise "Laughing at Taoism." (*Taisho*, V. 52, #2103). 甄鸞作笑道論．

569 CE. Wei Yüan-sung and others adapt Buddhist sutras to the Taoist Canon. Taoists use Buddhist *ching* and Taoist *ch'an* i.e., chants of merit and litanies of repentance, to create rituals aimed at popular religion and court ritual. 衛元嵩等,佛作道經

574-577 CE. Emperor Wu of the northern Chou dynasty supports Buddhism and Taoism. The Taoist encyclopedia *Wu-shang Pi-yao* is published, with complete *chiao* liturgies of renewal, used by the Taoists for court and popular village ritual. 北周時,無上祕要

581 CE. Founding of the Sui dynasty, and the re-unification of the empire. The Emperor supports Buddhism and Taoism. 隋朝建國

605 CE. Emperor Yang-ti builds a Taoist shrine in Lo-yang city, the *Yu-ch'ing Hsüan-t'an*. 隋煬帝建玉清玄壇

611 CE. Wang Yüan-chih, tenth Master of Mao Shan offers a *Chiao* ritual Emperor Yang-ti atop Mt. Sung (near the Shao-lin temple) 嵩山作醮

618 CE. Founding of the T'ang dynasty, by the house of Li. Taoists claim that the Emperor is a descendant of Lao-tzu. 唐朝建國.

622 CE. Publication of monk Fa Lin's *P'o-hsieh Lun*, a Buddhist diatribe against Taoism. (See *Taisho*, V. 52, #2109). 法琳作破邪論.

623 CE. Li Hsiang-feng composes the first Taoist manuals using *chen-yen* sanskrit seed words, mudras, mantras, the date-wood thunder block, and vajra-thunder magic. (TT. 631-636). 真言.雷法

624 CE. Court sponsored debates between Confucian, Buddhist, and Taoist. 儒.佛.道談論.

645 CE. The monk Hsüan-tsang returns to China from India with the Buddhist Canon. 玄奘歸長安

653 CE. Mao Shan Taoist Wang Yüan-chih dies, 125 years old. 王遠智化仙

666 CE. Emperor Kao-tsung performs the *Feng* and *Shan* sacrifices atop T'ai Shan, then proclaims that Buddhist and Taoist shrines must be built in each prefecture. 高宗在泰山作封禪記

668 CE. The *Lao-tzu Hua-hu Ching* (Lao-tzu converts the Barbarians i.e., becomes Buddha in India) burned at imperial order. 老子化胡經焚毀

705 CE. The *Lao-tzu Hua-hu Shuo* theory claiming that Lao-tzu is Buddha is forbidden by imperial order. 老子化胡說禁止

707 CE. Emperor Chung-tsung decrees that a Taoist temple be built in each prefecture. 中宗天下諸州建道觀

711 CE. Princesses Chin Hsien and Yü Chen become Taoist nuns at T'ai-ch'ing monastery, and receive Taoist *Lu* registers, listing all of the Taoist esoteric spirits, rituals, and meditations.

金仙,玉真二公主在太清觀收道籙

712 CE. Taoist Chang Wan-fu completes the *San-tung Ching-chieh Fa-lu*, (TT. 990), showing that the three major Taoist orders are unified under one system of investiture. 張萬福作三洞經戒法籙
735 CE. Szu-ma Ch'eng-chen, great master of Taoist meditation and ritual, resident of Mao Shan and Sung Shan, dies. 司馬承禎化仙

Works in the Taoist Canon show that he was familiar with the *Chuang-tzu Nei-p'ien* and the meditations of kenotic emptying. During the T'ang dynasty a marvelous unity of scriptures and teachings typifies religious Taoism. The ritual and registers of the three great traditions, Shang-ch'ing, Ling-pao, and Cheng-i Meng-wei are arranged in ascending order, with the Mao Shan Shang-ch'ing meditations of decentered emptiness ranked highest. The later Sung dynasty legal stipulations will license this process. A wide variety of Taoist orders and local sects are born during the Sung period (see below).

Besides the three major orders, the Pole Star registers of Mt. Wu-tang in Hupei province, and the Ch'ing-wei registers of T'ang dynasty thunder magic, attributed to a lady Taoist Tsu Shu, become popular during the T'ang and Sung period. See below.
738 CE. Emperor Hsüan-tsung decrees that a Taoist *K'ai-yüan* 開元 temple (the Emperor's reign title) be built in each prefecture. In 744 CE he commissions a 3,744 fascicle Taoist Canon. A school of Taoist studies is instituted; the works of Lao-tzu are made a part of the state civil service examination, and various titles are granted to Lao-tzu.[10]
755 CE. The An Lu-shan rebellion. Emperor Hsüan-tsung flees to Szechuan. Yang Kuei-fei, his favorite concubine, is executed on the way. The flight is commemorated in T'ang dynasty poetry 安祿山亂起
819 CE. Han Yü's famous memorial against the relic of the Buddha. He is exiled to Ch'ao-chou in southeast China, where he worships at the Ch'eng-huang temple, and performs a Taoist exorcism. The beginning of Neo-confucianism, and the borrowing of the *T'ai-chi T'u-shuo* chart from the Taoist caves of Hua Shan 華山太極圖說
845 CE. The mad emperor Wu orders the burning of Buddhist temples and the laicization of thousands of monks and nuns. Japanese monks bring back esoteric tantric Buddhism to Japan from Ch'ang an, Wu-t'ai Shan, and Mt. T'ien-t'ai, between 804-845. 武宗滅佛教
847 CE. Emperor Hsüan decrees the restoration of Buddhism.

889 CE. The lady Taoist Tsu Shu popularizes a tantric form of Taoist Thunder rites known as the *Ch'ing-wei* "Pure Subtle" form of thunder meditation. The new thunder sect was approved and adopted by the Cheng-i sect of Lung-hu Shan, Shang-ch'ing Mao Shan, and Wu-tang Shan's Pole Star Taoism. 祖舒成立清微雷法

901 CE. The Taoist master of Szechuan Tu Kuang-t'ing flourishes. Patronized by the court, Tu wrote many treatises on Taoist liturgy, the Chiao festival, and Thunder ritual. 杜光庭旺盛

906 - 907 CE. The end of the T'ang dynasty, and the beginning of the Five Dynasties period. 唐朝末年

947 CE. P'eng Hsiao's redaction of the *Chou-i Ts'an-t'ung-ch'i*, combining the Yin-yang Five Element cosmology with the *I-ching* and the meditative process of inner alchemy. 彭曉 周易參同契諧

952 CE. Chu Hsiao-wai builds an altar dedicated to the Taoist Canon in the Tung-po Kung on Mt. T'ien-t'ai.

955 CE. Emperor Shih Tsung of the later Chou dynasty outlaws Buddhism in China. 後周世宗廢佛教

3. *Li* 利 *Autumn: the Religious Reformation, 960-1912 CE*

Emperors support the formation of new Taoist sects, and fund wood block editions of the Taoist Canon.

960 CE. The Sung dynasty is established. Buddhism is restored. 宋朝建立

985 CE. The Taoist Canon in the Tung-po Kung on Mt. T'ien-t'ai is brought to the Sung dynasty capital. Sung emperors support publications of the Taoist Canon. 桐柏道藏運首都

990 CE. Hsü, Wang, et alii edit a 3,737 volume Taoist Canon. 徐王編修道藏

1011-1015 CE. Emperor Chin-tsung offers prayers in various Taoist temples, builds Taoist temples, and grants Lao-tzu the official titles *T'ai-shang Lao-chun Hun-yüan Huang-ti* (Great Highest Lord Lao One-with-primordial Emperor), sponsors Taoist books. 太上老君混元上德皇帝

1016 CE. Wang Ch'in-juo's 4,359 volume *Pao-wen T'ung-lu* Canon.

1019 CE. Chang Chun-fang's 4,565 volume *Ta Sung T'ien Kung Pao* Taoist Canon. Emperor Chen-tsung prays in the Taoist T'ai-i temple.

大宗天宮寶藏

1030 CE. The twenty-fifth generation descendant of Chang Tao-ling Chang Ch'ien-yao is granted the title "Master Void Peace." 張乾曜.

号作"虛靖真人"

1030 CE. Chang Chun-fang completes the *Yun-chi Ch'i-ch'ien*, a massive encyclopedia of Sung dynasty Taoist lore (TT. 677- 702). The collection lacks the ritual *Chiao* manuals of classical orthodox Taoism, and the rubrical instructions for liturgy, a part of the privately transmitted lore of the Taoist priest. 張君房編雲笈七籤

1037 CE. The Wu Yun Temple built at Mao Shan by the emperor. 五雲觀

1064 CE. The 4,500 volume Ch'ung-Tao Kuan Canon is collected by Yao Juo-yü and others, in Ch'eng-tu, west China. 成都府姚若裕編崇道觀道藏

1080 C + E. Mao Shan Taoists study and teach the *Tao-te Ching*, the *Tu-jen Ching*, the *Chuang-tzu*, the Yellow Register Chai and Gold Register Chiao rites, in the reformed Shang-ch'ing tradition.

1086 CE. Liu Hun-k'ang, Twenty-fifth generation Mao Shan master, heals the illness of Emperor Che-tsung's concubine. He is entitled *Tung-yüan T'ung-miao*, Master of Shang-ch'ing Temples 劉混康治哲宗妃之病

1093 CE. Official attempts to curb the growing religious reformation by forbidding private reception of Taoist orders. 道師私度禁止

1098 CE. The meditation Yüan-fu Monastery built on Mao Shan. 元符觀建作

1102 CE. Official approval of the popular cult to the Three Mao brothers atop Mao Shan. 茅山三君加封

1103 CE. Liu Hun-k'ang builds the Wan-fu Kung temple for popular pilgrimages atop Great Mao Shan. 劉混康建萬福宮

1105 CE. Emperor Hui-tsung grants the title "Master Void Quiet" to Chang Chi-hsien, Thirtieth Generation descendant of Chang Tao-ling, and master of Lung-hu Shan. 三十代天師号作虛靜先生 張繼先. 天師府.

1106 CE. Popular "Three Religions are One" images and devotions forbidden in official Taoist and Buddhist temples. 天下寺廟禁用三教像

1113 CE. Emperor Hui-tsung orders the gathering of Taoist books from throughout the empire, for a new Taoist Canon. 徽宗求天下道教仙經

1115 CE. Completion of the 5,480 Vol. Wan-shou Taoist Canon. The founding of the Liao Chin dynasty in north China 萬壽道藏完成, 北方建金國.

1116 CE. Lin Ling-su, (Wen-chow, Chechiang Province) favored at the court of Emperor Hui-tsung. The *T'ai-shang Chu-kuo Chiu-min Tsung-chen Mi-yao*, By Yüan Miao-tsung, is completed. Typical of modern "Redhead" Taoism, this reformation text teaches a Taoism totally involved in summoning and controlling spirits, without mention of "kenosis" meditation. Reformatiom Taoist texts are transmitted in brotherhood, not in master-disciple relation. 元妙宗編太上助國救民總真秘要

1117-1120 CE. The *Shen-hsiao* Taoist sect is founded and favored by the court. Lin Ling-su is at first patronized, then expelled from the court. His version of Shen-hsiao reform Taoism is rejected in 1120 CE. Lin returns to Wen-chow, Chekiang, 1119 CE. 神霄派成立. 林靈素遭放溫州.

1127 CE. Beginning of the Southern Sung period. The northern Chin capture and enslave Hui-tsung. Temples named after the Shen-hsiao movement are renamed. About this time Taoist ranks at ordination are regulated. 南宋建國. 天下神霄宮改舊名.

1138 CE. Founding of the reformed T'ai-i Taoist sect. 太一道派成立

1142 CE. Founding of the Chen-ta Taoist sect. 真大道派成立

1159 CE. Wang Chung-yang, founder of Ch'uan-chen reform Taoism, professes Taoism and is called an avatar of Lü Tung-p'in, a T'ang Taoist master canonized as one of the "Eight Immortals." 王重陽入道

1161 CE. Wang Chung-yang retires to a cave, and practices Zen like Taoist meditation. He places a tombstone over the cave where he meditates, declaring himself dead to the world. 王重陽穴居打坐

1164 CE. The *Kan-ying P'ien* treatise declaring that human acts are meritorious for freeing souls from Buddhist-Taoist hell, becomes one of the basic texts of the popular religious reformation. Devotional practices of lay men and women dominate Sung dynasty religious reforms. 太上感應篇作成

1166 CE. Hsiao Pao-ch'en founds the T'ai-i Taoist sect 蕭抱珍

1167-1169 CE. Wang Chung-yang establishes the first Ch'uan-chen communities of religious men, based on celibacy, simplicity, and Zen-like meditation. Ch'uan-chen values meditation first, acts of merit for souls second, and a simplified Chiao rite souls third, when requested by emperor or people. He dies in 1170 CE. Reformation Taoism allows celibate nuns and lay meditation until modern day China. 全真派成立

1171 CE. Completion of a Ch'ing-ching sect Taoist center. 淨明道派

1190 CE. The Chin Emperor (N. China) forbids Taoist and Buddhist private ordination without state approval. The 6,455 Vol. Sun Ming-tao Taoist Canon is completed. 金皇帝禁止僧道私度. 孫明道大金玄都寶藏完成

1197-1201 CE. The Chin emperor patronizes the Ch'uan-chen Taoists Wang Yu-yang and Liu Ch'ang-ch'un. They offer a Chiao rite for the Chang-tsung emperor in the T'ai-ch'ing temple (1201 CE) 王玉陽. 劉長生建醮

1200 CE. Death of the Neo-confucian scholar Chu Hsi. Completion of the *Wu-shang Huang-lu Ta-chai Li-ch'eng Yi*, a grand collection of Taoist rituals for all occasions. 無上黃籙大齋立成儀 編集

1205 CE. The Ch'uan-chen Taoist Ch'iu Ch'ang-chun performs the Chiao ritual at Lai-chou, for the emperor. 丘長春在萊州建醮，

1207 CE. The Chin emperor's concubine Lady Li gives a complete Taoist Canon to Ch'iu Ch'ang-ch'un. The T'ai-i Taoist master Hsiao Hsü-chi successfully offers two Chiao rituals for rain, and to curb an infestation of insects. 金章宗妃李氏下賜道藏於丘長春

1216-1222 CE. The Ch'uan-chen Taoist Ch'iu Ch'ang-ch'un is patronized successively by the southern Sung Emperor (1216), the Chin Emperor, and Chingis Khan. 宋、金、元皇召丘長春．

1224-1255 CE. Ch'uan-chen Taoism favored by Chinese and Mongol.

1257 CE. Debate at the court of Kublai Khan between Buddhists and Taoists. The Taoists lose, and Kublai orders that the *Lao-tzu Hua-hu Ching* (see 668 CE above, the text claiming that Lao-tzu went to India and became the Buddha) be burned. Some sources say that 28 Taoists were beheaded. 佛道論爭、道側敗

1269 CE. Kublai Khan declares the five ancestors and the seven founders of the Ch'uan-chen sect immortal *chen-jen*. 全真五祖七真加封真人

1271 CE. Beginning of the Yüan-Mongol dynasty. 元朝建國

1276-1280 CE. Kublai Khan brings the 36th generation head of the Cheng-i sect, the 43rd generation master of Shang-ch'ing Mao Shan Taoism, and other Taoist leaders to court for official approval and support. The Yüan dynasty holds to the policy of supporting all religions, for state blessing. 三十六代天師．四十三代茅山師朝見

1300 CE. Completion of the massive canonical collection of Ling-pao rituals, the *Ling-pao Ling-chiao Chi-tu Chin-shu*. 靈寶領教濟度金書

1368 CE. Founding of the Ming dynasty. 明朝建國

Emperor Ming T'ai-tsu attributed the success of the campaign to overthrow the Yüan and establish the Ming to the martial spirit Hsüan-t'ien Shang-ti, patron of Wu-tang Shan in Hupei province (1410-1425 CE). Later the Yung-lo Emperor built a beautiful monastic complex on the Wu-tang cliffs, and in the Cheng-t'ung reign years sponsored a woodblock edition of the Taoist Canon. The Ming rulers passed laws forcing Taoists to be licensed by the great Taoist centers. Grand Chiao rituals were still offered for the nation's blessing, but Taoism never again attained the official or intellectual status it held during the T'ang and Sung dynasties. Yet Taoism had a deep influence on Ming and Ch'ing dynasty thinkers, as seen in Liu Ts'un-yen, *New Excursions from the Hall of Harmonious Winds* (Leiden:1984).

1644 CE. Founding of the Ch'ing dynasty. 清朝建國

1580-1640 CE. Taiwan is settled by peasants and merchants from Fukien province across the straits. 福建省閩．客定居台湾．

Ming loyalists set up a kingdom in exile under Cheng Ch'eng-kung (Koxinga). Taoists come from Fukien and Kwangtung to serve the needs of the Minnan and Hakka speaking settlers. Taiwan submitted to Ch'ing rule in 1683, and becomes a subsidiary of Fukien province, then a semi-independent territory, up until the annexation by the Japanese Colonial Empire in 1895. During this period, especially after 1780 when Taoists came from Mao Shan, Lung-hu Shan, and the southern part of Fukien Province to north Taiwan, a very traditional form of classical Taoist Chiao ritual became popular in Hsinchu, T'ao-yuan, and Taipei.

1780 CE. The arrival of Chuang Ch'eng, a Taoist from Mao Shan who settled in Hsinchu city. 茅山道師莊誠定居新竹，北斗，清微法傳與台湾．

1823 CE. The arrival of Wu Ching-ch'un, from T'a Shan outside of Ch'üan-chou city, south Fukien. Wu's ancestors had studied Taoism at Hua Shan and Wu-tang Shan. 華山．武當山道師吳氏定居新竹，台湾。

1850-1868 CE. The Lin clan of Hsinchu city, military officials of the city, patronize Taoist ritual and poetry. Ch'en Chieh-san is appointed leader of the Taoist association. 新竹林家照顧道教

1886-1888 CE. Lin Ju-mei, fifth son of the Lin clan, leads an expedition to Lung-hu Shan, San-ch'ing Kung in Chianghsi, to purchase a 2,000 tael collection of Taoist books from the 61st Generation Celestial master. Upon returning to Hsinchu city, the Cheng-i Ssu-t'an (Heirs to the Cheng-i Tradition) was organized, with Ch'en Chieh-san as leader. 林汝梅訪閩龍虎山，正一嗣壇建立

1892-1896 CE. Lin Hsiu-mei, ninth son of the Lin family, lives at Lung-hu Shan, San-ch'ing Kung for four years, and learns the meditations of the Yellow Court Canon, the Ch'uan-chen Zen like meditations, and the Cheng-i rituals of emptying kenosis. 林修梅隱居龍虎山

1906 CE. The *Tao-tsang Chi-yao* (Essentials of the Taoist Canon) is published in Ch'eng-tu, Szechuan. 道藏輯要編集

4. Chen 真 *The winter of Chinese religion, 1912 to the Present*

1912 CE. Founding of the Republic of China. 中華民國建立

1913 CE. The Taoist Association of China established at the Pai-yun Kuan monastery (Ch'uan-chen sect) in Beijing. 中國道教總會組織与白雲觀

1919 CE. May 4th movement, the rejection of China's traditional past, and western democracy; Versaille treaty gave the colonial possessions of Germany in Shantung to Japan, for joining the allies in WW I. 五四運動
1921 CE. Founding of the Chinese Communist Party. 中國共產黨成立
1923-26 CE. Completion of the printing of the *Cheng-t'ung Tao-tsang* (Cheng-t'ung Taoist Canon), the Commercial Press, Shanghai.
1938 CE. The Japanese Army burns Mao Shan, the Ming dynasty woodblocks of the Taoist Canon, and executes the Taoists. 日軍燒茅山
1949 CE. Founding of the people's Republic of China. 人民中國建立
1950 CE. Beginning of the "Three Self" religious movement in China; Buddhist and Taoist Studies Association, and the United Front Bureau of the Communist Party established to watch over religion in the socialist state. 三自運動開始
1967-1979 CE. The Great Cultural Revolution. Religious freedom denied, and religious shrines closed. Mao Shan burned. 文化大革命燒茅山。
1975 CE. Publishing of the *Chuang-lin Hsü Tao-tsang*, books brought to Taiwan from Lung-hu Shan in 1886.[11] 莊林續道藏編集
1979 CE. Restoration of religious freedom in China. The state supports the restoration of religious shrines, and subsidizes the training of priests, monks, ministers, and mullahs. 宗教信仰恢復

II. Taoist Liturgy and Meditation
Arthur Waley's sensitive work *Three Ways of Thought in Ancient China* treats of Chuang-tzu the Taoist, Meng-tzu (Mencius) the moralist, and pragmatic *Fa-chia* legalists and their influence on Chinese political and cultural life style. The Chinese scholar Ku Chieh-kang further divided the thinkers of ancient China into six schools of religious-cultural thought:
1. Taoist nature———————————┐
2. Muo-tzu's universal concern—————————Religious Taoism
3. Yin-yang Five Element cosmos———┘
4. Confucian ethics———————————┐
5. 100 schools of logic———————————— Confucian state
6. Legalist politics———————————┘

Records of ritual in China's religious springtime are limited to the classical writings promoted by the confucian scholars and officials. The *Book of Odes*, the *I-ching* in the earliest 64 lines, and the *Shu Ching* Book of History record court sacrifices and seasonal rituals. The original line of Chapter 45, the *I-ching* reads:[12]

> *Ts'ui* 萃, A Large Gathering.
> *Heng* 亨 , (Spring, sacrifice)
> The King retires for an ancestral hall rite.
> It is beneficial to go see a Great Man.
> Offer sacrifice; benefit; contemplate/prognosticate.
> Use a *Ta-sheng* (large animal) for the rite.
> Good fortune! Beneficial to have a distant goal.

How the common people worshipped is only occasionally reflected, as in the Confucian *Lun-yü* where the master is seen holding his ears and protecting his ancestral shrine from the noisy *nuo* exorcisms and proto-lion dancers of popular religion. The scholarly stance of holding the ears and closing the eyes to popular ritual is not found in the Chuang-tzu, who is unafraid to rejoice rather than mourn death. Death is seen in the Taoist eyes as a passing to immediate awareness of Transcendent Tao. Taoists were called upon almost from the beginning of post Han-dynasty Taoist ritual, to refine the soul of a beloved departed in the alchemical fires of *Huang-lu Chai* (Yellow register Chai) burial ceremony, as will be seen below.

From the ancient religion of the Oracle Bones and the *I-ching*, when the in-out, motion-rest philosophy was first expressed in semiotic form, and the later Han dynasty Yin-yang based ritual system was created, lived two of China's most important religious philosophers. Lao-tzu's *Tao-te Ching*, and Chuang-tzu's *Chuang-tzu Nei-p'ien*, developed during the 5th-3rd centuries BC, became the formative texts for the Taoist system of internal alchemy (*nei-tan* 内丹) meditation. The inspiration for the meditative philosophy of empty center developed by later Cheng-i and Shang-ch'ing Taoists was inspired by these two works. The opening lines of the Lao-tzu express the philosophy of emptying thus:[13]

> Tao that can be walked is not the eternal Tao. 道
> Name that can be spoken is not the eternal name. 名
> *Wu* (Transcendent) name, is heaven and earth's origin. 無始
> *Yu* with name, is the myriad creatures' mother (ch'i). 有,母 .

43

Thus, be *wu* ch'i-empty, to contemplate it's mystery; 氣妙
Be *yu* ch'i-filled, to penetrate its utmost reaches. 徼
These two states (*wu* and *yu*) are internally one, 一
Externally only are they named differently. 同
Both are called *hsüan*, deep mystery. 玄
Mystery is itself empty of mystery, 妙
The gateway to all that is wondrous mystery. 門

To empty the mind of ch'i breath, i.e., the attention of intellect to the outermost extent of the Tao working in nature, and the intention of the will to acquire, are conditions for being aware of the *Wu* transcendent act of the Tao gestating. To do this, the Lao-tzu text teaches an attitude towards things that is freed from relativity in judgment, from the desire of possession, and from self-centered action.[14]

For everyone under heaven, beauty and its
Opposite are matters of mental judgment,
As are the "good" and "not good."
Thus, the judgment *wu* not to have (transcendent)
And *Yu* to have, (immanent) are related to the judger,
As are hard and easy, tall and short, high and low.
Sound needs a hearer; before demands an after.
That's why the sage serves *Wu-wei* (Non Act)[15]
And follows the teaching without words.
The myriad creatures do it without speaking.
They give birth and let go,
Do their work without fuss,
Succeed and don't dwell on it.
That's why (Tao) never leaves them.

In a humorous paradoxical manner Lao-tzu teaches the ruler and the ascetic to be freed from mental image and heart desires, to fill the intuitive powers of the belly with the Transcendent de-centered presence:[16]

Don't reward the worthy, and the people won't fight.
Don't value things hard-to-get, there'll be no thieves.
Don't look at desirables, and the heart won't flutter.
This is how the (Taoist) sage rules:
Void the heart, fill the belly;
Weaken willful desire, strengthen the bones.
Let the people cherish *Wu* empty mind and will,

And the knowledge-centered won't dare rule (act).

Act the *Wu* (Tao-transcendent) way,

And all will be well governed.

The doctrine of the empty non-center is taught in chapter six of the Lao-tzu. In this crucial text the term "Valley spirit" refers to the place in which the Tao eternally gestates *yüan-ch'i* i.e., the primordial female source of yin-yang and the entire cosmos. The valley in which spirit resides is an empty non-center. The word valley (ku 谷) refers to an empty, decentered place, which is able to respond to the cosmos, by producing breath and blessing equally to each of the myriad creatures, friend and foe, good and bad, because it is empty. The logico-centered intellect, the good-oriented will, even the most sacred of spiritual images may not penetrate this place.

In an analogy to Paul's "The eye has not seen, the near not heard, nor the mind conceived" (the vision of God), the Valley Spirit can give birth to yang and yin, heaven and earth, from within the de-structured non-center (the valley is "below" center, i.e., out of reach of the will and intellect), because it is empty. Tao dwells there and gives birth within it. The reason why this eternal female womb, the *hun-t'un* cosmic egg, can continually spin out the thread of life breath, is because it is gestated from the eternally present transcendent act, *Wu-wei chih Tao*.[17] The eternally gestating Tao is the focus of Taoist ritual and meditation in the religious Taoist tradition.

The valley spirit does not die,

That is, the mysterious female;

The gate of the mysterious female,

Is the source of heaven (yang) and earth (yin).

It spins and spins, from (Tao's) eternal presence.

Use it, it cannot be exhausted.

The interpretation of this cryptic passage of the Lao-tzu in the above manner, i.e., after the manner of the mystic prayer of kenosis or emptying, is proper to two of the above named Taoist traditions, i.e., the Cheng-i Meng-wei of Lung-hu Shan in Chianghsi Province, and the Shang-ch'ing Yellow Court Canon of Mao Shan in Chiangsu Province. In the Cheng-i meng-wei tradition, the body is seen to be occupied by not one but many spiritual energies, that must be ex-teriorized or sent out of the body during meditation in the Tao's presence.[18] In the Shang-ch'ing Yellow Court tradition, attributed to

45

the lady taoist Wei Hua-ts'un, the multitude of spiritual forces within the entire body are given names, visualized, and cast out from the body. In a prayer which totally decenters and destructures the microcosmic center of the meditator, a true kenosis or emptying of mind and heart is effected by color visualization and inner alchemy.[19]

To the Cheng-i meng-wei tradition and its *fa-lu* rite for sending even the most sacred spirits out of the body, can be attributed the beginnings of Taoist liturgy. To the Shang-ch'ing order and the meditating monks of Mao Shan is credited the founding of kenotic meditative Taoism. The third great order, the Ling-pao sect with its *new text* yin-yang style liturgy must be credited with developing and structuring the grand Chiao liturgies of renewal and chai rites of burial.[20] The development of these three movements took place between the third and sixth centuries CE, as seen in the following chart:

1000 BC to 300 BC
Lao-tzu   I-ching   Yin-yang 5 Elements   Inner Alchemy, Chuang-tzu
Healing, spirits   Ritual   Meditation
200 CE to 500 CE
Cheng-i Taoism   Ling-pao Taoism   Shang-ch'ing Taoism
600 CE to 900 CE
Pole Star, (martial arts) Taoism   Ch'ing-wei, Tantric Taoism
900 CE to 1300 CE
Shen Hsiao and popular Taoism   Ch'uan-chen monastic Taoism

Three major Taoist orders are seen in the above chart to come into existence from the end of the Han period to the end of the north-south period, i.e., between 200 CE through 580 CE. By the time of the T'ang dynasty a marvelous unity of Taoist ritual, meditation, and a written canonical tradition existed. Taoist ritual was popular at court and in the peasant villages. The Chiao rites of renewal were offered throughout China, wherever Taoists dwelled. Both monastic Taoists who lived on sacred hilltops and shrines, and fire-dwelling Ling-pao and Cheng-i Taoists who married and acted as village wine libationers (chi-chiu祭酒) performed these rites.

The semiology of the three sections of the macrocosm (heaven, earth, water) that correspond to head, chest, and belly within man, the multiple soul theory, the burial rites that hastened the alchemical purification of the *hun* soul in the fires of hell, and many other basically Taoist themes were a part of religious iconography found in tombs, temple friezes, and canonical writings of the north-south period and the T'ang. These same semiotic themes were acted out in Taoist ritual. Taoists were able to do these marvelous rites which emptied the village temple of its spirits and made the Tao present, because they knew the mind and heart emptying meditations of internal alchemy. Taoists thus became spiritual mandarins, who stood before the Transcendent Tao during Taoist ritual, to present the ordinary people's and the emperor's petitions to the Gestator of water, earth, and heaven, after exteriorizing (de-centering) the myriad spirits.

The ritual in which alchemical meditation is enacted, and the spirits of nature are sent out of the temple before an audience with the Transcendent Tao, is called *Chai-chiao*. Though the term Yellow Register *chai* eventually was used only for burial ritual, and Golden Register *chiao* for the renewal of life, in the beginning of religious Taoism the terms were used interchangeably. The ritual structure of the *chai* and the *chiao* are internally one. In its earliest format, the basic structure was as follows:[21]

Text   *Inner Alchemy meditation*

1. *Su-ch'i* 宿啟 The Night Announcement. During this ritual the Ling-pao Five True Writs representing the five elements in nature, can in the classical Taoist system, be planted in five bushels of rice (a pure ritual area) to hold audience with the Tao. The liturgy is analogous to the New text Ming-t'ang ritual.[22]

2. *Tsao-ch'ao* 早朝 The Morning Audience with the Tao. During this ceremony the green breath of east's wood and the red vapor of south's fire can be mixed in the meditative furnace inside the Taoist's belly, and refined into prime breath (purple).

3. *Wu-ch'ao* 午朝 The Noon Audience with the Tao. The yellow vapor of earth's center, a symbol of the willful soul-spirit, is purified in the alchemical fires of meditation. The soul, purified of willed desire, is visualized as bright gold.

4. *Wan-ch'ao* 晚朝 The Night Audience with the Tao. The white light of west's metal and the dark blue of north's water are refined by the interior fire's of meditation into a bright white aura, symbol of intuitive awareness of Tao's presence in the microcosm.

5. *Tao-ch'ang* 道場 Also called *Cheng-chiao*正醮the moment of total kenosis (hsü) in the Chiao. The three visualized vapors, purple ch'i, yellow shen spirit, and white intuitive awareness are totally burned away in the *Yellow Court*, the "valley" where Tao is present. Note that the five true writs, "planted" during the *Su-ch'i* rite are meditatively harvested and stored in the five internal organs during the Tao-ch'ang Cheng-chiao ritual.[23]

The Taoist liturgical tradition calls for a non-closure of textual meaning, in the interpretation of meditation texts. A wide variety of interpretative meaning is possible because the texts are *eidetic* in nature, i.e., moving, creative visions not bound by a dictionary definition or a single static experience. The meditations of the kenosis-emptying tradition are not taught, for instance, to the outsider or the novice in Taoist meditation. The so-called *k'ou-ch'uan* tradition, as will be seen below, permits the Taoist master to teach a simple method of visualizing spirits to the people and the novice, saving the meditations of emptiness to those men and women able to follow the ascetic tradition. Openness to textual meaning exists in the Buddhist Zen (Ch'an) *koan*, and in the tradition of the Asian and European storyteller. In the words of Roland Barthes:[24]

> In this way the Text is restored to language: like language, it is structured but decentered without closure... The text is plural. This does not mean just that it has several meanings, but rather that it achieves plurality of meaning, an irreducible plurality.

Jacques Derrida, in applying the principles of post-structural criticism to language, uses the term *différance* to describe the putting off definition or closure of meaning indefinitely, deferring to the experience of the language user.[25]

> Note that the word "writing" has ceased to designate signifier of the signifier, but... describes, on the contrary, the movement of language; in its origin, to be sure, but one can suspect , an origin whose can be spelled as "signifier of the signifier" (it) bolts off and effaces itself in its own production.

Much as Barthes defers to the story-teller, or the Zen master to the insight of the disciple who creatively solves the *koan*, the Taoist master in the best sense of the Lao-tzu teaches the disciple to suspend all judgment at the moment of kenosis, by a creative color visualization not depending on words for realization. But the text can also be taught to the unaware foreign scholar or lay people of the village, as a presenting of memorials to the spirits of the heavens, earth, and watery underworld.[26] Thus the wording of the *chiao* liturgical text is open to at least two distinct interpretative traditions, and the meditative tradition to even more orally transmitted meanings.[27]

Even though the Cheng-i, Ling-pao, and Shang-ch'ing Taoist masters shared the manuals, music, and sacred dance steps used in the above five rituals, not all of the masters taught the kenotic meditations concomitant with the external details of the rite. Only some masters of the Cheng-i and Shang-ch'ing tradition taught the Chiao rites as an external manifestation of internal alchemy, portrayed in the eidetic (creative) imagination of the Taoist master. Other Taoists, especially after the Sung dynasty reformation, taught the rites as 1) the establishment of a Taoist *t'an*壇 sacred area by planting talismans in five bushels of rice; 2) the sending off of documents to the spiritual rulers of the heavens, earth, and underworld, during the Three Audiences with the Tao; and finally 3) used the *Cheng-chiao Tao-ch'ang* liturgy to portray receiving a grand rescript from the heavens, granting blessing to the community of men and women offering the Chiao. Some masters used both traditions simultaneously.

In the dramatic ritual tradition, the five talismans planted in the bushels of rice during the Su-ch'i, were harvested during the Tao-ch'ang to renew the eternal cycling process of nature.[28] One and the same Taoist master could teach the five rituals as internal meditation to his disciples, and as the sending off of petitions and winning of blessing for the people of the community.[29] The many meanings assigned to Taoist meditation texts by masters were eventually regulated and licensed by the imperial government, from the Sung dynasty onward.[30]

The five basic *Chai-chiao* rituals listed above, i.e., the Su-ch'i, Morning, Noon and Night Audiences, and the Tao-ch'ang, (also called *She-chiao*, and *Cheng-chiao*) occur again and again in the earliest Canonical records.[31] The canonical texts of the five basic rites are standardized for all of China. Wherever the Chiao liturgy is performed in the Cheng-i Meng-wei, the Shang-ch'ing, or the Ling-pao tradition, the five rites are found. Many other rituals are added to these core Chiao liturgies, as follows:

49

1. The *Fa-piao* 發表 , announcing the Chiao-chai to the cosmos.
2. The *Ch'ing-shen* 請神 , inviting all spirits to attend the rite.
3. The *Chin-t'an* 禁壇 , to create and purify a sacred area.
4. The posting of flags and banners to signify the sacred area.
5. The *Wu-hung* 午供 , noontime offerings to assembled spirits.
6. The *Fen-teng* 分燈, acting out the 42nd chapter of Lao-tzu.[32]
7. The *Hsieh-shen* 謝神 , thanking and seeing off the spirits.

  Though elements of these rites, aimed at popular religion and
the needs of the people, are Taoist in origin, they differ in one important aspect from the basic five Chai-chiao rites of classical Taoist
liturgy. The five classic Chai-chiao rites all begin with the *fa-lu* 發爐
(Lighting the Interior Alchemy fires) meditation, in order to expel all
of the spirits from the body of the meditator. The refining of the five
elements, the three primordial breaths (purple *ch'i* breath, yellow *shen*
spirit, and white *ching* intuition), and the voiding of the microcosmic
center, all depend on the fires of internal alchemy for realization.
When the meditations of kenotic emptying are done, the Taoist
masters of the Three Mountain classical tradition close the process
with the converse *Fu-lu* 復爐 ritual, which restores the exteriorized
spiritual powers to their original places within the microcosm.[33]

  The above seven rites, on the other hand, do not use the *Fa-lu*
fire visualization as a means of exteriorizing and decentering the
body's intellectual, imaginative, and self-willed powers. The rites of
popular Taoism, reformed Taoism (such as the Ch'uan-chen sect), and
the lower grades of classical Taoist orders perform Taoist ritual in the
sense of controlling spirits, sending off memorials to the heavens, and
praying for nature's blessing. It can be stated, from the surface face-
value in fact, that the goals of the popular religion are *kataphatic*, i.e.,
self-fulfilling and rewarding, while the goals of the ascetic quest are
apophatic, i.e., aimed at kenotic emptying. The use of Buddhist style
rites by Taoists follows the kataphatic model.

  The third great influence in the making of popular Taoist
liturgy aimed at the needs of the people, was Buddhist ritual. The saf-
fron, grey, and black robed monks of Chinese Buddhism won the
hearts and imagination of the villagers and farmers of China. Missionary monks, among other *upaya* skillful means, created lengthy rites for
the dead. Though such burial ritual may have been far removed from
the teachings of the Buddha, in the millennium between original In-

dian doctrines and the transmitted Chinese form of popular devotional Buddhism, liturgies, philosophies, and grand monasteries were built on Chinese soil which deeply influenced Taoist practice.[34]

From the Buddhist missionaries and their scriptures the Chinese favored and patronized the chanting of *ching* 經 canons of merit and *ch'an* 懺 litanies of repentance. Taoist versions of the *ching* and *ch'an* soon appeared in the Taoist Canon, and became an essential part of the Chai-chiao.[35] Thus, a third genre of literary texts were added to the Chiao as follows:

1. *San-kuan ching*   Canons to the Three (Taoist) Officials, heaven, earth, water. 三官經

2. *San-yüan ching*   Canon of the Three Taoist origins. 三元經

3. *Pei-tou ching*   The Pole Star Canon. (East, South, West, North, and Center Canons also are used).

4. *Yü-huang ching*   Canon to the Jade Emperor. 玉皇經

5. *Shih-t'ien Pao-ch'an*   Litany of Repentance to the Ten Precious Heavens. 十天寶懺

6. *Yü-huang Ch'an*   Litany of Repentance to Jade Emperor. 玉皇懺

7. *T'ien-shu Ch'an*   Litany of Repentance to Thunder Spirits (Heavenly Pivot). 天樞懺

8. *Fang shui-teng*   Floating lanterns to summon all the souls from the underworld hell. 放水燈

9. *P'u-tu*   The ritual to free all souls from hell. 普度

It is therefore possible to identify at least three kinds of Taoist ritual, used in the villages and cities of China since the third and fourth centuries CE. These rites appear today in the Chiao rituals of mainland China, Hongkong, Taiwan, and overseas communities, very much a part of popular religious practice. The rites, when celebrated over a three day village festival, are used as follows:

A. Popular	B. Buddhist	C. Classical

The First Day
Fa-piao (Announce the Festival) 發表
Ch'ing-shen (Invite the spirits) 請神
Chin-t'an (Purify the Temple) 禁壇
                    San-kuan Ching 三官經
Wu-hung (Noon Offering)   午供

51

A. Popular	B. Buddhist	C. Classical
	San-yüan Ching 三元經	
Fen-teng (Lao-tzu, Ch. 42) 分燈		
		Su-ch'i 宿啟
The Second Day		
Re-invite (ch'ung-pai) 重白		
	Pei-tou ching 北斗經	*Morning Aud.* 早朝煉炁
Noon Offering 午供		*Noon Audience* 午朝煉神
	Shih-t'ien Pao-ch'an 十天寶懺	
	Floating the Lanterns 放水燈	*Night Audience* 晚朝煉精

(The Yellow Court Canon is chanted here by Shang-ch'ing Taoists).

The Third Day

A. Popular	B. Buddhist	C. Classical
Re-invite (ch'ung-pai) 重白		
	Yü-huang ching 玉皇經	
	Yü-huang ch'an 玉皇懺	
	T'ien-shu ch'an 天樞懺	
		Tao-ch'ang 道場煉虛 與道合一
Wu-hung (noon offering) 午供		
	P'u-tu (free all souls) 普度散花	
Community Banquet		
Hsieh-shen (Thank and Send Off the Spirits) 謝神		

The Chiao festival, as described above, was used in popular village festival and in the presence of the emperor of China from the fifth century CE. The format was not altered or seriously challenged until the Sung dynasty religious reformation. During this startlingly free and open period, the Chinese laity took over and usurped the controlling power in religious ritual practice. Classical Taoist priests were no longer required to chant the *ching* and *ch'an* canons of merit and repentance, or the popular rites of purification and summoning, used to control nature's spirits. Instead a whole new kind of Taoist religious expert sprung up from the countryside villages and provincial capitals, who did not refer to the classical orders for their *lu* registers or their *k'ou-ch'uan* oral instructions for ritual.

Of the many sects founded during the Sung and Yuan dynasties religious reformation, the most important from the historical religious viewpoint were the *Shen-hsiao* and the *Ch'uan-chen* movements. *Shen-hsiao* Taoists were popular at court only for a brief few years, i.e., from 1117-1120 CE.[36] Shen-hsiao style rituals are used in northern Taiwan and in southern Fukien province in the modern period, along with the popular local Lu Shan style rites peculiar to the "Redhead" mediums of Taiwan and Fukien.[37] Ch'uan-chen Taoists, on the other hand, are to be found in every province and city of mainland China.

III. Taoism and Popular Religion: Lay Reformation
Of the many Taoist sects that were founded from the Sung dynasty onward, the following movements remain popular and are flourishing in Chinese communities today:
1. The *Shen-hsiao* (Spirit Cloud) order, favored by Emperor Hui-tsung, 1116-1119; led by Lin Ling-su of Wenchow city, Chekiang, and later made a part of the Taoist teachings transmitted at Lung-hu Shan, Shen-hsiao style liturgies are popular with the redhead Taoists of north Taiwan. 神霄
2. The *Ch'uan-chen* sect, by far the most popular of the Sung dynasty reformed orders, observes strict monastic celibacy, vegetarian diet, Zen style sitting meditation, and breathing exercises from the inner alchemy tradition. The government of the people's Republic favors Ch'uan-chen style practice, and sponsors this sect in the city and mountain top shrines throughout China. 全真
3. The *Lu Shan San-nai* sect of Fukien province and Taiwan, that practices popular exorcism and healing, acts as interpreters for the possessed mediums (Minnan dialect: *tang-ki* 童乩; mandarin: *wu* 巫), and uses an ox horn to summon and expel spirits. The Lu Shan Taoists actually wrap a red cloth around the head when performing public ritual, and thus earn the epithet "redhead" (Hung-t'ou 紅頭) from the people.[38]
4. The popular *Cheng-i* 正一 Taoists of Hongkong, Taiwan, and the overseas communities of Chinese, who practice Chiao ritual with the same hand-written manuals of the Three Mountain Alliance Taoists,

53

but do not perform the meditations of kenosis-emptying. The *fa-lu* 發爐 rite, if used, is not interpreted to be an "emptying" of the spirits of the body but rather the summoning of spirits to the T'an sacred area.

With the exception of the Ch'uan-chen monastic order, all of the Taoist sects established during or after the Sung dynasty emphasize the kataphatic "filling" forms of visualization and the summoning of spirits. The Chiao festivals celebrated by post reformation Taoists do not contain the Su-ch'i ritual for planting the Five True Writs, or the Tao-ch'ang final meditation of apophatic emptying. The Taoists of the Three Mountain Alliance on the other hand, preserve the apophatic aspects of Taoist meditation. I.e., they practice the kenotic emptying of the microcosm of all spirits and the triple audience with the Tao, described in the above pages. Taoists of all orders could travel to one of the three sacred mountains, and learn the classical meditations by living with the monks and practicing meditation.

The recently published gazetteer of Mao Shan celebrates the rebuilding of that ravaged mountain after the burning by the Japanese and the pillaging by the red guard; among the details described by the surviving elderly Taoists are the rules for receiving traveling Taoists into the sacred mountain environment. Taoists who wished could remain in one of the monasteries, and learn the rituals, meditations, and music of Ch'uan-chen, Ling-pao, Cheng-i and Shang-ch'ing Taoism.[39] Taoists brought their manuals, meditations, and oral teachings to one of the Three Mountains for approval and licensing, from the Sung dynasty until the present. Some also learned the canonical meditations.

In order to verify the use of this system, manuals brought from Mao Shan to north Taiwan in 1780-1823, were returned to Mao Shan in 1987, by the author. The Taiwan manuals were compared word-for-word with the teachings of the Mao Shan masters. The Mao Shan Taoists not only used the same manuals, but acted out, danced, and described the *fa-lu* meditation for emptying the microcosm of spirits,[40] performed the *yü-pu* 禹步 sacred dance steps of Yu pictured in the manuals,[41] and taught the method of Pole Star meditation and Ch'ing-wei Thunder meditation described in the manuals.[42]

Later these same manuals were carried to Lung-hu Shan, San-ch'ing village in Chiangsi. Here too the manuals were examined minutely for any deviation from the Lung-hu Shan versions. Taiwan's classical Taoist liturgy was proven to be authentic when the Chiao texts were shown to be identical with the mainland versions.[43] Upon returning to Taiwan in the late Fall of 1987, the Redhead Shen-hsiao Taoists of north Taiwan spoke of making the same trip to the mountain, when state policy allowed Taoists to travel to the People's Republic. Taoism is a force which binds the religious consciousness of the Chinese into a single yin-yang system, balanced between the kataphatic "filling" with spirits by the redhead and medium, and the apophatic emptying and decentering of the blackhead and monastic traditions.

Though the influence of Taoism on Chinese popular religion is deep and lasting, there is another aspect of "Blue Dragon White Tiger" that proves a profound difference between the two systems. The monastic and classical Taoists are a contrast to the villagers, farmers, city merchants and housewives who patronize the temples, shrines, and festivals of China. Whether emptying or filling self with spirits, the Taoist does not have the same fear of the unknown, i.e., the spiritual forces of the cosmos, and the demons and ancestors of the underworld, that fill the imagination and the icons of the popular religion. For the people who hire Taoists and Buddhists to do ritual, the spirits are treated like public officials, to be cajoled, bought off, and kept as far away as possible from the lives of the ordinary folk.

For the devout practitioners of China's popular religion, there are three loci of access to the spiritual order, the city temple, the Buddhist shrine, and the family altar. For the people, the microcosm, i.e., the interior of lay person's human body is not seen to be as powerful as the Taoist's as a receptacle of spiritual power. The Taoist specialist is hired to cast off the spirits, souls of the departed, and demons because he or she is most adept at this role from the ancient past until the present. Thus a Taoist is hired to perform ritual in all three places for this special ability to address and expel spirits.

Since temple, shrine, and altar fulfill the symbolic function of relating humans with the invisible order, each of these places must have its own proper custodian and clientele. The city temple is organized and governed by a board of laymen. Lay custodians are elected by reason of leadership or appointed because of wealth to look after the temple and its ritual needs. Taoists or Buddhists are hired for special ritual occasions, but the daily care of the temple, the planning of festivals, and the handling of family ritual, prognostication, and the hiring of Buddhist or Taoist expert is totally the concern of the laity.

The control of liturgy by lay officials, the multiplying of popular Taoist orders, the creation of fraternal associations, and clan temples to promote business interests, became more and more popular from the Sung period into the modern era. The secret societies of the Ch'ing dynasty, founded to overthrow the Manchu usurpers, have become business associations in Hongkong, Singapore, Honolulu, San Francisco, and other Chinese communities of the modern industrial age. Modern temples and shrines are run by Chinese business associations. This is especially true of the Chinese overseas communities, such as the eighty or more Chinese *hui* of Honolulu, each of which supports a private shrine to Kuan-kung, the red faced patron saint of merchants, or public shrines to Kuanyin and Tin-hau (Ma-tsu).[44]

In Kowloon the massive *Yüan-hsüan Hsüeh-yüan* temple complex of Sam-dip Tam, is totally organized by lay men and women. The temple has trained married women to perform Ch'uan-chen style Taoist Chiao and burial ritual. Lay Buddhists are hired to perform funeral services, while the wealthy patrons of the organization perform Confucian style ancestral rites. Members of the organization pray for blessing in Taoist, Buddhist, and Confucian shrines, and provide mausoleum space for urns bearing the ashes of the deceased. Earnings from the temple rituals are donated to support homes for the aging, clinics, schools for the poor, and the rebuilding of Taoist and Buddhist shrines in neighboring Kwangtung province.

The spirit of reformed popular religion is summarized in the classic of the Chinese religious reformation, the *Kan-ying p'ien* (The Classic of Retribution) attributed to Lao-tzu:[45]

> Happiness and evil do not come spontaneously; it is men
> who bring them upon themselves. The consequences of virtue
> and vice follow each other, just as shadow follows form. Now
> there are spirits in heaven and in earth whose business it is to

investigate the sins of men, and who shorten their lives according as their transgressions are serious venial.

The text of the *Kan-ying p'ien* is profusely illustrated with wood block prints showing the punishment of evil, the rewarding of good, blessings sent down by smiling Buddhas and ageless Taoist sages on those men an women who acted generously. By loving family members, emptying the heart of selfish desires and caring for the needs of others, life is filled with good:[46]

> Accumulate virtue, and store up merit; treat all with gentleness and love; be loyal, be dutiful; be respectful our elder brothers and kind to your juniors. Be upright yourselves, in order that you may reform others; be compassionate to the fatherless and the widow. Reverence the aged and cherish the young. Do not injure even little insects or grass, or trees. he wickedness of others, and be glad of their virtues. Succor them in their distress, and rescue them in their danger. When a man gains his desire, let it be as though his good fortune were your own; when one suffers loss, as though you suffered it yourself.

The motive for doing these good deeds, the *Kan-ying p'ien* teaches, is to live out one's years in happiness. The three spirits in the handle of the Big Dipper, and the *Ssu-ming* spirit of fire in the hearth (and in the heart) record the good and bad deeds of humanity, and report to heaven once a month, and on the occasion of the sixtieth birthday (the completion of a five-times twelve year cycle, the Chinese method of counting years).[47]

> But if any person acts in opposition to what is right, turns his/her back upon the truth, ... injures the gentle and the good, abuses his sovereign and his parents in private, treats his elders with disrespect, ...(more than 200 prescriptions follow), if a man is guilty of any of these crimes, the spirit who rules over human destinies will, according as the sin is trivial or light, abbreviate his span of life... *and if any of his sins are left unatoned for, they will be visited on his sons and grandson.*

The way to gain merit and overcome the natural and spiritual punishment for social transgressions is to perform works of merit. 1,300 works make a heavenly immortal, while 300 virtuous acts give earthly powers to heal and help others. Grave offenses take twelve years off life, while lesser sins delete one year.

The ways of gaining merit are many. Printing and distributing free copies of the *Kan-ying p'ien* and other *shan-shu* "good books" that teach the doctrine of recompense for good and evil deeds became one of the most popular forms of meritorious work during the Ming and Ch'ing dynasties. *Shan-shu* and other forms of devotional books continue to be published and distributed free of cost in overseas Chinese communities today. The building of homes for the aged, hospitals, orphanages, contributions to monasteries and temples, the giving of lavish banquets on the occasion of festivals, weddings, and funerals, are all semiotic signs of the spirit of self-emptying and giving that wins blessing for the community.

Among the harmful deeds forbidden in the *Kan-ying p'ien* are the following:[48]

> accepting bribes for violating the law
> slaughtering those who surrender in war
> hindering physicians, diviners, astrologers, ...
> frightening birds at roost or on the nest
> injuring a foetus in the womb
> conceiving lustful desires at the sight of beauty
> acquiring wealth by robbery or extortion
> heeding wife and concubines, to neglect parents
> forsaking old friends for new ones
> singing or dancing on inauspicious nights
> spit, evacuate, or nose-blowing towards spirits (north)
> wantonly killing tortoises or snakes...

The most popular way of indicating to humans and spirits that merit for good deeds is offered to overcome the social guilt of one's ancestors, is to burn paper money in the temple furnace of under-world merit. By so doing, any harm that might come to the living for unatoned misconduct of an ancestor is neutralized. The burning of paper money is a true semiotic sign of atonement. The money is "deposited" in the Bank of Hell, and the interest accruing from the bank notes is used to "buy off" the corrupt officials of the netherworld, as well as pay for atonement.

The living can help free the soul of an ancestor from hell's prison, by performing good deeds of self-giving (self-emptying) in the present. Unlike officials in real government, hell's politicians are influenced by the good deeds, not the physical wealth of the living. The merits of the living, not the burning of paper money, win blessing. This premise of the *Kan-ying p'ien* is a broad extension of the Confucian ethic, to include all mankind in virtue which was once a sign of the Chun-tzu. It further opens to all the basic rituals of the Taoist. All of the villagers are now enjoined to officiate in the rites of offering paper money, incense, and lighted candles before the altars of the ancestors and the spirits.

The semiotics of the *Classic of Retribution* inspired a variety of popular responses to the doctrine of winning merit for good deeds performed by the populace. The burning of paper money became an expression of folk art and legend. Tales of virtuous men and women, miniature houses filled with wealth, paper Mercedes Benz's and bank notes worth millions of merit-dollars were burned as offerings to the ancestors. Paper money itself was open to the imaginative definition of each province and district. In the artistic expressions imprinted on the surface of the merit bills are to be found heroes and myths of all forms. Gold paper money for earth spirits, silver for the underworld, symbolic wealth and riches offered in ritual fires, taught that human deeds influence heaven, hell, and the visible world of nature.

The basic world view of popular Chinese religion, from the time of the Sung dynasty reformation (if not earlier) until the present, is defined in terms of self emptying merit. The purpose of prayers offered in the temple, petitions at the family shrine, liturgies celebrated by Buddhist and Taoist expert, is to integrate human social life, nature, and afterlife, through acts of giving. Hell, in this system of symbols, is an eidetic, semiotic image of a life lived without family love, friends, and society. The goals of Chinese life, expressed in the triptych *fu* 福 *lu* 祿 *shou* 壽 , are in practical everyday reality, the blessing of children, the wealth to make a family for them, and old age to enjoy a household filled with grandchildren. The means to attain these goals, i.e., good deeds done for family and friends, are within the

59

reach of every man and woman. A Buddhist or Taoist can offer prayers and rituals to free souls and win blessing, but cannot add or subtract on the personal level from the micro- and macrocosmic effect of human deeds and their retribution.

Thus the popular religion and its expression from the Sung dynasty onward grew out of the practical need of the laity to express religious fervor on the personal, family, and village level without the mediation of a priest or monk expert. Taoist and Buddhist were necessary at such times as the funeral, and village renewal (Taoist Chiao festival). But the people were and are the officiants at birth, puberty, marriage, and annual festival. In this sense, the visible world is the domain of the people, while the invisible world that of the spiritual experts. Taoists were called on to serve the world of the spirits, and Buddhists to offer lengthy chants for the deceased. On all other occasions, the laity relied on local talent, such as healers, mediums, herbalists, lion dancers and martial arts, among many other functionaries, for the practice of festival and customs.

The prayer of the laity offered for the good of family and friend is based on emptying self for the good of the other. The prayer of kenosis for the Taoist is by analogy an act of self-emptying by living for the people. The teachings of Lao-tzu and Chuang-tzu thus are at the core of popular beliefs as well as classical Taoist ritual meditation. This analogy is reflected in the immense respect the Taoist priest always shows to the beliefs of the local populace, customs of the village temple, and practices of a district festival. Taoism adapts to the demands of each village and district in China, not for the "convenient skill-in-means" (*upaya*) reasons of the Buddhist, but because both systems (Taoist and reformation popular practice) are firmly rooted in Yin-yang five element cosmology, and the spirituality of emptying found in Lao-tzu and Chuang-tzu. In this spirituality based on the workings of yin and yang in nature, men and women are equal before the Tao. Men and women therefore can both perform Taoist ritual, meditation, and healing.

Before describing the rituals of popular religion associated with birth, puberty, marriage, healing, burial, and annual festival, we must first speak of the influence of Buddhism on the spirituality of Taoism, and all of China. At the philosophical level, we can contrast its teachings with those of the Taoist ascetic. Nevertheless, ideas from

Buddhism influenced Taoist and popular religious practice at the deepest conscious and sub-conscious levels. Sutra chanting, the imagery of a subterranean hell with its punishments, and lengthy post-burial rites to free souls from hell are obvious proofs of Buddhism's influence throughout China's history into the modern present. Less obvious are the influence of Buddhist spirituality in the form of Madhyamika philosophy, Ch'an (Zen) practice, and notions of the void and empty center. Taoism as well as popular religion owe much to the ascetic ideals of Buddhism.

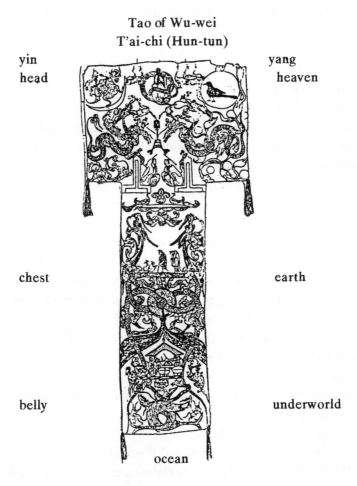

Tao of Wu-wei
T'ai-chi (Hun-tun)

yin · yang
head · heaven

chest · earth

belly · underworld

ocean

The Ma Wang Tui burial robe, 2nd Cent. BCE.

NOTES

1. See Kubo, Noritada, *Dokyo Shi*, (A History of Taoism), Tokyo: Yamakawa Press, 1977, pp. 8-20. Yoshioka, Y., *Eisei e no Negai*, (The Quest for Eternal Life), Tokyo: Dankosha, 1971, pp. 248-55.

2. See Keightley, David, "Shang Divination and Metaphysics," in *Philosophy East and West*, Honolulu: University of Hawaii, 1988, Vol. XXXVII, No. 4, Oct., pp. 367-375.

3. See Saso, Michael, *Taoism and the Rite of Cosmic Renewal*, Pullman: 1990 (2nd edition), Ch. 2 and 4.

4. See Ch. 1, p. 18, and note 27 for *fang-shih*.

5. See Seidel, Anna, *La divinization de Lao tseu dans le Taoïsme des Han*, Paris: EFEO, 1969 for a definition of Huang-lao.

6. See *Yun-chi ch'i-ch'ien*, Ch. 104.

7. See Saso, M., *Taoism and the Rite of Cosmic Renewal*, (TROCR) (Pullman:1990), and John Lagerwey, *Taoist Ritual in Chinese Society and History* (New York:1987).

8. The *Huang-t'ing Ching* Lung-hu Shan edition, 1868. The read "T'uo chu shen" (get rid of, or exorcise all spirits) instead of "shuo chu shen" explain all spirits. The text is read in north Taiwan during the Chiao ceremony, over a loud speaker.

9. See Seidel, Anna, *The image of the perfect ruler in early Taoist messianism: Lao-tzu and Li Hung*, in *History of Religions* Chicago: 1969-70, vol. 9.2/3, Nov., Feb., pp. 216-247.

10. Charles Benn, *Taoism as Ideology in the Reign of Hsüan-tsung (712-755)*, Ph.D. thesis, 1977. In press, 1990.

11. The collection is in the process of publication, 1987-1990.

12. *I-ching*, Ch. 45, Kao Heng commentary.

13. Lao-tzu *Tao-te Ching, Tao-tsang Chi-yao* edition, vol. 16, p. 388; Ming: Shih Te-ch'ing commentary.

14. Ibid., p. 383.

15. The word *shih* here means to serve or to offer ritual to a spirit.

16. Ibid., p. 396.

17. Lao-tzu, Ch. 42; see Ch. 1, pg. 8 above.

18. See Ch. 1, figure 9, the Hun and P'o souls.

19. The Yellow Court Canon is translated in M. Saso, *Taoist Ritual Meditation*, Asian Spirituality series, Vol. 4, Honolulu: 1990.

20. See Schipper (1968), and Lagerwey (1986) for the distinction between Yellow Register *chai* and gold register *chiao* ritual.

21. *Wu-shang Pi-yao*, Taoist Canon (TT) 768-779, HY 1130.

22. See Ch. 1, note 10.

23. Ch. 1, Fig. 1, above.

24. Roland Barthes, "From the Work to the Text," in *Textual Strategies*, ed. J. Harari, Ithaca: Cornell Univ. Press, 1979, pp. 75-76.

25. Jacques Derrida, *Positions*, Chicago, Univ. of Chicago, 1981, p. 27

26. See Lagerwey, (New York:1986) for a layman's view of the Chiao.

27. The *Huang-t'ing Wai-ching*, (Yellow Court, Outer Chapters) is interpreted in three ways, a) as kenosis meditation by the Shang-ch'ing masters; b) as breath circulation by kung-fu, t'ai-chi and other martial arts teachers; and c) as sexual hygiene in the secret society traditions.

28. *Taoist Rites of Origin*, Honolulu: University of Hawaii, Religion Dept., 30 min. videocassette, 1980, 1986.

29. See Michael Saso, *The Teachings of Taoist Master Chuang*, New Haven: 1978, pp. 211-214.

30. Ibid., p. 213-14.

31. *Wu-shang Pi-yao*, 561-581 CE. See footnote 18 above.

32. Ch. 1, note 15.

33. Saso, *The Teachings of Taoist Master Chuang*, (TOTMC), New Haven: 1978, p. 225-233. Note the different interpretations of Lagerwey (1986) and Schipper (1968) who do not find kenotic prayer in Tainan forms of Taoist practice.

34. Cf. Ch. 3, the development of Buddhism.

35. Saso, M., *Chuang-lin Hsü Tao-tsang*, (CLHTT) Taipei: 1975, for the *ching* and *ch'an* texts used in Chai and Chiao ritual.

36. Saso, M., *Dôkyô Hikestu Shusei*, (Tokyo:1979) Pt. 1, p. 36a-b for Shen-hsiao registers transmitted by the Taoists of Lung-hu Shan.

37. Saso, M., (Taipei: 1975), Vol. 20-25 for Shen-hsiao style rituals.

38. Kuepers, John, "A Description of the Fa-ch'ang Ritual as Practiced by the Lu Shan Taoists of Northern Taiwan," in *Buddhist and Taoist Studies, I*, Honolulu: Univ. of Hawaii Press, 1977, pp. 79-94.

39. *Tao-chiao Tsa-chih*, Mao Shan commemorative issue, June, 1988.

40. See note 30, above. The Taoists of Fukien, Kwangtung, and Taiwan traditionally went to Lung-hu Shan in Chianghsi for licenses.

41. See CLHTT, (Note 35) Vol. 20, pp. 5835-6 for examples of Yü-pu.

42. Ch'ing-wei Mi-chüeh manuals, San Shan Ti-hsüeh collection, 1990.

43. Saso, M., *Religion in the People's Republic*, *China News Analysis*, Hongkong, Dec. 15, 1987, #1349.

44. See Naquin, Susan, *Millenarian Rebellion in China, The Eight trigrams Uprising of 1813*, New Haven: Yale University Press, 1976, and Overmeyer, Daniel, *Folk Buddhist Religion. Dissenting Sects in Late Traditional China*, Harvard: 1976.

45. *T'ai-shang Kan-ying P'ien*, TT. 834-839.

46. See Balfour, Henry, translation, *The Book of Recompense*, in *Taoist Texts*, London: Trubner & Co.; Shanghai: Kelly and Walsh, 1880, pp. 103-118. Author's woodblock copy with illustrations, 1655, reprinted in Shanghai from the original blocks, 1923.

47. Ibid., p. 103.

48. Ibib., p. 104-105.

Refining the Five Elements. Ch'ing dynasty woodblock, *Hsing-ming Kuei-chih*.

3. THE SPIRITUAL QUEST
Buddhist and Taoist Ascesis of Emptiness

Two foreign belief systems above all others, Buddhism and Marxism, have had profound success in influencing Chinese culture. The Marxist influence on Chinese religion and culture are studied in the last chapter. Here we shall examine the coming of Buddhism to China, and its acceptance into the popular religious tradition. In this process Buddhism became an integral part of Chinese ascetic as well as popular religious practice. The term *San-chiao kuei-i* (Three religions, one culture) expresses the openness of popular religion to practices that conform to the Yin-yang cosmology. Buddhist practice has influenced reformed Taoist movements such as the Ch'uan-chen order, rituals for the dead, and the celebration of festivals of in communities, temples, and households throughout China.

In this sense, Confucianism can be called the head, Buddhism the heart, and Taoism the belly of China's post-Sung dynasty religious culture. Confucian ethics, the domain of logic and the logico-centered intellect, dominates the Chinese legal system. Buddhist compassion, on the other hand, moved the heart of the Chinese by its ritual care for souls in the afterlife. Taoist harmony with natural process, and the meditations of centering and decentering in the belly (called the *hsia tan t'ien*, lower cinnabar field) helped formulate Chinese healing, martial arts, and the celebration of nature's festivals. In this threefold cultural system Buddhism plays a crucial role in burial and commemorative services, and in the quest for a life of spiritual ascesis. To understand how Buddhism effected Chinese religious practice, we must now follow its path across the northern silk road through the steppes of central Asia, and the southern sea route through southeast Asia and the southern coast into China.

In this section we shall attempt to outline the major doctrines of Buddhism in China. We shall divide the study into five segments: 1) The *founding* of Buddhism in India, from the sixth century BCE to the second century CE; 2) the *canonization* of Buddhism in China, from the second to the sixth century CE; 3) the *diversification* of Buddhism into many sects, sixth to ninth century CE; 4) the *reformation* of Buddhism and the unification of practice, tenth to twentieth century CE; and 5) the *rebirth* of Buddhism in modern China (see Chapter Eight).

65

By canonization is meant the forming of the Buddhist canon with its codes, biographies, and bibliographies of Buddhist works. By diversification is meant the founding of many orders and movements of Buddhist monks based on specialization in one or more sutra and the practices associated with them. The Sung and later reformation of Buddhism, parallel to the reforms of Taoism and popular religion, admitted laity into *Nien-fuo* Buddhist chant and *ch'an* (zen禪) sitting combined. Buddhism in China today is unified by these two practices, i.e., chant and meditation.

I. Buddhism in India

The life of the historical Buddha, surrounded in legend and myth, is thought to have been lived between 563-483 BCE. Born in northeast India, in an area now on the Nepal-India border, Buddha belonged to a wealthy Ksatriya caste (landowning-kingly) family, of the Sakya tribe. The capital city of the tribe, Kapilavastu, lies inside the Nepal border, whereas the small countryside Lumbini park where he was born is in India. The sources for studying Buddha's life depend on traditions preserved in much later commentaries, including the reports brought back to China by the pilgrim-monks Fa-hsien (399-414 ACE) and Hsüan-tsang (629-45 ACE). Sanskrit, Pali, and Chinese language texts bear different versions of Buddha's origins.

Two canonical sources, the Sanskrit texts of the northern Mahayana tradition, and the Pali Canon of the southern Theravada tradition derive from dialects spoken during and after the time of Buddha. The teachings of Buddha were transmitted in perhaps five early languages, i.e., Magadhi (the language spoken by Buddha), northwest Indian Prakrit from the Gandhari area, the southern Pali (western Prakrits of the Avanti and Kathiawar regions), hybrid sanskrit (Siddham), and standard sanskrit. The present Pali and Sanskrit texts were written down more than 500 years after the oral traditions of the Buddha's life and teaching were first propagated in these five spoken dialects. They did not become "canonical" i.e., accepted as a fixed scripture, until the second century ACE.[1]

From these varied sources we learn that Buddha's father Suddhodana ("He who has pure rice") was a wealthy landowner and ruler, and that his mother died seven days after Buddha's birth. He was brought up by his maternal aunt Mahaprajapati. Legend says that he took seven steps at birth, a sign of stepping out of the six paths of recycling, and announced that he was a Buddha (i.e., an enlightened person, from the root Bodhi, enlightened).[2] Legend says that a prophet told Buddha's father that if the boy ever left the pleasure park in which he was born, he would forsake his kingly inheritance and become a great religious leader. For this reason he was made to marry (at age 16), raise a son (Rahula), and lead a life of luxury within the family estate.

At the age of 29, Buddha rode his white horse Kantaka out of the city gates, and was rudely awakened by four sights: an old man, sick man, dead man, and monk (sadhu). Chinese, Tibetan, and other Asian versions of the story influenced by the Yin-yang five element cosmology, see Buddha riding successively out of the four gates of the city: 1) east gate, to see an old man; 2) south gate to see a sick man; 3) west gate to see an dead man, and 4) north gate to see a monk-sadhu. Leaving behind the world of luxury, Buddha crosses the river (i.e., paramita, crossing to the other shore of enlightenment) and spends six years of extreme austerity in the wild forests. Emaciated but still unenlightened, he decides to adopt a middle way, between the extremes of austerity and acclaim as a saint. Sitting under the tree of enlightenment, (the Bo tree), the tempter Mara comes with a bevy of lascivious dancing maidens to lure Buddha back to his life of luxury. Calling on the earth (earth goddess, Prthivi) to witness his purity of intention, Buddha experiences enlightenment.

Fig. 1. The Historical Buddha

Vision	Truth	Sanskrit	Chinese
1. Old man: life is conditioned by suffering	Duhkha	K'u 苦
2. Sick man: selfish desire makes suffering	Trsna	Chi 集
3. Dead man: annihilate selfishness	Nirodha	Mieh 滅
4. Monk-sadhu: the Way has eight steps	Margha	Tao 道

The enlightenment of Buddha is not that of a great religious leader preaching a way of universal salvation. It is a simple response to the four visions at the gateway to the pleasure palace of his imprisonment. All of life is conditioned by suffering, brought on by selfish desire. To stop suffering, the first step is death to selfishness. The way to stop selfishness has eight simple stages:

The Eight Steps to enlightenment (i.e., annihilate selfishness):

1. Co-dependent origination (Yin-yüan, pratityasamutpada): everything I have is received from another, nothing is my own. Prayer of thanks. 因緣, 正見

2. Right judgments: no malice, no negative judgment. 正思

3. Right speech: no negative words. 正語

4. Right karma: (karma means deeds); do only good to others. 正業

5. Right livelihood: live my life to serve others (compassion). 正命

6. Right thoughts and images only in the mind. 正精進

7. Right concentration: (Samatha, Zen), keep one thought only. 正念（止）

8. Right samadhi: no thought, intuitive wisdom (Vipasyana). 正定（觀）

The second of the four noble truths, that is the realization that selfish desire is the cause of internal suffering, is further elaborated into twelve causes or nidanas. The first of the eight steps to enlightenment re-directs these twelve causes into the source of compassion and love of others. The epistemological origins of this causal system are an essential part of the Buddhist experience. Based on the act of judging (karman), conditioned by passion (klesa), the karmic act which brings retribution must be conscious, reflected on, and deliberate. Thus the Buddhist system does not reprove acts (karma) arising from the unconscious or animal-vegetable reflexes of man. In terms of modern studies of the brain and its functions, it is not the reptilian (life sustaining) or the mammalian (instinctual) activity, but the reflective intellectual and willed acts that bring about the chain of twelve causes and effects. The Twelve Nidanas are as follows:

(past causes)

1. Avidya: ignorance of the four truths; klesa, passion. 無明
2. Samskara: predisposition to like and dislike; karma, deeds. 行

(present causes)

3. Vijñana: initial consciousness, embryo. 識
4. Namarupa: name and form, mind and body distinct. 名色
5. Sadayatana: six powers to know; 5 senses and mind. 六入
6. Sparsa: contact between senses and thing. 觸
7. Vedana: act of sensing the thing. 受
8. Trsna: thirst and desire for the thing. 愛
9. Upadana: holding on to the thing. 取
10. Bhava: the act of producing existence. 有

(future cause-effects)

11. Jati: rebirth, bearing again and again. 生
12. Jara-marana: old age, sickness, death. 老病死, 憂悲苦惱.

The third truth, the annihilation of suffering, is defined by the term *nirvana*, which means the state wherein all selfish desire is neutralized. By taking the eightfold steps, doing away with negative judgment, and approaching the "one thought" of the seventh and "no thought" of the eighth step, the monk of the Theravada tradition and the Bodhisattva of the Mahayana tradition attain to the eradication of selfish desire. The emphasis on the Vinaya rules of disciplined monastic life (Theravada) are balanced and complemented by the vows of compassion (Mahayana) of the Bodhisattva, as means to liberation from selfish desire. Both systems lead to liberation from deeds (karma) motivated by attachment, hatred, infatuation. Action done with perfect insight into the true nature of the world, without attachment, and for the good of others, does not produce the cycle of rebirth. The Buddha compares this second act to sewing seeds that have been fried and made barren. They do not bear new life.[3]

Nirvana therefore does not mean the extinction of personality or ego, but rather the liberation from selfishness and suffering caused by the continual rebirthing of desires, unrequited goals, and reasoning. The view that the soul must seek bliss in the afterlife as well as the view that there is no afterlife to seek are both contrary to the Buddhist notion of Nirvana. Nirvana is a condition of non judgment and non-attachment, rather than of non-being. Attachment to any real or ideal good is a part of the chain of twelve causes that prevent enlightenment.

The third noble truth teaches the kenotic emptying of intellect and will of all selfish desire. In this sense, we can state that the Buddhist path is similar in some way to the "dark night" of the western mystic tradition and the "sitting in forgetfulness" and "fasting in the heart-mind" of Taoism; all three are kenotic or emptying meditative experiences.

The life of the Buddha after enlightenment is depicted in myth, temple murals, popular art, and literature throughout Asia. At Benares he preached his first sermon on the "marks of non-soul," and at Gaya (the place of his enlightenment) he preached the "sermon on fire." Besides the Sangha or community of monks, lay men and women soon became disciples. When monks and disciples reached sixty in number, Buddha sent them out to preach his doctrines. The chief among these were Sariputra, Maudgalyayana, and Änanda, whose names appear in many early Buddhist texts. Buddha predicted his death three months before dying. It is recorded that Änanda did not ask him to remain in the world. He died of food poisoning, from eating soft pig's foot (one text says "magic mushrooms"). His last words were recorded as "Now then, monks, I address you: subject to decay are all compound things. Strive with earnestness."

According to the *Vinayapitaka* section of the Pali Canon, the first council of monks occurred shortly after Buddha's death, at Rajagrha. Legend says that the disciple Änanda recited Buddha's sermons on doctrine, while Upali (Buddha's barber) read the Vinaya (disciplinary) regulations. A second general council was held at Vaisali ca. 386 BCE to condemn certain practices. During the reign of King Asoka a third council was held at Pataliputra (Patna), ca. 250 BCE to condemn heretical doctrines and expel offending monks. Only the Pali version of the Canon mentions these councils. The compilers of the later written version of the Pali Canon probably wrote about these councils to verify the authenticity of the written Pali texts, a witness to the need of the early Buddhists to create an authentic, stable version of the Buddha's teachings.

Conflict and dispute over the Buddha's doctrines brought about a schism between the Arhat monks of the strict observance, on the one hand, and the laity and popular monks on the other. Two early schools of Buddhism were formed from these arguments. The Sthaviran school of monks claimed to be faithful to Buddha's austere practices, while the Mahasanghika promulgated Buddhist practices more compatible to devotional practice, the source of the Mahayana canon. These and other disputes, schools, and schisms, brought about the writing of the Pali Canon of the Theravada school, in 35-32 BCE.[4]

Lifetime of the Buddha, 563-483 BCE

1st Council, Rajagra, ca. 483 BCE

2nd Council, Vaisali, ca. 383 BCE

2nd 2nd Council, Pataliputra, ca. 340 BCE

first sectarian split

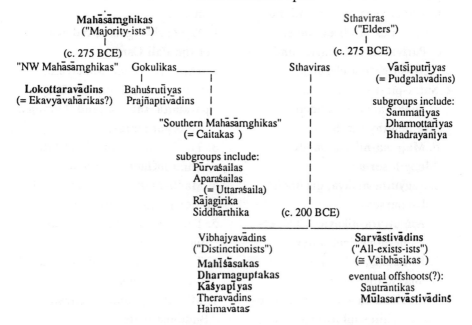

Though the Mahayana school of northern India existed by this time, the first sanskrit Canon was probably written at the Council of Jalandhara in Kashmir, between 128-151 CE. The Mahayana Canon accepted the Hinayana-Theravada scriptures, and added the later Mahayana scriptures and interpretations, an *upaya* sanctioned from the beginning of the Mahayana tradition. Thus the distinction between the two great schools of Buddhism is one of practical emphasis rather than basic doctrinal difference. Even though scholars and scholar monks bitterly argued philosophical differences in writings produced by the schools, in actual practice the East Asian continent, especially the Chinese form of Buddhism, accepted all forms of Buddhist discourse as *Upaya* (Chin: Fang-pien; Jpn: Hoben方便), convenient, skillful means to attain enlightenment.

71

The two forms of Buddhist practice formulated in the early centuries after the Buddha's death can be summarized as follows:

Pali Canon, Southern Buddhism	*Sanskrit, N. Buddhism*
Tripitaka, Three Baskets or arcana of Buddha's teaching:	The most complete version of the Sanskrit Canon exists in Chinese today. The Taisho period Japanese printing of that Canon (1923) contains the following sections:
1. Vinaya-pitaka, rules of the Buddhist community, Sangha.	
a. Suttavibhanga, 227 rules.	
b. Khandakas, major and minor rules of observance.	1. The early Agamas-Nikayas of the Pali Canon.
c. Parivaras, summaries and classification of rules.	2. The texts of the Mahayana tradition, including the Prajña-paramita, the Garland, Nirvana, and other sutras.
2. Sutta-pitaka, Sermons.	
a. Digha-nikaya, collection of lengthy sermons.	
b. Majjima-nikaya, medium length sermons.	3. The Tantric manuals of late Hindu influenced ritual.
c. Sugyutta-nikaya, grouped discourses.	4. Madhyamika, Yogacara, and other philosophical texts.
d. Anguttara-nikaya, 2308 suttas in numerical order.	5. The various Chinese forms of Buddhist practice.
e. Khuddaka-nikaya, smaller concise discourses.	6. The Biographies of famous Buddhist monks.
3. Abhidhamma-pitaka, commentaries, philosophical treatises, school Buddhism.	7. Miscellany, and Japanese Buddhist texts.

From the above summary outline, differences in the two canons can be seen. Other Chinese versions, and the Tibetan Mahayana Scriptures contain different structural arrangements, and more complete texts than the 1923 Japanese-Taisho edition of the Canon. There is no sacred scripture in religious history that has developed a lengthier body of texts, than the canons developed by Buddha's disciples. Inspite of the distaste Buddha felt for doctrinal and philosophical argument, the followers of the Buddha elucidated, explained, and developed Buddha's simple sermons into one of the most complex and variegated philosophical and religious systems in history. A religion for export, Buddhism died out on native Indian soil, only to flourish worldwide as a faith fulfilling perennial needs in human nature.

Nikaya or Theravada Buddhism flourishes today in South and Southeast Asia, i.e., Sri Lanka, Burma, Thailand, and is dormant in Laos and Cambodia. Mahayana is dominant in China, Japan, Korea, Vietnam, and communities of Buddhist practice in the west. Tantric Buddhism, the last, ritual-meditation oriented form of Buddhist practice which developed as a reaction to folk practices in India and mountain Asia, flourishes in Tibet, Mongolia, and Japan, and more recently in Europe and North America. The differences in the three regional variations of Buddhism today are geographic and political, rather than philosophical and doctrinal. Unlike Christians in the west, Buddhists in the modern world usually agree on basic doctrine, and differ only in philosophical discourse, *Upaya* prayer methods, and ritual practice, (Japanese Buddhist schools are an exception).

In summary, even though the southern Theravada tradition of Buddhism approved a canonical scripture earlier than the northern Mahayana monks, both traditions seem to have developed from equally early roots. Within the first 300 years, Buddhism split into 18 separate schools, the most important of which were the Theravada, Sarvastivada, and Mahasanghikah. From these last two schools arose the Mahayana tradition, influencing Chinese, and most of East Asian Buddhism. The Mahayana tradition does not record the third Council of the Theravada tradition, and places the birth and death of the Buddha 100 years later than the Theravadins, (i.e., Buddha died in 383 BCE, in some Mahayana sources). A different set of masters or teachers (Acarya) are listed in Theravada and Mahayana lineages:
Theravada: Upali, Dasaka, Sonaka, Siggava, Moggaliputta, (Asoka),
                Mahinda (who brought Buddhism to Sri Lanka)
Mahayana: Mahakasyapa, Änanda, Sanakavasi, Upagupta, (Asoka)

Thus both traditions claim direct descent from Buddha, and both agree on the four noble truths, the eightfold path, the twelve nidanas, and other basic teachings of the Buddha. The difference in the two early forms of Buddhism, the Theravada, the Mahayana, and later Tantrayana are as follows:

1. *Theravada*: (Hinayana, "little vehicle"), the way of the monk or Arhat, emphasizes individual striving for enlightenment, and strict observance. It is cominant in south and southeast Asia.

2. *Mahayana*: ("great vehicle"), the way of the Bodhisattva, who vows to give up parinirvana, i.e., "reaching the other shore" of final enlightenment, until all sentient beings are saved. Universal salvation through invoking Amida Buddha becomes a common doctrine of Mahayana Buddhism, in East Asia.

3. *Tantrayana*: (Vajrayana), Tantric mountain Buddhism, a way of total body (body-mudra, mouth-mantra, mind-mandala) meditation as means to enlightenment, is practiced in Tibet, Mongolia, Japan, and influences Chinese Buddhism.

Whether in its southern, east Asian, or mountain form, Buddhism always contrasts enlightenment with the state of this present life, and therefore is seen in the eyes of the common folk to be focused on the afterlife, rather than present day needs and necessities. For this and other reasons, Buddhism always functions hand-in-hand with one or more popular religions, whose rituals and festivals are either assumed into the Buddhist system, or exist side-by-side with Buddhist practice. Such is the case of the folk religions of Sri Lanka, Burma, Thai, and the Bon religion of Tibet. the Mudang-shaman of Korea, Shinto in Japan, and Taoism in China are seen as religions for the "living" while Buddhists assume the function of offering lengthy salvational chants for the dead (Burial Buddhism in Japan). Thus, though the devout Buddhist monk may or may not approve, most of Asia considers Buddhist practice to be compatible with other beliefs, and to be especially effective in prayers for the deceased.

The tolerance of Buddhism to folk customs and beliefs acted as a convenient means (upaya) on the one hand to the conversion of China and other east Asian countries, and a diminishing influence within India that eventually led to the end of Buddhism on its native soil, on the other. In the same period of time, that is between the second and the tenth centuries ACE, Buddhism entered China, and became an essential part of Chinese life and culture, but died out in India. The Chinese proverb, *San-chiao Kuei-i*, the Three religions (Buddhism, Confucianism, Taoism) are one culture, refers among other meanings, to the syncretism of the Chinese religious system during this period.

The development of Tantric Buddhism in the 5th and 6th centuries deeply influenced medieval China, Tibet, and Japan. In India, however, Tantrism effected the purity of Buddhist practice, so that it became indistinguishable from the new cults to Siva, Krsna, and Kali.

Further, many of the most influential Buddhist schools in northwest India were inundated by the Islamic conquests of the Seventh century, and later. Buddhism no longer exists on Indian soil, except as a new religion of the lower castes, an expression of social equality in a culture that is based on caste exclusion. Buddhism on Indian soil has sometimes been called a "religion for export." It has become popular in the western world in the twentieth century, where it has both made converts, and moved christians to emulate Vipasyana and Zen forms of prayer, in the monastic and lay context.

II. The Buddhist Canon Comes to China

By the canonization of Buddhism is meant the translation of Sanskrit, Pali, and other Buddhist texts into Chinese, the making of these translations into a bibliography of approved (i.e., canonical) writings, the establishing of a code to be followed by monks, nuns, and laity who practiced Buddhist teachings, and finally the writing of bibliographies of "saints" who followed the way of Buddha. The process of canonization lasted from approximately the second to the sixth century CE.

Many excellent books are found in English and other European languages that exhaustively study this period. E. Zürcher's *The Buddhist Conquest of China*, Arthur Wright's *Buddhism in Chinese History*, Kenneth Ch'en's *Buddhism in China*, and Derk Bodde's inspiring translation of Feng Yu-lan's *History of Chinese Philosophy* (Vol. II, pp. 237- 292) can be found in most bookshops, and provide detailed accounts of Buddhism's entrance and acceptance into China. The French works of Étienne Lamotte and La Vallée Poussin summarized in the brief monograph of Paul O'Brien *Buddhism in India and China* are used in conjunction with above works for the following brief outline.[5]

The northern route of Buddhism touching the Altai mountains and the Caspian sea, the central route through Chinese Turkestan north or south of the Tarim basin, were ruled from the second century BCE through the Han dynasty by kings that favored Buddhism. Tokharian speaking Kashgary, Sogdian speaking merchants from Transoxiana, the Yüeh-chih, an Indo-scythian tribe from Kushana brought knowledge of Buddhism to China through trade and warfare. Legend says that when the Han Emperor Ming-ti (58-75 CE) saw a sixteen foot high "golden man" in a dream, it was indeed a sign from the Buddha. An ambassador was sent to India to inquire about Buddhism. Two monks returned from India in 67 CE, Mo-teng and Chu Fa-lan. Chu Fa-lan translated the Sutra in 42 Chapters into Chinese for the imperial library.[6]

The Forty-two Chapter Sutra taught the legend of the birth of the Buddha, a summary of his preaching, the way of Buddhist ascesis, meditation, and the doctrines of karma and metempsychosis. The Parthian monk An Shih-kao and the Indo-scythian Liu Chia-ch'an translated the Sutra of Infinite Life (Wu-liang Shou Ching) and the Sutra of infinite Purity (Wu-liang Ch'ing-ching ching) at Lo-yang, between 148-186 CE. From the End of the Han in 220 CE until re-unification under the Sui Emperor in 581 CE, China was divided into three, then into ten southern and sixteen northern kingdoms. Both Buddhism and Taoism flourished and grew during this period of disunity. Buddhism especially was popular as an oasis of peace and tranquillity during a time of intensive war and instability.

The reasons for Buddhism's early success have been variously described by Asian and western scholars. Five causes are generally agreed upon as factors for Buddhism's popularity:
1. Mahayana Buddhism taught general salvation for the masses.
2. Buddhist metaphysics intrigued the intellectual scholars.
3. Buddhist monasteries offered havens of peace, prayer, and refuge during war. Some note the parallels with western monasticism in Christian Europe during the same period.
4. Buddhist rites for the dead appealed to popular practice.
5. Buddhism was favored by emperors as a power for order, peace, production and prosperity. Note the parallels with the restoration of religious practice in modern China (chapter seven).

During the period of division monks from central Asia translated the Nirvana Sutra, the Lotus Sutra *Miao-fa Lien-hua Ching* (Fa-hu, i.e. *Dharma Raksa* first translated the work ca. 266-317 CE), and the Ullambhana Sutra, that taught the need to free all souls from the fires of Buddhist hell. Along with the Mahayana doctrines of Universal Salvation, the Chinese villager was encouraged to offer rites for all souls, i.e., spirits other than family ancestors. The Ullambhana Sutra had a profound effect on popular religious practice, and on Taoist ritual for the people. It's Chinese equivalent, The *Yü-lan P'en* rite for Freeing of All Souls became an annual pre-harvest festival celebrated throughout East Asia during the seventh lunar month.[7]

Taoism too had a profound influence on the translation of early Buddhist texts. Taoist notions of *wu* transcendence were used by Buddhist translators of the early "Six houses" and "seven schools" of Buddhist thought.[8] Tao An (312-385 CE) taught that "non-being (*wu*) lies prior to the first evolution, and emptiness is the beginning of the multitudinous shapes.. if (man) could rest his mind in original non-being (*pen-wu*本無), heterodox thoughts would then cease."[9] Early Buddhist schools treated by Chi-tsang include:

1. *Original non-being*, Tao An, 312-385 CE.
2. *Variant non-being*, Chu Tao-ch'ien, d. 374 CE. Non-being generates all of nature, (influenced by Lao-tzu, Ch. 42).
3. *Matter as such*, Chih Tao-lin, 314-366, influence of Chuang-tzu.
4. *No mind* (Wu-hsin), Chu Fa-wen, (d.?), influence of Chuang-tzu.
5. *Stored impressions*, Yu Fa-lan, (ca. 370), what is seen by the mind is illusion; empty the mind, awaken to the highest truth.
6. *Phenomena are illusion*, Tao-yi, d. 401 CE. Dharma is illusion. Spirit and mind are real; when empty, find the highest truth.
7. *Combined cause*, Yü Tao-sui, of Tun-huang; (d.?), being is made by multiple causes; relational cause is the highest truth.

The earliest Buddhist schools, as known from the fragmentary texts quoted by Chi-tsang, are metaphysical in nature, and closer to the theory of transcendent causation (gestation) taught in chapter 42 of the Lao-tzu. Later Buddhist schools, however, are closer to *upaya* "skill-in-means" epistemology that empties mental image and destructures the process of cognition. The non-reality of mental image, not the non-reality of the outer world, are emphasized in many Buddhist sources. Thus Buddhist enlightenment consists for these early schools in emptying or destructuring mental images. *Empty mind intuits non-being* is a theory shared by Buddhist and Taoist of this period.

The purification of mind, ie, the de-causation of word in the mind by non-judgement i.e., non-formation of predicated causal concepts, is common to early Buddhist and Taoist practice. The conscious separation of Buddhist and Taoist terminology, and subsequently the influence of the emptying *sunya* philosophy of the saintly Indian monk Nagarjuna brought about a clearer distinction between the two forms of practice. The most influential Buddhist scholar responsible for these changes was the eccentric monk Kumarajiva (344-413 CE), who was captured by the northern Liang kingdom in 384 CE, then by the Ch'in kingdom in 401 CE. Brought to the capital city of Ch'ang-an, Kumarajiva was given a large body of monks to help translate the Buddhist scriptures of India and Inner Asia into Chinese.[10]

Two of Kumarajiva's most important disciples were the Chinese monks Seng Chao and Tao Sheng. Seng Chao (384-414 CE) was born in Ch'ang-an, and earned his living as a calligrapher (text copyist).[11] Turning from *hsüan-hsüeh* neo-Taoism to Buddhism, he read the *Vimalakirti Sutra*, and decided to become a monk. He joined the group of Kumarajiva, and wrote an influential series of treatises now known as *The Book of Chao* (i.e., the Book of Seng Chao).[12] Seng Chao explained, in these writings, the Buddhist philosophy of the middle way, (Sanskrit: *Madhyamika*; Chin.: *San-lun* 三論), as understood from the teachings of Kumarajiva. Chao taught that the judgement of movement and quiescence, real and "empty," being and non-being must be suspended for Buddhist enlightenment. *Prajña* or wisdom, i.e., ultimate truth (*martha satya*, Chen-ti 真諦) cannot be an object of knowledge, since knowledge is dependent upon relation of mind to objects mediated by the senses. That is to say, knowledge by the very process of cognition is meant to deal with things. Absolute truth, therefore, cannot be known by the process of cognition.[13]

Tao Sheng 道生 (360-434 CE) was born in Suchow, Chiangsu province, central China.[14] He became a Buddhist monk, and in 406 CE traveled to Ch'ang-an to become a disciple of Kumarajiva. His writings had a profound effect on the development of Chinese Buddhism. Tao Sheng taught the important notion that words were but semiotic symbols, to be discarded once ultimate truth had been encountered. The theory of retribution for good or bad deeds, so essential to the Vedic system out of which Buddhism developed, even the words of the canonical scriptures themselves, were among the words to be discarded. "A good deed entails no retribution," and the doctrine of instantaneous enlightenment, both essential parts of later Ch'an (Zen) Buddhist practice, were first enuntiated by Tao Sheng. Learning, knowledge, and ascesis are only means towards the goal of enlightenment, Tao Sheng taught. Intuitive understanding, a state of mirror-like voidness, was a condition necessarily without stages. Enlightenment must therefore be instantaneous (Tun-wu 頓悟), i.e., without verbal content.

Summarizing Buddhism during the period of division, i.e., from the fall of the Han dynasty to the beginning of the Sui (220 to 569 CE),[15] the following chronicle of monks and their translations of Buddhist canonical works can be made:

252 CE. The Dharmakala school at Lo-yang, under the Wei kingdom, translated the entire *Vinaya* rules for monks, and re-edited the *Amitayus sutra* (The act of faith in Amida Buddha saves all).

241 CE. Kang Seng-hui and Chih Ch'ien translate the Amida Sutra.

266-317 CE. Dharma-rak ʃ sa, supported by the Ch'in, translates the *Saddharma Pundarika Sutra* (Lotus Sutra), and the *Ullambhana Sutra* (the *Yü-lan P'en Ching*盂蘭盆); beginning of the seventh month fifteenth day Yü-lan P'en festival to free all souls from hell.

335 CE. The T'o-pa Hun rulers of the north issue an edict of tolerance for Buddhism, due to the influence of Fu-t'u-teng, a Mahayana monk from Kusha in Kashgary.

384-413 CE. The dissolute monk Kumarajiva translates the major Mahayana canons into Chinese at Ku-tsang, and then at Ch'ang-an; these included the works of Asvaghosa, Vasubandhu, and Nagarjuna's Madhyamika (San-lun) theory of emptiness and suspended judgement.[16]

399-414 CE. The monk Fa-hsien travels from Ch'ang-an via Kashgary to India to bring back Buddhist scriptures. He returns by the sea route, via Sri Lanka, Indonesia, and Shantung.

414-520 CE. Carving of the great Buddhist statues at the caves of Yunkang in Shanhsi, and at Lung-men near Lo-yang. The first texts of Tantric Buddhism (mantric dharani) come to China.

518-521 CE. Queen Hu of the northern Wei (Tungus) sends the monk Sung Yun to Gandhara and Udyana in India; he returns with 170 scriptures as yet unknown in China.

502-550 CE. The Emperor Wu of the southern Liang dynasty favors Buddhism, and sponsors the first Buddhist Canon, with 2,213 works.

546-569 CE. The monk Paramartha from Udjayana arrives in China, and translates the "Awakening of Faith," *Vajraccedika*, and *Abhidarma-kosa*, among many other works.

The period of division between the northern and southern kingdoms came to an end with the formation of the Sui empire, 589 to 618 CE. During this period of intense social and political change, Buddhism and Taoism grew and flourished. The mutual influence of the two great religious movements brought about profound spiritual changes in China as well. The tetralema of Madhyamika Buddhism (neither affirm or deny the real or the mental image) and the emptying philosophy of Lao-Chuang seemed hardly distinguishable to the mystics and ascetics who followed one or the other practice. With the establishment of a permanent unifying rule in China, the period of religious creativity too came to an end. Buddhism in China developed its own schools of practice during the Sui and T'ang periods.

III. Diversity: The Buddhist Schools of China
A diversity of Buddhist schools developed in China between the fifth and ninth centuries CE. From the period of disunity, when Hui Yüan founded the Pure Land School (at Lu Shan, ca. 402 CE) until the suppression of Buddhism by the mad emperor Wu-tsung in 845 CE ten major Buddhist movements arose. The Chinese schools were in many ways analogous to their Indian roots, and in others were adapted so thoroughly into the Chinese religious system as to be viable only in Chinese cultural idiom. The ten schools and their founders are listed as follows:[17]

Name of School	Founder	Date
1. *Pure Land* (Ching-t'u 淨土)	Hui Yüan 慧遠	402 CE
2. *Ch'an* (Zen 禪)	Bodhiharma, Hui Neng 慧能	520, 713 CE
3. *T'ien T'ai* (Tendai 天台)	Chih I 智顗	575 CE
4. *Hua Yen* (華嚴)	Ta Fa Hsun, Hsien Shou	640, 712 CE
5. *Fa Hsiang*, (Wei-shih 法相唯識)	Hsüan Tsang 玄奘	648 CE
6. *San Lun* (Madhyamika 三論)	Kumarajiva 鳩摩羅什	408 CE
(Absorbed by T'ien T'ai, basic to all Chinese Buddhism)		
7. *Chen Yen* (Tantric 真言)	Vajrabodhi	719 CE
8. *Ch'eng Shih* (Theravada 成實)	Kumarajiva	408 CE
9. *Chu She* (Abhidharmakosa 俱舍)	Paramartha	556 CE
10. *Vinaya* (Ritual 律)	Tao Hsüan	ca. 650 CE

Unlike the Buddhism of Tibet or Japan, which developed into various schools and sects, Chinese Buddhism of the T'ang dynasty emphasized the use of a text or a practice, associated with a specific monastery or a specific master. By the Sung dynasty (960-1281 CE) and the period of religious reformation the ten schools were assimilated into a generic Chinese Buddhist practice. From the period of the reformation onwards, Buddhist monks and nuns favored the chants of Pure Land and an adapted form of Ch'an (Zen) meditation, as will be seen below. Five of the above schools, Pure Land, T'ien T'ai, Hua Yen, Ch'an (Zen), and Chen Yen (Tantric) Buddhism had a lasting impact on Buddhism in China, Japan, and abroad. The other schools, whose influence is still felt within Chinese Buddhist practice, became absorbed in the popular form of Buddhist ascesis after the reformation.

1. *The Pure Land School.* Ching-t'u 凈土(Jpn.: Jodo).

The teachings of the Pure Land school base enlightenment on an act of saving faith in Amida, the Buddha conceived of as measureless compassion and light. Three early texts are the source for the practice of invoking Amida:

a. The Greater Sukhavati Sutra, *Wu-liang Shou Ching*, first said to have been translated by An Shih Kao between 140-170 CE. The translation of Chih Ch'ien (222-253 CE) points to a lost sanskrit text of the 1st-2nd century CE.

b. The Lesser Sukhavati Sutra, *A-mi-t'uo Ching*, translated by Kumarajiva in 402 CE, and later by Hsüan Tsang, 650 CE.

c. The *Amitayurdhyana* sutra, "Meditation on Amitayus," *Fuo-shuo kuan wu-liang shou fuo ching*, translated by Kalayasas in 424 CE.[18]

The legend of Amida as told in the Greater Sukhavati Sutra tells of a king-monk named Dharmakara (Dharma storehouse) who makes forty-eight vows before becoming a Buddha. Of these the eighteenth is recognized as the most important:

> When I become a Buddha, let all living beings of the ten regions of the universe maintain a confident and joyful faith in me. Let them concentrate their longing on a rebirth in my paradise. Let them call upon my name, even ten times or less; then provided they have not committed the five henious sins, have not slandered or vilified the true religion, the desire of those beings to be born into my paradise will surely be fulfilled. If this be not so, may I never receive the perfect enlightenment of a Buddha.

Though the earlier texts of the Pure Land tradition do not reject good works, the Lesser Sukhavati sutra states clearly the doctrine of salvation by faith alone:

> Beings are not born in that (Pure Land) Buddha country as a reward and result of good works done in this life. No, all men and women who hear and bear in mind for seven days,

81

or for only one day, the name of Amitayus, when they come to die, Amitayus will stand before them in the hour of their death. They will depart this life with quiet minds, and will be reborn in paradise (Pure Land).

This act of saving faith in Amida, the prospect of a second chance to reach nirvana from the peaceful lotus filled Pure Land by envisioning and invoking the name of Amida, became the single most popular form of Buddhist practice in East Asia. China and Japan both accepted the doctrines of Pure Land Buddhism as the simplest and most easily understood form of Buddhist practice. Buddhism no longer needed to rely on Taoist notions of the empty center or non-cognitive awareness for acceptance. Though the distinction between the two great religions was not always clear in the popular mind, Buddhists and Taoists themselves were more and more aware of their differences. Emperors were swayed to recognize one or the other system as superior, from the North-south period onward, through Chinese history.[19]

The Pure Land devotion to Amida took two forms. The first, more popular form, was a simple invocation "Namu Amitabha," made in the pure faith of Amida's saving power. The second, enshrined in art throughout China until the present day, is the triple invocation of Amida, *Kuanyin* (Avalokitesvara), and *Ta-shih Chih* (Mahasthama). The latter two bodhisattva represent the compassion and wisdom of Amida, respectively. These three statues are found in the western hall of Buddhist temples throughout China. Kuanyin, or Avalokitesvara (Avalokita-isvara, *Kuan Tzu-tsai* 観自在 the Lord who looks down with compassion on all humans) became an object of devotion that rivaled and surpassed that of Amida.

By a misunderstanding of the foreign sanskrit transliterated into Chinese, the word Avalokitesvara was taken to mean *Avalokita-svara*, (Kuan shih-yin 観世音) He/she who sees the cries or sounds of the world. The compassionate Bodhisattva gradually transformed from a T'ang dynasty young man into a Sung dynasty woman (960 CE). Pure Land mandalas pictured a female Kuanyin as well as a male Amida coming down to bring the soul into the pure land, at the moment of death. The saving powers of Kuanyin were further described in the 25th (26th) *P'u-men P'in* chapter of the Lotus Sutra, promoted by the T'ien-t'ai school. By the Eighth Century and the coming of Tantric Buddhism to China, there were some 27 forms of Avalokitesvara honored in the Lotus World Mandala alone, a rich source of later iconography.

2. The *T'ien T'ai School*. Also called *Fa-hua Tsung*, Lotus school.

The T'ien T'ai school was founded by Chih I (pronounced Jr Yee, 538-597 CE). An ascetic of Mount T'ien T'ai (Platform of Heaven) in Chekiang province, he made a grand synthesis of Buddhist sutras and teachings based on the centrality of the Lotus Sutra, and the Ch'an-Zen meditations of the Madhyamika tradition. Chih I drew his teachings on Zen meditation and Madhyamika from the monk Hui Wen (d. 550 CE) who practiced a form of Zen based on Kumarajiva's translation of the Chung-lun (Madhyamika) "Middle Way." This form of Zen (dhyana) was called *chih-kuan* (samatha-vipasyana). *Chih* (jr) was taken to mean the suspension of all judgement and will, i.e., neither affirming or denying the phenomenal or the real, the relative or the absolute. *Kuan* meant to look outward from the void center of the body, i.e., toward the other shore of prajña-wisdom, or to look toward the suffering world with compassion.[20]

Chih I formulated a grand synthesis of Buddhist doctrines that became a hallmark of Chinese Buddhism after his time. The teachings of the Buddha were placed into five "historical" periods, as Chih I conceived them to have been taught by the Buddha himself. The five periods are as follows:

a. The *Hua Yen* 華嚴 period, taught by Buddha for the first three weeks after his enlightenment under the Bo tree. The *Hua Yen* (Avatamsaka) Sutra contained the fullest, most advanced teachings of the Buddha on sudden enlightenment, but was too difficult for humans of that period to understand.[21]

b. The *A-han* 阿含 period. For twelve years Buddha taught the doctrines contained in the Agamas, i.e., the Theravada-Nikaya tradition of the Arhat or the way of gradual enlightenment.

c. The *fang-teng* 方等 period. For the next eight years Buddha taught the Vaipuyla sutras, a period of expansion i.e., teaching the gradual Theravada to some, and the sudden Mahayana methods to others. The secret mind-mouth-body tantra is assigned here.[22]

d. The *P'an-jo* 般若 period. For twenty-two years Buddha taught the Prajña-paramita scriptures, and the distinctive doctrines of the Madhyamika, the empty middle way of wisdom.

e. The *Fa-hua* 法華 period. For the last eight years of his life Buddha taught the *Fa-hua ching*, (with its 25/26th chapter emphasis on the saving power of Kuanyin), the Pure Land sutras, and the Nirvana Sutra (Nieh-p'an ching 涅槃), a complete doctrine.

The synthesis of Buddhist doctrines proposed by Chih I, though highly uncritical from the viewpoint of the modern hermeneutic scholar, nevertheless wielded profound influence on later Chinese and Japanese Buddhism.[23] His teachings are found in twenty-two works in the modern Taisho Canon, attributed to Chih I himself, or composed from notes taken by his disciples during his lectures. Among these are the Great and Lesser Vipasyana meditations, and treatises explaining the Lotus Sutra.[24] Chih I taught that Ch'an (Zen) could be practiced not only while sitting, but while walking, working, and by acts of compassion in everyday life.

The philosophy of T'ien-t'ai is based ultimately on the San-lun (Madhyamika) school of *sunya* emptiness and non-judgement. The monk Chi Tsang, (549-623 CE) of Nanjing, though not himself a T'ien-t'ai follower, wrote lengthy commentaries on the Madhyamika, and developed the theory of the double truth, which became an essential part of Chinese Buddhist practice. The double truth theory holds that worldly and ascetic or perfected judgement are different. Worldy judgement either affirms or denies the existence of being, i.e., by judging a thing to exist, be true, or not. Perfected i.e., madhyamika ascetic practice neither affirms or denies being and non-being. In this latter state, the affirmation of either being or non-being is taken to be a worldly truth. To affirm or deny life, death, nirvana, or the Buddha's teachings is to take one or another side of an extreme. To neither affirm or deny is to take the "middle path."

In an even higher meditative state (Chi Tsang's third or highest form of ascesis), all categories of judgement are to be abandoned. The middle path itself, a destructured and decentered *sunyata* or emptiness, in the final state, must eventually be discarded, since it too is empty. Thus the void, the real, and the illusory (i.e., sunya-k'ung 空 the void middle path, *shih* 事 the real, and *hsiang* 相 the mental image) are not affirmed or denied. This ascesis of suspended judgement is epistemologically similar to the way of Chuang-tzu, but metaphysically quite different from Taoist ascesis. The forty-second chapter of the Lao-tzu (see Chapter Two above) affirms that the Tao does give birth to the One (the entire cosmos), the one to the Two (yin-yang), and the Two to the Three (Heaven-earth-water), and the myriad creatures. The decentered suspension of judgement in both Buddhist and Taoist meditation may be analogous, but the metaphysical position is significantly different.

3. The *Hua Yen* 華嚴 Avatamsaka Sutra, and the *Fa Hsiang* school of idealism.

After the Madhyamika school of empty or decentered judgement, the next most influential Buddhist philosophy in China derives from the Indian schools of *Yogacara, wei-shih Lun* 唯識 that attribute reality to illusory manifestations of the mind. The monk Hsüan Tsang (596-664 CE) traveled across the silk route to India beginning in 596 CE, and returned to Ch'ang-an and a hero's welcome in 645 CE. Hsüan Tsang brought back to China 657 Buddhist texts. Among these were the major works of the idealist philosopher Vasubandhu, the *Abhidharma-kosa* and the *Vijñaptimatra sastra*. Hsüan Tsang spent the rest of his life translating the Yogacara idealist texts from sanskrit into Chinese, including the theory of *Alaya* 阿賴耶 or storehouse consciousness.

According to this theory, there are eight stages or modes of consciousness: i.e., the five senses feed data to the sixth sense-center of the brain that integrates the data into a single unified experience. The seventh stage of intellection, called *manas* (末那 muo-na) creates the false notions of ego, self-belief, ignorance, conceit, and self-love. These seven stages act as seeds that "perfume" and fertilize the eighth *Alaya* inner consciousness. The *Alaya* mind is a storehouse (tsang-shih 藏識) that creates the mental illusion of outer reality. As long as one believes in the reality of the self (atman, wo 我) or the truth of the dharmas, i.e., doctrines, facts, reality, enlightenment and the escape from suffering-recycling is impossible.[25]

Hsüan Tsang's *Fa Hsiang* 法相 school of Yogacara idealism as described in the *Ch'eng wei-shih lun*, The Completion of the Doctrine of Idealism (All Reality is Mere Ideation) taught that enlightenment was to be realized by not fertilizing the alaya-storehouse with the seeds or perfume of the seven prior stages of consciousness. Non-attachment to the real world or the dharma intellect world consists in a choice or a judgement that the suffering of the real world, the transition from life to death, and the doctrines-dharma of the intellect are illusion. The enlightened one judges that all things, real and mental, are non-existent of themselves. The unenlightened judge things, ego, and dharmas to be real. The enlightened take them to be unreal, illusion. The only real is the Bhutatthata, i.e., the *chen-ju* 真如, truly constantly thus. Yogacara teaches an unchanging ultimate reality, that does not arise.

85

Hsüan Tsang's doctrines of pure idealism were contrary to practical Chinese Buddhist philosophy in two ways: 1) he held the theory that man and nature are an illusion, and 2) he taught that not all sentient beings had the Buddha nature, i.e., the potency for enlightenment. These views were opposed by Hsüan Tsang's major disciple Fa Tsang 法藏 (643-712 CE), who is considered to be the founder of the *Hua Yen* 華嚴 school. Based on the Avatamsaka sutra and the philosophy of idealist monism, Fa Tsang taught that a permanent immutable mind was the basis for all reality, a kind of objective realism. This objectivizing of the ideal world re-affirmed the basic Chinese assumptions denied by Hsüan Tsang. The five periods of Buddha's doctrines taught by T'ien-t'ai Buddhists had affirmed that The Hua Yen sutra was the highest and most difficult of Buddha's teaching. The Hua Yen school of Fa Tsang now taught that indeed the Avatamsaka sutra was the most perfected form of Buddhist practice.

The Hua Yen Ching teaches four objects of knowledge, i.e., the real or noumenal world (shih 事), the phenomenal or mind reflected world (li 理), non-distinction or oneness between the real and the phenomenal (shih-li wu yi 事理無異), and no differentiation between real and real (shih-shih wu yi 事事無異). The basic insight of Yogacara idealism, in the teaching of Hua Yen school, is that there is no difference in the world of the real and phenomenal, and the absolute ideal Buddha mind. To affirm the oneness of all phenomena with the absolute ultimate is the source of enlightenment. Thus the Hua Yen school of Fa Tsang and his followers accepted the doctrines of Yogacara idealism and the eighth alaya consciousness, and at the same time affirmed the oneness of all things with the absolute mind.[26] The influence of Hua Yen idealism on the founding of later Ch'an (Zen) Buddhism and its practice was profound.

4. The *Ch'an* 禅 (Zen) school of master-disciple meditation.

The Ch'an (Zen) school of Buddhist meditation is the most widely recognized form of Buddhist practice outside of Asia. Bookshops, libraries, and magazine racks throughout Europe and America carry a wide variety of translated of Zen texts. Zen meditation centers, Zen masters, and university courses studying the phenomenon of Zen in the west abound. A concise summary of the origin and transmission of Ch'an-Zen teachings is found in David Chappell's "Hermeneutical Phases in Chinese Buddhism," under the title *The Ch'an Tradition*.[27]

Many excellent works in English concerning Ch'an-Zen are available. A list published in 1980 by Laurence Thompson covers eight double column pages, 227 titles on Chinese Ch'an alone, exclusive of the popular Japanese forms of Zen meditation popularized by D.T. Suzuki.

A dialogue between western monks and nuns of the Christian monastic tradition and Zen Buddhists of Japan has proven the practical use of Ch'an meditation outside of a doctrinal-sectarian context. The methods of concentration taught by the Ch'an-Zen masters are applicable to all forms of religious prayer, as well as to the martial and literary arts. Ch'an-Zen can be used to quiet the worried mind, eliminate distractions during prayer, and concentrate intellect, will (heart), and body on the work at hand, whether secular or sacred. Thus Ch'an-Zen meditation, along with Pure Land chant are the two most popular forms of Buddhist practice in China today. Zen practice in its western form is often quite different from the Chinese use of Ch'an techniques, combining Pure Land chant with quiet meditation.

In China after the Sung dynasty (960 CE) all Buddhist monks and nuns sought a license of ordination in a Ch'an lineage because the legends of 1004 CE *Transmission of the Lamp* Ch'an classic (Ching-te ch'uan-teng lu) taught that Ch'an had been transmitted directly from Buddha himself to Rahula, Nagarjuna, and Boddhidharma (a Scythian monk credited with bringing Ch'an-Zen to China in the early 6th century). Thus a monk or nun ordained in the Ch'an tradition could claim direct spiritual descent from Buddha, as well as from a later master. Ch'an was also popular because it allowed for an open, direct, inspired interpretation of a text, adapted to the needs of the disciple, rather than a closed, single meaning assigned to the written word.

Ch'an-Zen practice inspired a series of poetic phrases and dialogues between master and disciple, (Yü-lu 語錄) in which the teachings or sayings of an expert were interpreted in a different way by each follower. These sayings were recorded as poetry, as *kung-an* conundrum to be solved individually, or as dialogues between master and disciple. The non-closure of text, and the creative or eidetic interpretation of meaning were common to Taoist as well as Ch'an Buddhist practice in China.[28] Modern hermeneutic and post-structuralist scholars in the west have recently taken note of this openness to interpretative meaning, a hallmark of the Chinese ascesis of emptiness and the spiritual quest. Whether in its earlier Madhyamika or later Yogacara form, Ch'an Buddhist meditation left defining of words open in order to awaken intuitive awareness in the disciple.[29]

The legendary origins of Ch'an in China begin always with the coming of Boddhidharma to the Liang kingdom centered in Nanjing, south China, and later meditative residence in the Shao-lin temple of Mt. Sung, central China, ca. 520-549 CE. The use and spread of the Lankavatara sutra, and the *Treatise on the Two Entrances and Four Practices* (Er-ju ssu-hsing lun 二入四行) are attributed to this famous master. Works by Tao Hsin (580-651 CE) and Hung Jen's sayings (600-674 CE.) are early examples of the doctrines of sudden enlightenment, non-reliance on text, and the "perfection of wisdom" by direct intuitive rather than logical or discursive reasoning.

The Vimalikirti sutra, Heart sutra, Diamond sutra, Nirvana sutra and the Awakening of Faith are all mentioned in the writings of the Ch'an masters.[30] Early Ch'an practice does not rely on a single scripture, emphasizes non-closure of word and definition, points directly to the heart-mind for enlightenment, and seeks to awaken prajna or intuitive awareness of the Buddha nature from within. But Ch'an did not become a systematized movement until the eighth century CE, after the founding of the Hua Yen school and the influence of Yogacara mind-only philosophy on Buddhist practice. Hua Yen masters such as Ch'ing Liang Kuo-shih (738-839 CE) and Kui Feng (780-841 CE) had deep connections with the development of Ch'an in the T'ang period. The three distinct kinds of Ch'an practice that developed during the T'ang, i.e., the southern school of Hui Neng based on the Platform Sutra, the northern school of Shen Hsiu, and the Oxhead school of Ma Tsu, (named after Mt. Oxhead near Nanjing) all rejected a logical intellectual approach to Buddhist enlightenment.

The history of Zen practice popularized in the west emphasizes the legend told in the Platform Sutra, extolling the poetic school of Hui Neng over the sitting school of Shen Hsiu. Though neither monk were probably ever together in the Shao-lin temple of Sung Shan, the widely accepted mid T'ang myth found in the Platform Sutra tells the following story of the Hui Neng's appointment as Sixth Patriarch, a tale often taken literally in the west. When Hung Jen, the fifth successor of Bodhidharma felt that death was approaching, he decided to hold a contest to appoint his successor. His eminent disciple Shen Hsiu wrote:

The body is like the Bodhi tree,
The mind is a mirror bright;
Carefully we cleanse them, hour by hour,
Lest dust should fall upon them.

Hui Neng, a Cantonese cook (monk) in the kitchen took a piece of charcoal and wrote on the wall next to Shen Hsiu's work:

Originally there was no Bodhi tree,
Nor was there any mirror;
Since originally there was nothing,
Whereon can the dust fall?

The Platform Sutra legend says that Hung Jen appointed Hui Neng to be his successor, making Hui Neng Zen's Sixth Patriarch. Hui Neng returned to south China, and founded the Ch'an (Zen) school of sudden enlightenment, through the use of poetic conundrum for intuitive awakening. Shen Hsiu went north, and was patronized at the court of Empress Wu. The Oxhead school of Ma Tsu used the method of master-disciple dialogue, to break logico-centered reasoning, and awaken intuitive awareness. All three forms of practice, joined with meditation on the vision of Amida, or the invoking of Amida's name, became a part of Ch'an (Zen) practice from the Sung dynasty (960 CE) until the present. The *Transmission of the Lamp* records composed ca. 1004 CE. show that the Ch'an school held to the tradition of master handing on the light of intuitive awareness to the disciple from the mid-T'ang period onward. Chinese Buddhism, unlike the Buddhism of India or later Japanese sectarianism, did not develop any new schools after the widespread popularity of Ch'an practice. The Buddhism of China until today focuses on the teachings of a master, and his or her choice of Buddhist sutra for enlightenment. Ch'an and Pure Land practice remain the most popular forms of Buddhist practice in both mainland and maritime China today.

IV. The Sung Dynasty Reformation
Much as in Europe more than 400 years later, the religious reformation of China was a movement away from a priestly towards a lay liturgy, regulated by the needs and adaptations of provincial and local customs. China never had a centralized religious system such as the southern Roman form of Christianity, nor kingly patronage for reform as in the northern European protestant movements. The central government

controlled the ordination and licensing of Buddhist and Taoist priests, from the Sung dynasty onward. The spirit of provincial and local self-reliance in religious, economic, and private family affairs was balanced by the central government jurisdiction over public rites of passage. The duty of the local mandarinate, besides overseeing the collection of taxes, the trying of court cases, and the administration of local justice, was to report on the deviations in local customary practice in perfunctory manner to the throne.

The basis of the religious reforms of the Sung dynasty and after, i.e., from the Sung dynasty through the founding of the Republic of China in 1912, was the doctrine of merit taught in such popular manuals as the *Kan-ying p'ien* (The Classic of Retribution) as described above in Chapter Two, and lay participation in rituals that won benefit for the living and freedom for ancestors from punishment in the underworld. The proliferation of such manuals, and lay involvement in their reading constituted a radical change in religious direction.

No longer were Buddhist monks and Taoist priests alone hired to chant sutras and canons to free souls from afterlife punishments. The laity too could perform the chanting, even conduct services in private temples and family altars without summoning priest, nun, or monk to perform the ceremonies. Since family members officiated at the state recognized rites of passage, the same family members, temple keepers, and lay devotees could now be used to chant canons of merit and repentance during privately conducted ceremony. Religion became the concern and the domain of the laity.

Lay Buddhist and Taoist societies, clan and guild associations, and the places of worship connected with such organizations thus became the focus of ritual activity during the autumn period of Chinese religious history. Lay associations took on a wide variety of forms and functions. Martial arts and Kung-fu clubs in the villages, trade guilds in the cities, clan associations, secret societies, and wayside shrines governed their own internal affairs. Shrine members burned incense, offered paper money, and sponsored ritual to win blessing for their families or other club members. Festivals depended on laity for performance, who in turn elected village leaders (t'ou-chia 頭家) and temple accountants (lu-chu 爐主) to handle the liturgical as well as the financial affairs of the temple. Buddhist monks and/or Taoist priests were selected by contract to perform ritual.

The performance of the reformed lay-oriented rituals, based on the Yin-yang five element system, were enriched by private, local, and provincial variations. Thus the theme of merit, so important to reformation liturgy, was expressed in a variety of symbols and signs. Paper money, symbol of merit won by human deeds of compassion and giving, reflected the tastes, myths, and whims of local custom.[31] The general Yin-yang rules mentioned in Chapter One were thus applied in a creative, innovative manner. As noted above, golden paper money in varying sizes was burned for the earth and the heavenly spirits, while silver paper money was reserved for the dead and demons of the underworld. Miniature paper houses, paper carriages (in modern days, paper Mercedes-Benz; see ch. 2.37) and other symbols of generous giving to the members of one's living family were burned as offerings, to symbolize care for the soul of deceased relatives in the afterlife.

The burning of the paper houses and paper money usually took place in conjunction with the chanting of canonical texts and sutras. The act of the lay person's burning of paper offerings and the act of chanting the Buddhist or Taoist text were seen as a single, related process. The one was not complete without the other. The role of the laity as a mediator in the liturgical process was more far-reaching and radical than the Protestant reformation in the west. Devout lay Buddhist practice, the openness of liturgical and meditative texts to lay interpretation, and the right of local temples and organizations to hire Buddhist or Taoist experts to perform ritual, to determine the content of ritual, to literally "do it oneself" transcended by far the Christian reformation in northern Europe.[32]

Furthermore, the act of providing paper houses for burning during ritual commemorating the dead was itself a semiotic sign (i.e., a true science or systematic use of signs) of a person who in reality provided well for his or her living family. Only the person who lived the Confucian virtues to the fullest, by caring for family, friends, and village society, was able to win merit for the deceased, chant Buddhist sutras, and burn paper money. Paper offerings were thus meant to be semiotic signs of a truly generous, family oriented life. The lay reformation taught that without the practice of Confucian virtue, the chanting of Buddhist texts, the dancing and meditating of Taoist liturgy, and the burnt offerings of the laity were meaningless.

91

The religious reformation of the Sung dynasty lasted well into the modern period, and continues in the winter of rebirth in the People's Republic and modern overseas China. During this long period, which we summarize here, Buddhist monastic practice was simplified. The chanting of Pure Land sutras, devotion to Amida and Kuanyin, and a form of Ch'an (Zen) sitting that emphasized visualization as well as Samatha-vipasyana emptying, became standardized practice throughout China. Almost all Buddhist monks and nuns sought an ordination or transmission of teachings from a Ch'an-Zen master, because of the myth that Buddha passed on his teachings of sudden enlightenment directly to the Zen lineage.

If asked today about lineages, most Chinese Buddhists will claim to follow Zen, Pure Land, the Garland Sutra, Lotus Sutra, Awakening of Faith, Vimalakirti, and whatever other teachings were received from a famous master. Two distinct kinds of teachings are transmitted to the faithful, i.e.: 1) the strict teachings of the Buddhist monastic tradition for those able to follow the path of celibacy, abstinence from meat and spicy foods, and a life of strictly regimented discipline, and 2) the *upaya* doctrines of skillful means, whereby the reading of fortunes, burning of paper money, chanting of sutras for releasing souls from hell, and other folk practices are allowed in order to invoke an act of faith in the saving powers of Amida.

The absorption of the second sort of Buddhist practices into popular folk belief and custom, which was typical of Chinese religion from the Sung reformation onwards, is depicted in a wide variety of folk manuals, *shan-shu* books distributed for merit, and folk art hung in temples and homes during funeral ritual. An examples of art depicting the punishments of Buddhist hell are found in such *shan-shu* books as the ever popular *Yü-li Pao-ch'ao* (Shanghai:1891), which is widely distributed in Hongkong, Taiwan, and southeast Asia. The opening pages of the manual bear the following inscription:

> The heart-mind is (seat of) spirit;
> Spirit is (seated in) heart-mind.
> Heart without remorse is spirit without remorse;
> To deceive the heart is to deceive the spirit.
> The hell of underworld punishments
> Is the hell in our hearts.
> If man's heart has not the fruits of hell,
> The hell of punishments will be empty.

92

The manual then depicts a kitchen scene, with the men and the women of the household standing around the stove gossiping.

Fig. 2. The Hearth spirit reports to heaven

The Ssu-ming guardian of destiny/keeper of the hearth carefully records the good and bad deeds of the family, while listening to the gossip. The records of the hearth spirit (tsao shen灶神 the *ssu-ming* keeper of destiny) are brought before the Emperor of the Eastern Peak, whose minister holds up the decree:

Let good deeds be rewarded, evil punished.

The next ten scenes depict the punishments meted out to human beings for the offenses and evil deeds committed against fellow men and women of the community. A variety of scrolls depicting hell's punishments are used to decorate the walls of the room where funeral rites are being held, temples halls dedicated to freeing souls from hell, and *shan-shu* , distributed freely to win merit. Wood block prints depict the ten stages of hell, where every possible offense is punished in gory detail. Thieves arms are cut off, liars tongues impaled, male chauvinists sodomized by the saw-like beak of giant swordfish, gossiping women boiled in a bloody pool, and (in modern versions) bad drivers eternally run over by Taipei taxicabs.

The last two woodblock prints show 1) the karmic wheel of fate, recycling hell's liberated into one of the six paths of human existence, deva (spirit), human, animal, *preta* orphaned soul, *asura* angry demon, and *kuei* vengeful ghost, and 2) the tale of Meng Chiang-nü who gives a cup of forget potion to each person who is recycled into a new exis-tence. This latter scene is an expression of the Chinese reluctance to

93

accept the notion of Buddhist recycling. Chinese belief from primordial times has held that the soul, once out of the underworld, ascends to the pure Yang world of the heavens. To insure the safe journey of the soul out of hell into a happier form of afterlife, Taoist funeral rites and Buddhist memorial services are often both observed, or a Christian and Buddhist funeral performed contiguously.

This preoccupation of the Chinese religious mentality with winning blessing, longevity, and wealth through Buddhist and Taoist rites for the ancestors, is an honest expression of the goals of the human condition. As will be seen in the final chapter, after the 1979 restoration of religion in China, concern for ancestors in the afterlife was one of the first functions to be restored to Buddhist temples. The hiring of Buddhist monks and nuns to chant sutras for those who died during the long years preceding and during the cultural revolution became one of the first goals of the restoration.

All of these practices common to Chinese religion throughout modern mainland and maritime China are at surface level almost impossible to relate to the ascetic goals of the Taoist and Buddhist tradition. Yet we shall see in Chapter Seven that numbers of young men and women are choosing lives of ascetic celibacy and prayer in the people's Republic of China. More attend Christian services and Masses in mainland Chinese churches than in Taiwan, secular Japan, or much of Europe. The blend of common sense practicality and the needs of daily life with the deeper drive for mystic experience, solitary prayer, and the life of the ascetic was and is very much alive in China.

The methods and goals of Taoist and Buddhist ascesis are different, when seen from the viewpoint of ritual semiotics. The Buddhist sense of karmic cycling, pictured in the ten scrolls that are shared by Taoist and Buddhist funeral rites, is overcome by the Taoist semiotics of alchemical refining. The shen-spirit in the traditional Chinese philosophical (cosmological) system is charged at birth with breath (ch'i) and vital essence (ching). Upon death, when the soul separates from the body, the charge of ch'i and ching are used up. The soul is separated from the body, i.e., death occurs when the cycle of yin and yang are completed. The soul descends to the Buddhist underworld to be purified in nine stages (i.e., a magic square, as explained in chapter one). Once purified and released, the soul ascends to Taoist heaven.

This process of refinement is pictured on the silk robe of the Han dynasty princess whose tomb was discovered at Ma Wang Tui in 1974, proving that the concept existed in a clear triple-world form by the early Han dynasty, i.e., by the writing of the Huai-nan-tzu (ca. 180-169 BCE.). The princess is pictured in the famous burial robe as being on earth, then in hell, and finally in heaven, standing in audience before the Tao.[33] This process is unmistakably portrayed as a kind of spiritual alchemy of refinement. From the visible world of yang and yin in balance the soul descends first to the underworld realms of yin, then is cycled upwards to the realms of pure yang, and audience with the Tao.

All of the saints, holy men and women, and heroes whose statues are revered in Chinese temples are portrayed as humans for whom this process was somehow reversed or truncated. Whether death occurred by sickness, violence, or outstanding service in the Chinese community, the statues in Chinese popular and Taoist temples represent humans for whom the process of yang's decreasing presence (ch'i and ching used up) and yin's dominance was reversed or interrupted. Such figures as Kuan Kung, the red-faced general of the Three Kingdoms who was strangled to death, is canonized as patron of martial arts and merchants. Ma-tsu or T'ien Hou, the young woman of Fukien province who died in her twenties is canonized for serving her family, farmers, and fishermen. Ch'ing-shui Tsu-shih, a T'ang dynasty monk of Anhsi in Ch'üan-chou prefecture, is patron of the helpless, the outcast, and the weak.[34] Wang Yeh, spirits of pestilence, are local mandarins who died or committed suicide in office.

The common denominator for Taoist and popular heroes depicted in temple friezes and statuary is therefore the utilization of the overweening yang powers left with the soul at the time of death. Taoist sages who practice the refinement of breath and *ching* vital essence ascend to the heavens in broad daylight (pai-jih sheng-t'ien白日升天). Popular heroes and saints are depicted as humans who die before their time, i.e., with a supercharge of yang power in their bodies. Because of the need to use the superfluous charge of ch'i and ching, such heroes are enfeoffed in local temples, and spend their energies in the service of mankind. Ordinary men and women who die in old age must be sent to the fiery realm of hell-purgatory, where the alchemical furnaces of the cosmos purify the shen-spirit and allow the soul to be wafted upwards to the immortal fairyland of Taoist bliss.[35]

95

The men and women of China's villages employ the powers of the Buddhist monk and nun to offer prayers and chant sutras in order to release the last kind of soul, i.e., the deceased who are being punished and purified in the underworld. They also hire Taoists to officiate at funeral services that enact the process of cosmic alchemy, that is, speed up the process of refinement in hell.[36] As state above, increasing numbers of the laity, from the Sung dynasty onwards, practice the chanting of Buddhist texts and invoke Taoist and folk heroes themselves for blessing, to release souls from the underworld, and practice personal ascesis.

The laity can choose from a wide variety of Buddhist and Taoist practices, for personal ascetic goals. The writing out of Buddhist sutras, chanting of the Twenty-fifth chapter of the Lotus Sutra, the Heart Sutra, and the *Ta-pei Chou* dharani (sanskrit seed words invoking Avalokitesvara-Kuanyin) are popular lay Buddhist exercises. The Taoist tradition, on the other hand, encourages the laity in breath meditation, physical exercises such as kung-fu, t'ai-chi, and ch'i-kung that extend energy and breath for healing, and village participation in the grand retreats for spiritual renewal called Chiao.

Thus the Buddhist and Taoist traditions of personal ascesis that teach monk, nun, and priest to be generous, outward looking for the community, decentered in the ascetic meaning of that word, have had a deep and lasting influence on popular laity based religious practice. The Taoist meditations which empty the mind and heart to achieve awareness of union with the Tao, and the Buddhist four-fold truth that teaches the annihilation of selfish desires are in fact the guiding principles for lay ascesis within the Chinese family. The ascetics of the parents who give their lives for their children, and children who center their life around their parents and extended family, are the means whereby the Tao is made present in the center of Chinese life.

NOTES
1. Lamotte, Étienne, *History of Indian Buddhism*, Louvain-Paris: Peeters Press, 1988, pp. 607-647.
2. The names of the Buddha and their meanings are as follows: 1) Siddhartha, he who has accomplished his purpose in coming; 2) Gautama, family name; 3) Buddha, the enlightened one; 4) Sakyamuni, sage of the Sakya clan; 5) Tathagata, thus come and thus gone; 6) Bhagavan, lord; 7) Cakravartin, universal monarch.

3. Anguttara-nikaya, III, 33; and Majjihma-nikaya, 26.

4. Taken from Nattier, Jan, The *Candragarbha-sutra* in Central and East Asia: Studies in a Buddhist Prophecy of decline, Ph.D. thesis, Harvard: 1988. Quoted with permission of author.

5. See the bibliography for these titles. Paul O'Brien, S.J., *Buddhism* (Baguio: 1963) lecture notes used with permission of the author.

6. O'Brien, X.1. Note that Pelliot, TP XIX, 255-433, denies the authenticity of the Ming-ti legend. Buddhist monks and believers were in Yang-chou valley by 65 CE.

7. See Chapter Seven, Seventh Month, Fifteenth day, for this festival.

8. See Feng Yu-lan, Bodde, D., *Chinese Philosophy*, Princeton: 1953, Vol. 2, pp. 243-292, for a thorough treatment of the "original non-being" and other early Chinese Buddhist treatises on *wu* notions of the transcendent that compare with Taoist treatises. We know of these early schools mainly through the *Chung-kuan-lun Su*, a treatise by the monk Chi-tsang (549-623).

9. Ibid., p. 245, quoting Chi-tsang, 3b.92.

10. See Fung Yu-lan, Bodde, D., *Chinese Philosophy* Vol. II, pp. 245, footnote 4, brief biography of Kumarajiva.

11. See Fung, Bodde, pp. 258-260.

12. See the Taisho Buddhist Canon, Vol. 45, #1858, pp. 150-161, translated by Liebenthal, W., *The Book of Chao, Monumenta Serica*, Monograph XIII, 1948.

13. Fung yu-lan, Bodde, Vol. II, pp. 267-9.

14. Ibid., pp. 270-84.

15. After the fall of the Han, 220 CE, China was split into three kingdoms, the Wei (220-265 CE) whose capital was at Lo-yang; the Wu (220-280 CE) at Nanjing, and the Shu-Han (221-264 CE) at Ch'eng-tu in Szechuan. The Ch'in dynasty defeated the Shu-han in 264 CE, the Wei in 265 CE, and the Wu in 280, uniting China for a brief period with Lo-yang as capital. But the T'o-pa (Mongol-Turks) pushed the Ch'in back to Ch'ang-an (317 CE), then south to Nanjing (317-420). Buddhism developed during this period of division, roughly at the same time as Christianity in Europe.

16. The dominance of Mahayana Buddhism in China seems to date from this period, due to the influence of the two monks from Kashgary where Mahayana was prevalent. See Nattier, Jan, *Buddhism in Central Asia: Basic Sources*, AAR Annual Meeting, Conference Paper, Nov., 1988.

17. O'Brien, p. XI, 1.

18. Ibid., p. XV, 1.

19. Kuang Hung Ming Chi, Taisho Vol. 52.

20. Lu Kuan Yu, *The Secrets of Chinese Meditation*, York Beach: Weiser, 1984, pp. 109-162.

21. Note that the Hua Yen school later used this typically Chinese synthesis of Chih I to declare their school the highest of Buddha's teachings. See #3, below.

22. Chinese tantric Buddhism was brought to Japan in the early Ninth century by the monks Saicho and Kukai.

23. Chih I's formula for integrating many forms of Buddhist practice stands as a high point in religious thinking. Japanese Tendai Buddhism, following this model, trained the founders of distinct Japanese schools, including Pure Land, Zen, and Nichiren.

24. Chappell, D., edit., *The Fourfold Teachings of Tendai*, Honolulu: 1983.

25. Fung, Bodde, Vol. II, p. 315.

26. Ibid., pp. 383-4.

27. Chappell, D., *Buddhist Hermeneutics*, Honolulu: University of Hawaii Press, 1988, pp. 190-98.

28. See Ch. 2, note 27 for the various interpretations given to Taoist meditation texts.

29. See Odin, Steve, "Derrida and the Decentered Universe of Zen Buddhism," *Journal of Chinese Philosophy*, Spring, 1989, for a treatment of the post-structuralists Derrida and Roland Barthes of the Kyoto school of Zen philosophy.

30. see Chappell, op. cit., p. 191-198, and Fung, Bodde, pp. 386-406 for detailed descriptions of Ch'an Buddhism's development.

31. See Ch. 2, p. 59.

32. "Do it yourself" manuals for ritual, geomancy (feng-shui, ti-li), and prognostication still abound in the bookshops of Taiwan, SE Asia, and Hongkong. Recently village markets in China are doing a brisk business in reprints of older self-help manuals.

33. See the illustration, the Ma Wang Tui burial robe.

34. See Chapter 6 for the hagiographies of popular spirit heroes.

35. The Chuang-tzu Nei-p'ien Ch. 1.

36. See Ch. 6 for the Taoist funeral.

4. THE RITE OF MARRIAGE
Building the Chinese Family

The first chapters of *Blue Dragon White Tiger* proposed the hypothesis that the Rites of Passage and the Annual Cycle of Festivals are structured by the Yin-yang Five Element theory. For Taoist and Confucian expert, the common factor of all rituals in the Chinese religious-cultural system is the Yin-yang pattern. Peasant, merchant, and other casual informants may not recognize these underlying principles, due to the meticulous care for detail imposed by local practice and custom. Taoist and other local experts who are hired to enact the rites, however, and the ritual textbooks that give instructions in how to do ritual are very explicit about how Yin-yang and the Five Elements guide the execution of ritual performance. The Yin-yang philosophy provides an archetypal system for easing the human rites of passage.

When marriage, birthing, puberty, burial, and ancestral rites are performed, the men and women of the Chinese community know exactly what to do because of two sources of help and expertise at their disposal. The first local authority for ritual performance is the Taoist or Confucian scholar, who by profession knows how to perform the rite. The second fountainhead of assistance are the written sources, i.e., manuals available in bookshops and streetside bazaars that tell the people of the community how to perform the rites without expert assistance. From the *Li Chi* Book of Rites (Han dynasty ca. 200 BCE to 200 CE) onwards, books of approved ritual have been carefully monitored by the State, and officially approved editions promulgated in each dynasty. The popular manuals widely used in China today derive from these traditional state approved texts.[1]

The books used in the following chapters to describe the Rites of Passage are Lin Po-t'ung's *Kuan, Hun, Sang, Chi,* (Canton: 1845, Puberty, Marriage, Burial, Ancestral Rites), the popular *Chia-li Ta-ch'eng* (The Complete Home Rituale), that can be found throughout Taiwan, Hongkong, and southeast Asia, and the detailed ethnographic descriptions Japanese scholars in China and Taiwan. The details translated from these texts has been augmented by oral information from Chinese of Honolulu, as well as from Chungshan district, Kwangtung Province, Hongkong, and Singapore. The saying of the *Li-chi* Book of Rites must always be kept in mind, when reading about Chinese customs: Laws at the National level are augmented by local customs and household taboos. Even though customs and taboos vary everywhere in China, the law of the Yin-yang Five Element system is everywhere the same.

The first and most fundamental Rite of Passage is marriage, the act which establishes the Chinese family. The family is the center of Chinese social and cultural life, and therefore every precaution and care is taken that the ritual establishing the family is done properly. Without the Chinese family the rites of passage and the annual cycle of festivals cannot be celebrated. Children cannot be cared for, food prepared, the aged cared for, the ancestors remembered, unless the family is first established. To do this the Chinese allow for many variations in the mode of marriage. A major marriage between adults, a minor marriage arranged from childhood, an uxorilocal marriage where children may be given the wife's family name, and concubine arrangements, i.e., the legal recognition of paternity, are all to be found within the Chinese social condition.[2]

The only time that a full marriage ceremony, described in these pages, is allowed is on the occasion of a major marriage, i.e., a ritual joining an adult man and woman into a new family. It is the major rite of marriage that is described in the following pages. The other forms of marriage named above are simply registered in the city offices. The details of the marriage rite described below are valid today. They can be used in the Taoist, Confucian, or purely secular tradition. Local custom and family preference decide what material objects are used. The steps of the ritual are more-or-less the same for all of China.

The standard rite of Chinese marriage remains structurally unchanged since the Han period, from 200 BCE to the present. Its various forms, embellished by the addition of local customs and family traditions can be reduced in essence to the bare bones of the Confucian ritual defined in precise terms by the Han dynasty "new text" liturgists. Taoist, Buddhist, and Confucian alike accept the structural influence of the Yin-yang Five Element cosmology in the ritual. The bride's family are given the role of Yin, and the groom's family the role of Yang. Positions taken by the actors on the stairs of the bride's residence, the main hall of the groom's household and all other subordinate actions and positions are governed by rules developed during the Han dynasty systematization of ritual.

100

The marriage ritual is divided into six liturgical stages, as follows: 1) *Na-pien*, fixing the betrothal date and obtaining the bride's consent; 2) *Na-pi*, exchange of gifts and formal engagement, betrothal; 3) *Ch'ing-ch'i*, deciding the banquet date and sending of invitations; 4) *Ch'en-lien*, bride's dowry sent to the groom's residence; 5) *Ch'in-yang*, bridal procession to the groom's house; 6) *Ho-chin*, the marriage banquet, followed by: a) venerating the groom's ancestors, the morning after, and b) returning to the bride's natal home as a guest, three days later. No matter what the local customs may dictate at each of the six stages, the underlying structure of the Chinese wedding follows the yin-yang rules of the Confucian classics. Thus yin-yang structure, not locally defined detail, is the universal element found in Chinese wedding ritual.

1. Na-pien 納采 Fixing the Betrothal Date with the Bride's Consent
The lengthy process of choosing a bride for the son of a family begins often with the boy or girl seeing each other at a public festival. Since boys and girls were not allowed to associate freely after puberty, nor were girls of good families allowed out in public except on certain festive occasions, traditional days were set aside by Chinese custom for meeting or viewing prospective husbands or wives. These days were: the lantern parade and dragon dance on the First Lunar month, fifteenth day, the cleaning of the graves and picnic on Ch'ing-ming festival in spring, and the ladies' festival on the Seventh Month, seventh day. When a family became aware that their son or daughter was ready for marriage, and that a suitable partner was available, the very first arrangements took place between the boy's and the girl's parents.

Lin Po-t'ung in a manual popular during the Ch'ing dynasty insists that the girl must first agree to the wedding before any further steps be taken.[3] To assure that the girl's wishes may be heard, an announcement written on a red slip of paper is first exchanged through a go-between. The red slip of paper is in fact a brief note from the groom's family to the bride's parents bearing the year, month, day, and hour of their son's birth. The "red slip of paper" on which these numbers were written was also called "the eight characters" (pa-tzu) because the year, month, day, and hour of birth were filled in with eight written characters; e.g., (19)48-03-26-06 in modern script, or by the traditional classic characters in ancient times. A go-between was carefully chosen to carry the eight characters to the brides family, and return with the girl's eight characters to present to the groom's family.

The slip of red paper with the eight characters written on it was placed by the ancestor tablets of both families, for a period of three days. If any unfortunate events or dissenting words were heard during those three days the wedding was called off. The girl who did not wish to marry the prospective male could at this point cry, break pottery, or otherwise express her discontent in more subtle ways, while the boy in his turn could also hint to the inadvisability of the match.[4] In the case of an unwanted marriage, the girl's last two numbers could be altered, so that the sum of the boy and girl's figures would come out an even, or "yin" number. If the numbers when added together came out uneven, for "yang," the bride's family thereby signaled that the arrangements could continue.

Rubrics for receiving the red slip within the family are as follows:

a. On a propitious day the eight characters of the boy are written on a red slip of paper.

b. A master of ceremonies from within the boy's family, either a brother of the father, an older brother of the groom or a close relative is selected.

c. Besides the MC, a go-between may be chosen (mei-jen), to accompany the MC.

d. The groom's father, the master of ceremonies, and the go-between light incense at the ancestor shrine, announce the intent of exchanging red slips for marriage, and in formal attire of office, see off the master of ceremonies and/or go-between at the front gate.

e. The groom's MC arrives at the bride's home. The bride's master of ceremonies, either her father, an uncle, her older brother, or a relative, dresses in the proper robes of office (matching the groom's official rank), and goes outside the gate to welcome the groom's party.

f. The bride's MC leads the groom's MC up the stairs of the house from the east (the groom's side is yang, therefore east).

g. They enter the main hall of the household, groom's MC on the left (east) and bride's MC on the right (west).

h. The groom's MC offers the letter of engagement with the eight characters while facing east. He then places gifts on the main table of the guest hall, facing north.

i. The bride's MC faces north, bows twice, and receives the letter.

j. The groom's MC avoids the bow, and asks to withdraw to another room. This is done to prevent embarrassment to the bride's family while the letter is being read, and the eight characters placed by the ancestor shrine.

k. The bride's MC takes the letter, enters the ancestor shrine (or goes to the shrine, if it is in the main hall), and prays before the box containing all of the ancestral tablets. The wedding proposal is announced formally to the ancestors, and to the family.

l. The bride's MC then composes a letter in response, containing the girl's eight characters, and the name of the proposed groom.

m. The letter is held before the ancestor shrine and incense is burned. Then the girl's MC goes out of the main hall by the west (yin) side, and presents the answer to the groom's MC. He bows twice, and again the groom's MC avoids the bows.

n. The bride's MC invites the groom's MC to a "brief collation." The words "new wine" and "brief collation" are used out of politeness (N.b., li, sweet plum wine made overnight, is actually a euphemism used to avoid embarrassment to the groom's party). To serve poor wine would of course be an act of rudeness. The word *Li* is used as a polite subterfuge to convince the guest to stay. The best aged wine and a fine banquet are served.

o. The groom's MC refuses three times, pretends to leave, and finally accedes. A banquet is laid out. Toasts must be made by both sides three times (once each for blessings from heaven, earth, and water, in the Taoist tradition).

p. The groom's MC finishes the banquet, announces his departure, and now at last exchanges the formal bows twice.

q. The bride's MC sees off the groom's MC outside the gates.

The Na-pien ceremony, though simple, is pregnant with the symbols of Yin-yang cosmology. The groom's messenger or master of ceremonies (MC) always enters and leaves from the east or yang side of the family altar. The bride's MC always remains in the west. Offerings are made to the north, the place of respect (T'ai-chi, the immanent Tao, the heavenly pivot). The groom's MC refuses all bows until the banquet has been finished, showing that no burden or obligation is placed on the bride's family to accede to the groom's demands. The subtlety of behavior, always exquisitely proper on both sides, makes for extreme smoothness and comfort in a difficult situation. The refusal of the proposal can be seen as the will of the ancestors, not of the living. Whether the marriage is arranged or not, good relationships must continue between both families. The host always suggests a "simple banquet" of "uncured wine" so that the guest may not feel embarrassed about accepting. But only the very best wine is served. The guest, in this case the groom's MC, must refuse the traditional three times. After the triple toast of wine, performed by each side, feelings are warm and complete. Now the groom's MC accepts and returns the bow. A banquet is always the vehicle for closing a contract and a friendly relationship. The first stage of the wedding ceremony is completed.

Upon returning home to the groom's side, the MC must be again banqueted, but this time "like a family member." The details of the exchange of red slips are carefully recounted. Finally, while burning incense and praying, the bride's red slip containing the eight characters is laid by the groom's ancestor tablets. The three day waiting period has begun. Either prospective bride or groom may refuse the wedding. If modesty or shame prevents expressing true feelings, there are still other occasions for conveying dissent.

2. *Na-pi* 納幣 Exchange of Gifts and Formal Engagement

The second stage of the wedding rite consists in the sending of gifts to the bride's family by the groom. In many parts of China a bride price is also sent to "pay for" the upkeep of the bride from the time of her birth until her betrothal into the groom's family. The bride price is refused or not observed in areas which pride themselves on scholarly learning, an abundant life, or generosity when faced with life's cares. It is most probable that the majority of farming villages in China paid a price for the bride, yet there are strong feelings in many areas and certainly within the literatus tradition that the money publicly offered for the bride should not be accepted. Hsinchu city in Taiwan, parts of Canton city, and some of the districts within Chungshan in Kuangtung province, for instance, refuse the bride price. Custom does demand, however, that cloth for a bridal gown, the complete bridal outfit, and certain prescribed jewelry be given by the groom as a sign of formal engagement. The ritual is as follows:

104

a. The presents for the bride are prepared. These must include: 1) one set of woven damask silk clothes for the bride; 2) four bolts of embroidered silk cloth, arranged so that the middle sections are folded over each other, i.e., joined in the middle (the cloth folded in the middle and entwined with a second bolt symbolizes marital union and bliss); 3) four bolts of fine cloth for lining, intertwined as above; 4) ceremonial red robes embroidered with a four toed dragon (mang); 5) the four traditional jeweled ornaments, *chai* hairpin, *ch'uan* bracelet, *tsai* hairclasp, *erh* earrings; 6) four plates of edible delicacies: tea, pin-nang nuts, dates (tsao-tzu is a homonym for early birth), tangerines (etc).[5]

b. On a propitious day determined by the daily almanac, the gifts are brought by the groom's MC and his entourage to the bride's residence.[6] In the family of higher status the MC himself does not bring the gifts, but brothers and friends are sent in his stead, with a letter from the MC or go-between. The letter brings greetings and the announcement that the engagement is now formal.

c. The head of the bride's household receives the gifts, announces to the ancestors that the gifts have arrived, and composes a letter of acceptance in reply.

d. A banquet is given to the members of the groom's family who have brought the gifts. Respect and ceremony shown as in the na-pien banquet is again governed by the yin-yang rules, with the bride's emissaries always sitting or standing to the west, and the groom's family to the east of the altar, banquet table, and entrance.

The groom's family must use great discretion when sending gifts to the bride's family. If too many gifts are sent, the bride's family will be embarrassed, and unable to match the generosity of the groom's good intentions. If the groom's family does not choose gifts that are worthy of the bride, or if the bride's dowry is especially munificent, the groom's family in return will be embarrassed. Since the gifts are sent publicly, the whole village sees and talks about the expense. In many communities, the groom's family sends a large cash gift with the presents, knowing that it will be seen by the village and in some cases returned. The jewelry and ornaments sent to the bride especially must match in value the gifts soon to be sent by the bride's family to decorate her new home and her own room, providing the basic needs of a new family life.

Such delicate matters are seen to by the go-between, a discreet person who acts as liaison between the two families and is usually well rewarded for his or her assistance to both sides.

Local custom dictates what items are to be included in the gifts, what foodstuffs are used, and what the significance of the various dishes are according to the provincial dialect. The names of the gifts signify good luck and blessing in the locally spoken dialect, and so cannot be predetermined by the Confucian scholar in the ritual manual for common use. In all cases it is the local expert, i.e., usually the temple custodian or Taoist priest, who is called upon to arbitrate ritual questions at the village or community level.

3. *Ch'ing-ch'i* 請期 Fixing the Wedding Day and Sending Invitations
A propitious day for the wedding is determined by the groom's family, after consulting the *T'ung-shu* daily almanac. When the day has been decided upon (the bride's family must, of course, be consulted for final approval), the groom's family sends the MC with a formal letter called *chien*, and a live goose or a pair of mandarin ducks, and wine to the bride's home. Wedding invitations are then sent out by both sides. These invitations are accompanied by a large box of sweet cookies, similar to the round mooncakes used for the Autumn Full Moon festival. Any person or family receiving an invitation is expected to give a monetary gift at the time of the wedding banquet. The money gift is used to alleviate the great expense of the wedding. The bride's dowry is now prepared, and the day set for sending all of the bride's furniture, refrigerator, TV, automatic laundry machine, and so forth to the groom's home; in traditional China, the bride often brought with her a waiting maid or two, as well as all the necessities for her own private life in the new family.

4. *Ch'en-lien* 陳匲 Sending the Bride's Vanity Box
Two or three days before the wedding the bride's possessions, as a dowry, are sent to the groom's home. The most important items of the dowry are a jewelry and make-up box called *Lien* (vanity box) which is often simply the top drawer in a dresser sent with the bride's bedroom furniture. With the dowry comes a small key to open the box. The groom is expected to find the key and open the vanity box, a symbol for a successful marriage and collaboration between husband and wife. The

village closely watches the arrival of the dowry and counts the items sent by the bride's family, comparing them with the gifts sent previously from the groom's family to the bride.

In modern times it has become a custom to present the bride with gifts. Friends hold showers or pre-marriage parties, and in other ways convene the bride's childhood and school friends for moral and economic support before the passage into a new family. Working conditions in Taiwan, Hong Kong, and Singapore, among other industrial communities of overseas Chinese, allow the girl of the family to earn her own dowry and come to her husband's home laden with gifts, a bank account, and some degree of economic independence. Such would have been the privilege of only wealthy girls in the past. The modernization of the economic system has meant in many cases the possibility of confirming many of the traditional aspects of the major marriage, and strengthening the woman's role in the family.

A study of the marriage ritual confirms the strength and power of the Chinese woman inside family circles, a fact confirmed in Chinese novels. The Chinese family from within the *uterine*[7] or inner family circles, has always been matriarchal (ruled by the woman in inner economic and organizational matters) and patrilineal (children deriving the clan name from the father's side). The marriage rituals affirm the rights of the bride, including limited economic self-determination and the bringing of a dowry to confirm her strength and ability to form a new nuclear family in the groom's clan.

5. *Ch'in-yang* 親迎 Welcoming the Bride; the Bridal Procession
The traditional rules for a Chinese wedding demand that the groom arise at dawn, the daily rebirth of Yang, to welcome the bride into his home. In modern times wedding processions by taxi are frequently held in the afternoon, before an evening banquet. Strict custom, however, demands that the procession begin before dawn, or at the break of day, when the sun, symbol of Yang, begins to appear on the horizon. The *Hsin-lang* or groom arises, dresses in the robes fitting his status or the official rank of his family, and prepares to mount his horse (in modern times, a taxi) to lead the procession to the bride's house. The bridal sedan chair is decorated according to the social status (shen-fen) of the groom's family. The groom provides a live goose as an offering, two lanterns, and twelve musicians to accompany the procession to the bride's door.[8]

The bridal procession is formed as follows: a) two lanterns; b) the groom on horseback; c) the goose, carried by a servant or friend; d) the bridal sedan chair, decorated according to the family's rank; e) the twelve musicians. As the bridegroom prepares to leave his home, he first goes to the ancestor shrine, presents lit incense to the ancestors, and announces his intentions to the ancestors and his parents to bring a new bride into the household. The father of the groom, or the MC, reads the marriage manual aloud, following the instructions for the procession and the following banquet.[9]

The father and the MC then bow four times, while the groom kneels before the ancestor shrine, facing north. The MC takes a cup of wine, turns around facing the south or exterior of the house, and pours out wine three times (once each for blessing from heaven, earth, and the watery underworld). The cup is then filled, and offered to the groom. The groom bows, takes the cup, bows again, and kneels. The MC or the father of the household announces to the son:

> Go and bring your bride to our home, in order to continue our clan. Respect your elders, be kind to the younger family members, be diligent in your work, and create a good family life for your wife and children.

The groom bows, downs the wine, and responds to his father:

> I consent to the advice you have given me, only fearing that I am not able to fulfill it adequately; I promise to be filial and never violate your instructions.

The groom then bows four times and arises; as he walks towards the sedan chair procession outside the house, a winnowing basket is held over his head. On the winnowing basket's convex exterior has been painted the eight trigrams, in the Lo-shu configuration, for the chart of earth's blessing.[10] The basket is used to shelter the groom from the rays of yang sunlight until he mounts his horse (or sits in the taxi). It is then tied to the back of the bride's palanquin, or to the back of the taxi, as a talisman of blessing for the marriage procession. The groom then begins the trip to the bride's family.

Meanwhile, at the bride's home similar preparations have begun at dawn, the hour for beginning a wedding procession. The rite begins with a solemn announcement at the ancestor shrine that the bride will go forth from the home that day to be a wife in another family. The father of the bride reads the following:

Our beloved daughter, sister of (brother's names) will
his day be taken to her new home as a bride. We solemn-
ly announce these rites to our ancestors.

The bride is then led into the ancestor hall, with her master of
ceremonies, older brother or father standing in the east, and her lady
teacher (hairdresser) in the west, with the bride in the center. Her hair
is put up as a bride, as in the rite used for a girl's coming of age,
described in the next chapter (maturation). The jewelry given by the
groom is put on, along with the bride's own selections.

When her hair is done, and the wedding garments put on, the
bride stands in front of the MC, facing north, and bows twice. The wine
is then taken by the MC and poured out three times, as above. Another
cup is then given to the bride. She takes it and bows four times, signifying respect to the four seasons, and the four stages of life (see Chapter
One, the structure of life and nature's cycles). She touches the wine to
her lips, but does not drink it. The MC finally instructs the bride to be a
good and loyal wife, to be obedient to her new parents, raise a good
family for her husband, and be a kind and loving mother. The bride
does not respond verbally, but "assents in her heart," vowing to follow
the ways of her new family.

The father and mother of the bride then counsel their daughter
to follow the social rules of the Chinese family system. The father says:

Be obedient to your husband, respect his parents, and
follow the good counsel of your new elder sisters (i.e.,
the wives of the clan into which the bride marries).

The mother adds:

Learn to do things their way, respect them, and care
for your new mother-in-law even if it means staying up
late at night. Remember to observe the rules of the
ladies quarters in your new clan family.

Again custom forbids that the bride respond verbally, the tears
and emotion of parting being enough to indicate interior assent to the
fond farewell of the parents. A red veil is prepared to put over the
bride's face, covering the hairdo and wedding crown. The veil is call
shen-ming, "hiding the face, a homophone, for *shen-ming* to offer
one's life for a new family. The bride again silently assents to the veil-
ing. Meanwhile, the groom's procession has arrived at the front door of
the bride's home.

A strict order of ritual precedence is now observed:

a. The bride's MC comes outside the gates to welcome the guests.

b. They bow, and the groom is invited inside.

c. The groom's party climbs to the top of the east side of the stairs, while the bride's MC goes to the west.

d. The groom lays the goose on a special table at the top of the stairs, placed there to receive the gifts. He then bows twice. The bride's family do not return the bow.

e. Meanwhile the bride's veil is adjusted so that it covers her face, and she is led out to be seated in the sedan chair. The groom maintains his place at the top of the stairs on the east side, while the MC is on the west. The bride comes out from the main hall, and the groom escorts her down the stairs, first bowing, then leading the way. The bride's MC does not come down the stairs.

f. The bride's lady teacher, the same who did her hair for the wedding, helps her to be seated inside the sedan chair (taxi).

g. Two lanterns from the bride's family, carried by two assistants are now placed at the head of the procession next to the lanterns from the groom's family, followed by the sedan chair and musicians. The lanterns are called *Lung-teng*龍灯, dragon basket lights.

h. The groom mounts his horse, and the procession begins. The groom traditionally rides ahead, and is waiting at the gates of his home when the bride's party arrives.

i. The bridal procession arrives at the groom's front gates. The groom assists as she alights from the palanquin, and proceeds through the front gates.

j. Various local customs govern the bride's passage through the gates and up the pathway to the home. In general, the bride must pretend to be weak and faint, as she walks into the new home. A saddle for peace (saddle: *an* = peace) under the pommel of which is placed an apple (apple: *p'ing kuo* = peacefully passing over) and so forth, are put in the bride's way to step over. The stumbling steps of the bride recall the days when women's feet were bound, a custom begun in the Sung dynasty and discarded in the modern period.[11]

k. As they enter, the bride's retinue stands in the west, and the groom's attendants in the east. i. The bride and groom entourages mutually exchange bows. The bride and groom prepare to exchange cups of wine, and affix their seals (han) to the marriage document.

6. *Ho-Chin* 合卺 Exchange of Wine Cups; the Marriage Ceremony
The Ho-chin or pledging the cup of the betrothed, is accompanied by a
banquet. The wedding banquet is always an elaborate affair, and is
governed by the rules of local custom. In general, the guests include all
of those who have given gifts to the bride, any of the city officials related to the bride or groom, and all acquaintances. To leave any village
member out of the banquet is a failure in propriety, and leads to a life-
long grudge. Due to the great expense, each guest brings along a red
envelope (*hung-pao* or *li-hsi*) as a gift to present at the door of the
banquet. The wedding ceremony itself is brief, as follows:
a. The bride's teacher, or in rural villages the groom lifts the veil of the
bride, revealing her face.
b. A banquet is laid out, and the guests are invited to be seated. The
bride and groom sit in the place of honor, the bride on the west and the
groom on the east.
c. A tray bearing the betrothal cup is placed in front of the groom and
bride. They drink from the cup. The bride's retainers present the cup to
the groom, then the groom's best men present the cup to the bride.
d. Groom and bride mutually bow. A document of marriage is signed or
"sealed" at this time with the *han* or chop of both sides.
e. The marriage banquet begins, during which time the bride and
groom must toast each table of guests. The attendants see that the
bride and groom's cup is, in fact, filled with wine colored tea, to avoid
intoxication.[12]
f. After the banquet and speeches are finished, and the bride has been
teased by old friends, the couple retire for the first evening together.
They toast each other with three cups of wine, and enter the bed cham-
ber.
7. *Post Marriage Customs*
a. *Pai-t'ang,* 拜堂 First Respects to the Ancestors
The traditional marriage in China was not considered to be legally
binding until the new bride worshipped at the family ancestor shrine on
the morning after the wedding. Court cases in the Sung period show
that girl's dissenting at this time were considered to be legally free from
the obligations of wifehood and the married state, and still eligible for a
first marriage. Since the consent of the couple was ultimately bound up
with the bearing of offspring in the traditional legal system, the Chinese
bride who refused to bear children, symbolized by refusing to burn in-

cense at the ancestor shrine, separated herself from the family's fortunes. The morning after the wedding, therefore, was an extremely important moment for the entire clan. Strict rules governed the actions of
the new bride and new groom leading up to the actual burning of incense at the shrine. The bride retained her lady teacher and brides-
maids to prepare a special banquet for the new parent's breakfast, and
assist at the offering of incense. The rules are as follows:

i. The new bride arises before dawn on the first day after her marriage,
dresses, and goes to the ancestral hall.

ii. There she awaits the arrival of the new parents-in-law, who also arise
early, dress, and take up their ceremonial positions, the father-in-law to
the east and the mother-in-law to the west of the breakfast table. All
face south in anticipation.

iii. The new bride enters, and stands in front of her parents-in-law, offering them gifts brought especially for the occasion. The new parents
sit to receive the gifts, to the east and west side of the table, respectively.

iv. The gifts consist of dried fruits, dates, and chestnuts, symbols which
represent the bearing of children quickly. The fruits have been very
carefully arranged in a basket with a cloth underneath for artistic
effect.[13]

v. The new bride bows twice, approaches the table which has been carefully prepared beforehand, with the gifts laid out, and offers the basket
of fruit to her new father-in-law. He pats the basket, as one would pat a
child's head, and deliberately disturbs the order of the dried fruits.

vi. The new bride takes the basket, rearranges the fruits, bows twice to
the mother-in-law, and presents her with the basket. The mother-in-law
in like manner pats the basket as if it were a child, "rumpling the hair"
or disturbing the order of the fruit.

vii. The mother and father now both arise, and retire for a moment to
their own room, while the new bride's teacher and waiting ladies lay out
a morning banquet. The banquet includes wine, congee rice, pickled
vegetables, all provided by the bride, including bowls and chopsticks.

viii. The parents then re-enter, and take their places at the table,
mother on the west, father on the east side of the center table. When
they have finished eating, the bride toasts them with wine, bowing
twice.

ix. A table is now set on the east side of the hall for the bride to be served her breakfast. She sits on the east side of the table, facing west, that is, the cosmic direction of the ancestors' final rest. The parents invite the new bride to eat, remain with her during the banquet, and toast her with wine, also bowing twice. The bride now enters and exits from the east side of the ancestor hall.

x. The parents wait until the bride has finished, then exit from the west side of the hall. The bride is now an official member of the family. The grandparents to be, (parents-in-law) by exiting from the west (joining the ancestors) relinquish the care of the family to the new bride. The bride then offers incense and wine to the ancestor tablets, and exits through the east door to her own apartments .

b. *The Third Day Visit* 廟見

On the third day after the marriage, the bride visits her natal home for the first time "as a guest." The marriage ritual does not symbolize a complete break between the bride and her natal home. Ritual custom demands presents of the bride's family at the time of children's birth in the bride's new home, and presence to the third degree of affinal relation at the bride's funeral. Smooth relationships between the bride and her natal home are therefore established on the third day after marriage.

The visit to her parent's home begins with the presenting of morning incense, wine, and food offerings before the ancestor shrine in her new home. The third day after the wedding is therefore the first time that the new bride officiates at the morning food offerings before new husband's ancestor shrine. The ritual is as follows:

i. Early in the morning the family's ritual experts prepare the morning offerings to be placed before the ancestor shrine. Local custom determines what these objects are. The most common food offerings consist of the items prepared that morning for the family's breakfast, plus wine, tea, and incense.

ii. The offerings are arranged on two tables, one placed at the foot of the stairs leading to the east side of the shrine, the other to the foot of the stairs by the west side of the shrine. The groom stands behind the table to the east, and the bride behind the table to the west. All bow twice .

iii. The groom then ascends the stairs from the east, enters the shrine, offers incense and wine, announces the ceremony to the ancestors, and returns to his place in the east.

iv. The bride (as officiant) comes to the center of the stairs, faces the north, and bows twice. According to local custom, the bride also burns incense, and pours tea and wine into cups on the altar.

v. The bride returns to her place. All bow twice, and then set out on the visit to the bride's home. In many parts of China the bride visits her parent's home separately from her husband, or even without her husband, the bride's visit being the most crucial event on the third day. But by strict official custom, the groom too must visit the ancestral hall of the bride, greet the parents, and thank them for the privilege of marrying their daughter. Gifts are brought at this time as a token of gratitude.

The ritual for receiving the groom's gifts is as follows:

i. The bride's parents welcome the groom at the front gate, and bow twice.

ii. They lead the groom to the ancestral hall where the gifts to the bride's family are laid on a table.

iii. The parents stand behind the table, with their backs to the north, facing south.

iv. The groom approaches the table from the south, facing north. The gifts are offered towards the north, after which the groom bows twice.

v. The bride's father responds with bows to the west, twice.

vi. The groom pays his respects to the mother-in-law (mother of his bride), by bowing twice.

vii. The groom then goes outside the hall, turns, and bows twice to the ancestor shrine from the doorstep, outside the hall.

viii. The bride's father responds by bowing twice from within the door of the ancestor shrine. They both leave the shrine, and a banquet is prepared for the groom (son-in-law) by the bride's parents.

Meanwhile, the bride is allowed to visit her mother, tell the story of the wedding to her parents, brothers and sisters, and spend the day at home enjoying herself as she wishes. The marriage is therefor seen not only to be the beginning of a new nuclear or hearthside family, but also as an alliance between the bride and groom's two families. Marriage is such an important event in the life of the individual within the family, that all possible means are employed by Chinese social custom to ensure that the young man and woman, whatever the social status, successfully establish a nuclear family. Once established, the ties between the two families of the groom and bride could develop into a close working or business relationship with gift exchanges and visits. The bride's personal welfare, happiness, and success in the new household are a continual concern for her natal family. Ritual custom therefore assures that the bride's feelings and welfare be cared for.

The above description of marriage found in popular manuals available in most bookshops, is shared by the Buddhist, Taoist, and Confucian traditions. The order of events and the material details are often changed by local custom. Some families increasing the minutiae of ritual detail, or shorten the six stages into a more pragmatic set of rules. Thus many modern manuals telescope the marriage process into three steps, simplifying the exchange of gifts and the wedding day formalities in the following bare format:
1. The exchange of eight characters, leading to engagement.
2. The exchange of gifts and sending of invitations.
3. The wedding day, procession by automobile, and banquet.

The propitious time for a wedding has always depended upon the agricultural cycle. Relative freedom from work and relief from household chores were needed for villagers to attend a wedding. The Confucian state's legal prescriptions bowed to the peasant's convenience in such matters. Marriages were avoided from the fifth month through the busy summer season. Yin-yang cosmology justified the farmer's nonattendance at ritual acts by assigning the fifth and sixth month intensive farming period to the "birth of yin," cosmically inappropriate for a marriage liaison. The farmers of the villages and the merchants of the cities continue to favor the late autumn and winter months as the best time for a marriage. The winter solstice, the annual celebration of the rebirth of yang in nature, theoretically coincides with the principle of union and gestation at the cosmic level. Thus popular local custom, yin-yang cosmology, and Confucian approved ceremony are operative simultaneously in the marriage rite. The structural principles of yin-yang ritual are visible through the camouflage of local custom, no matter what the area or condition of China.

The traditional marriage manuals contain a wealth of homespun lore and counsel for the newlyweds. The parents are warned by such awesome scholars as Chu Hsi and Szu-ma Kuang that their daughter must be asked repeatedly if she really wants to go through with the

115

wedding match. A girl from a higher social status will have a very hard life with a boy of less refined tastes or lower economic interests. Therefore marriages from within the same district or village are preferred, because the two have been brought up in the same value system, and cherish the same sorts of things. Ideally there should be moral, economic, and physical proximity for the marrying couple. Yet, practically speaking, the person of pure and unalloyed motives makes the best mate. The building of a new family, the raising of children and grandchildren must be the primary goals of the marriage rite.

If physical and economic proximity are impossible, moral agreement as to goals (children and family) is the over-riding factor in choosing a mate, Lin Po-T'ung tells his readers. Marriage is blessed when the relationship of the two couples is based on mutual respect. Love, therefore, must be based on respect for the other rather than passionate feelings. Chinese novels unanimously bewail the fate of a young couple who mate or marry out of sexual passion alone. The characters *ching-ai* 敬愛 (respectful love) therefore typify the relationship which will be most blessed and happy in marriage. *Hu-hsiang ching-chung*, mutually filled with respect, and *pu-kan ch'ing-shih*, never feeling even the slightest disrespect for the other, must be the basis for *li* 禮 (the confucian word for respect and proper social behavior). No matter how many gifts are exchanged, how many polite phrases expressed, a marriage not based on respect is wasted labor. When love is based on respect, the marriage will be long-lasting .

The aging Cantonese scholar Lin Po-t'ung insists that the first duty of the parents is to educate their children (chiao er-nü wei hsien) in respectful social relationships. The four sets of social relationships are the primary object of instruction for children. These are:
1. The relationship of child to parent, filial love (hsiao 孝).
2. The relationship of brother to brother, and by transferral reciprocity of friend to friend (yi 義).
3. The relationship of loyalty to state/community (chung 忠).
4. The respect of young for old, the basic respect that all men and women must show to their fellow human beings (jen 仁).

Children who have not been taught these virtues should not be allowed to perform the rites of maturation (kuan 冠 , the capping ceremony) or to marry (hun 婚) . The story is told of a scholar named Chin, who chose a bride for his son from a well-placed local gentry family. The girl was truly beautiful, well brought up, and learned in the classics. There was no better match by public agreement, than between the intelligent and promising son of the scholar Chin and the neighbor's beautiful daughter. On the night of the marriage, the bride was brought to the banquet in tears. All during the toasts and speeches, she continued to cry and wail. Moved by her grief, the good scholar Chin asked the girl to explain her tears. In truth, she said her lover was a boy named Ti in a distant village. She had been forced by her parents into this prestigious wedding. Immediately the father called for the lover, Mr. Ti and saw that the bride's gifts were escorted with full honor to the neighboring village of her chosen love. The marriage was performed in Mr. Chin's residence and the bride given away by Mr. Chin to the man whom she truly loved.

Through this touching story, the parents of the future bride and groom are warned that a couple not well matched will forever bear resentment to each other. The scholar Chin was wise to assist both the beleaguered girl and his own son in avoiding an unhappy marriage. The parents must therefore investigate the new family. If a girl is married to a boy and covets another kind of life, whether because of wealth, a former loved one, or unfulfilled dreams of her family, it is the parent's fault if the marriage subsequently fails. When choosing a daughter-in-law, better to pick a virtuous one rather than beauty. When choosing a husband for one's daughter, prefer a man of character rather than wealth. A boy who has been brought up without discipline and strict training can be filled with excuses, easily putting the blame for his failures on others. A woman brought up without learning how to get along with her own brothers and sisters will not get along in her new family with the wives of her husband's brothers.

Therefore, the parents on both sides should not rely solely upon the go-between, but should get together and talk about their children's likes and dislikes. The bride to-be should be seen at home by her future parents-in-law, and the groom too should be seen by the bride's father. A flattering go-between or ambitious parents can often hide the true personality of bride or groom.

Village chatter provides an easy access to knowing the inner problems of the family into which one's daughter is marrying. Since the young bride is usually taught the rules and customs of her groom's family by the older wives (of the older brothers' marriages) it is just as

117

important to know the condition of the clan into which one's daughter is marrying as the moral qualities of her husband-to-be. The bride's parents are therefore given counsel to look into the affairs of the groom's entire clan. Only after understanding the problems of the intended family should the parents decide on the propriety of the daughter's marriage.

The alliance between clans worked out by marriage goes far beyond the giving of a bride or taking a daughter-in-law. Business, investment, temple and market associations, good relationships within the village, the proper care and attention given by the new family for the bride, are vital concerns of the entire village community. Custom therefore demands that the bridal procession be given preference over the royal progress of an emperor or the visit of a great mandarin to the district, a rule perhaps never tested beyond the telling of local folk tales. The importance of marriage is related directly to the central place of the family in the Chinese system, and the right of each individual to build a family to ensure social, economic and psychological stability in the passage through life and death.

Certain excesses in the celebration of the marriage rite, and in the treatment of the bride may occur during and after the wedding ceremony. The official manuals bewail these local aberrations, and discourage their practice among the common folk and the wealthy. Three less desirable forms of hazing during marriage are sometimes seen in southeast China, including parts of rural Kuangtung, Fukien, and Taiwan. The bride is sometimes unwillingly subjected to teasing and "staring" by the children and unrelated strangers during the difficult period of waiting for the procession or banquet to begin. Children crowd to the windows of the home where the bride is being dressed for the wedding, or the groom's home where she waits for the banquet to commence. The bride is terribly embarrassed by such unwanted attentions. To the refined observer, the "staring" seems cruel and uncalled for. Custom, Lin Po-t'ung and the other commentators warn, demands that the bride be seen by and greet her new in-laws, but not that the entire village stand at the door and watch.

Lin Po-t'ung and other authors condemn the custom of public "staring at the bride." Yet the very structure of the Chinese farm house and the closeness of village and city community make the bride's plight very real. The temptation to come and watch the wedding, if even from a neighbor's window, is a popular pastime for the western world, as well as for Asia. The thoughtful family protects the bride's welfare in the difficult process of the wedding day.

A second form of literary hazing took place in the traditional past when the younger generation were conversant with popular or classic poetry. The bride and groom were expected to memorize books of (wedding-banquet) poetry, as mentioned above, and forced to down a cup of wine at the banquet when friends challenged them to finish a line of verse and the newlyweds failed to respond. Manuals of wedding poems abound in the local Taiwanese and Fukienese book shops, and were an important part of the bride and groom's preparation for the banquet. The best men and maids in waiting strove to supply the bridal party with bottles of supposed rice wine actually filled with tea, so as to prevent complete intoxication of bride and groom. The custom of teasing the bride by quoting segments of poems, however, died out with the coming of modern education. Neither the newlyweds nor their friends in today's world are knowledgeable enough in poetry, to quote or respond to the demands of classical scholarship. Manuals of wedding poetry are still sold in temple bookshops, however, as a relic of the literary past of southeast China's upper class families.

A third custom is sometimes still heard of in parts of China, which allow the bride-to-be to express her anger and sorrow at being "married out" from her natal home. The plight of the girl in the Chinese family is legendary, the subject of a myriad novels, folk tales, and ballads. On the last night in her parent's home, the bride-to-be is allowed to express her sorrow freely at parting from her natal family. Her feelings of resentment for the inferior manner in which a girl is brought up, the favoring of the boy over a girl child, and whatever else may be pent up inside are given free expression on the night before the wedding. Though the ideal custom calls for the filial expression of daughterly sorrow, the evening before marriage sometimes ends in a high-volume expression of resentment to the parents and older brothers for being sent out of the family by marriage. The display of emotions in what the social psychologist calls a "blow-off" pattern can be a healthy release of tension.

The greatest blessing, Lin Po-t'ung concludes, comes from a marriage in which respect for the person is foremost. The elderly scholar ends his treatise on marriage with the touching reminder that

119

the woman is not to be oppressed or mistreated before or after marriage. To do so would be to destroy human feelings, all that is best in building the foundations of a family, the center of cultural, religious, and social life. The success of a family depends on the woman's bearing and mothering of children. Burial ritual and Ancestor Memorial are symbols of the importance of the family as China's basic social unit. The saying that "a boy is worth more than a girl" is, in fact, wrong. The family is blessed and made wealthy in the spiritual as well as the economic order by the hard work and careful accounting of the wife and mother. The strength of the wife from within the household lies in her ability to create and maintain the structure and values of the Chinese family system. For this reason, the choice of a bride, or the choice of a husband for one's daughter, is one of the most important events in life. At every stage, the marriage ritual reflects the significance of this first step in building the family, the core of Chinese society.

NOTES

1. *Ta T'ang K'ai-yüan Li*, Ikeda Jun, ed., Tokyo: Toyo Bunka Press, 1972. The T'ang Dynasty K'ai-yüan Period Ritual Manual
2. Saso, Michael, *The Chinese Family*, in press, 1990.
3. Lin Po-t'ung, *Kuan, Hun, Sang, Chi*, The Rites of Passage, Canton: 1844. Woodblock print, Toyo Bunka Library, Tokyo.
4. The word for pear *li* is a homonym for *li* profit. To remove the pear from the altar signifies that the marriage has no profit.
5. The words are homonyms for children, wealth, and prosperity.
6. The *T'ung-shu* Almanac, purchased annually in Chinese bookshops.
7. See Margery Wolf, *Women and the Family in Rural Taiwan*, Stanford: 1972. See pp. 159-70 for the "uterine" family.
8. See Lin Po-t'ung, *Hun-chi*, op. cit.
9. *Chia-li Ta-ch'eng*, The Complete Home Ritual, Hsinchu: Chu-lin Press, 1962.
10. See Saso, M., TROCR, (Pullman: 1990), Ch. 3.
11. Foot binding was made illegal in China in 1911.
12. Books of wedding poetry can still be purchsed from the Chulin Press, Hsinchu, for traditional Chinese wedding ceremonies.
13. "Dates," *tsao-tzu*, is a homonym for quick birth to children.

5. BIRTH AND CAPPING
Childbirth and Initiation

The purpose of the marriage rite is to found a new nuclear family, the center and core of Chinese cultural and social life. Once married, the young couple establish their own embryo family focused around a doorway (hu) to their own apartment (fang), whether alone or within the family or clan complex, and a stove (lu) where the family meals are cooked. Once the marriage ceremony is over, and the daily routine established, the traditional Chinese wife was expected to become a mother as soon as possible, in order to continue the family line, provide heirs and workers in the family business, (whether farmer, merchant, or literatus), and fulfill the ideal of the extended (fang 房) and grand (tsu 祖 clan) Chinese family.[1]

The *Complete Home Ritual* manuals have explicit instructions concerning the *kuan* capping ceremony for a boy and the first hairdo for a girl, but do not attempt to give directions for ritual at the birth of a child. The customs and practices at the time of childbirth fall completely under the jurisdiction of local usage and household taboo. So personal are the rituals and customs surrounding birth, and so dependent are the ritual items used at birth on the woman-controlled household culture, that rules were not formulated by the male dominant Confucian mandarinate to regulate this basic rite of passage. Customs observed in southeast China, i.e., Fukien, and Kwangtung will be described here, without attempting to compare practices found in other parts of China concerning the care of mother and child.[2]

The birth of a first child is of course a most traumatic experience for the newly wed couple. Intense pressure was put on the young bride to bear a son for the sake of family inheritance and continuity. In order to alleviate some of the duties imposed on the young bride, upon whom the burden of washing dishes, cleaning the household, and cooking for the extended or even grand family were imposed, a young girl was often adopted or brought in to be raised as a bride for a future son, even before a first child was born. Female adoption, or more exactly the buying of a child in her tender years to be a bride when she matured, or the purchase of a servant or slave girl, were common practices in traditional China.[3]

Farming communities especially practiced the custom of adopting out girls to be servants of their future mother-in-law from a tender age. This custom, called *t'ung-yang hsi* in mandarin (child brought up to be a bride) or *simpua* (child-bride) in southern Fukien and northern Kwangtung Min dialect, has been practiced since at least Sung dynasty times in imperial China.[4] Farmer's households vied among themselves to procure daughters-in-law, and trained them from tender years within the groom's family. Such girls indeed had a hard and thankless childhood, but often exerted much more influence than brides married into the family as adults, who, it was thought, tended to be more independent and unconcerned about clan affairs.

Besides the adoption or procurement of a girl child to be a mini-bride and servant, girls were also bought to be bond-servants, or even slaves in wealthy families. Since Ch'ing dynasty law and later the Japanese colonial government in Taiwan discouraged bond-servants or slaves, the legal fiction of adopting a child-bride was often used instead. A legal contract was drawn up in which the receiving family promised to see the girl married somehow or other, upon reaching adulthood. Such a legal ruse covered the real purpose of child-bride purchase, which in many cases was to acquire an extra hand, a maid-servant, or a girl to be sold into prostitution in order to provide extra funds for educating the sons of a lower middle class farming or merchant family. The girls sold into city red light districts from nearby farming communities were often called filial daughters.[5] Their earnings helped put a boy of the family through an expensive college education, or provide for an elderly couple, who would otherwise have been bereft of support.

Boys too were adopted in the Chinese family system, in one of two fashions , depending upon consanguinal relationship within the adopting family. If one branch or *fang* of a Chinese family had many boys, and another clan branch had none, it was frequently arranged for a boy from one *fang* to be passed over or adopted into another branch of the family with the same surname. This practice is called *kuo-fang-tzu,* i.e., a boy child passes over from one *fang* or branch of the clan to another. If a poorer family had many boys and wealthy family was in need of male heirs, It was also allowed to adopt a boy from a clan with no consanguinal ties. Such a boy was called *Ming-ling-tzu,* after the ming-ling moth which laid its eggs in the nest of another insect, to be brought up by other parents. The Kuo-fang-tzu boy had the right to a full share of the family inheritance, while the ming-ling-tzu received only a half share.

The birth of a child into a Chinese family was therefore an extremely important event, which the entire clan took a close interest in ministering to. Sibling position in the family, i.e., whether a first boy or girl, a second or third child, the need to adopt boys or girls within branches of the clan, and many other factors entered into the thoughts of the mother as the birth of the child drew near.

I. The Tao of Birthing

The birthing process in Taiwan and southeast China is divided liturgically into three stages; 1) the period preceding birth when certain tasks which might prematurely terminate the pregnancy or harm the mother are forbidden; 2) The birth itself; and 3) the post birth period when all attention is given to the health of the new mother and her child. The rituals and taboos used during the three periods are aimed specifically at aiding the mother in the difficult process of birthing, by providing mythical and religious justification for a healthy life style, the eating of proper food, and recuperation.[6]

The period before birth is governed by a special spirit called T'ai-shen (womb-foetus spirit), whom popular mythology appoints as the guardian of the foetus. T'ai-shen becomes angry if the wife is disturbed by her in-laws or clan relations during the months of pregnancy. The location of the T'ai-shen in the house is not constant. He (or she) may be in a cabinet, a closet, or under a bed. It is therefore not allowed to move furniture or otherwise move heavy objects which might disturb T'ai-shen or harm the unborn child within the mother's womb. If the wife who is pregnant becomes ill, feels stomach pains, or is in any way indisposed, the women of the family blame T'ai-shen, and summon a Taoist to read soothing prayers to quell his anger, *An T'ai-shen.* 安胎神

Movements and work forbidden the pregnant woman, lest T'ai-shen be offended include the following:
1. Tying of heavy bundles inside the home, lest the child be born deformed.
2. To use a large knife to cut objects, lest the child be born without ears.
3. To use an awl to bore holes, lest the child be born blind.

4. To burn waste objects, lest the child be born with a burn or scar on the face.

5. To lead a water buffalo by a rope, lest the child be born after a twelve month or extended pregnancy.

6. To hang out a large wooden wash tub at the time of the Ullambhana festival (7/15), which will enrage the spirits of hell, and bring bad luck to the family. (The Ullambhana, or Yu-lan-p'en festival, of the Seventh Month Fifteenth day, means symbolically the emptying out of the basin or tub of hell, thereby freeing all souls from the punishments of the underworld in the bowels of the earth. By semiotic meaning it also implies the emptying out of the womb; thus a woman who is pregnant is not allowed to empty buckets, lest a miscarriage occur).

7. Attendance at a funeral or the public drama often provided at funerals brings bad luck to the mother. (I.e., pregnant women are exempt from funeral processions and other stressful funerary ritual).

8. To go out late at night, lest the pregnant mother meet the dark tiger spirit (*Hei-hu shen*, the spirit of night or yin) or otherwise be frightened.

9. To move or help carry a coffin, lest the child be born a beggar. (Only beggars and the coolie class are hired to carry the heavy Chinese coffin in a traditional funeral).

Even though work at home and the carrying of heavy objects are banned, the pregnant woman is not forbidden such tasks as work in the fields if a farmer, marketing, and other movements which help rather than impede the actual birthing and labor process. Some kinds of physical exercise are beneficial for the mother in labor. Folk sayings affirm that the farming mother often gives birth more easily than the wealthy urban socialite who abstains from all kinds of physical labor. Only those actions are made taboo by ritual custom which might cause miscarriage, or otherwise harm the child and mother.

Local custom changes the meaning and selection of taboo objects according to material culture (objects used in the household) and the homophonic patterns of the local dialect. Thus in parts of Taiwan, Fukien, and northern Kwangtung province that use the Min dialect, sewing or the use of a needle is forbidden because piercing or blinding the eye sounds similar to piercing the cloth with a needle. Similarly, to step over a rope tied to a water buffalo, empty buckets filled with waste matter, or use of the units of measure on a scale can become liturgically taboo signs for protecting the mother and child because the semiotics of language and material culture allow such open semiosis to have ritual meaning. Thus local custom defines that using a scale for which the measuring unit is 16 liang, will make the pregnancy last 16 months. The practical role of such customs is to keep the family from imposing work on the pregnant mother which might cause a miscarriage.

The most important spirits invoked before and after the delivery of a child are, besides the womb-foetus spirit T'ai-shen, the popular *Chu-sheng Niang-Niang*, the spirit mother who gives aid at childbirth, and the medium spirit *Ch'en Nai-ma*, Mother Ch'en. Many of the popular temples of Taiwan, Fukien, Kwangtung, and southeast Asia have shrines and statues dedicated to these benign female spirits who are believed to assist the mother during birth. Chu-sheng Niang-niang is often pictured with twelve attendants, one for each month of the year, to assist the mother in labor. Mothers pray to the lady spirits during the nine months of pregnancy, and offer gifts at temple shrines such as new robes, shoes, and other decorations for the statue when the delivery of the new baby is over. Some shrines add layer after layer of red silk robes to the statues of Ch'en Nai-ma and Chu-sheng Niang-niang, proving the efficacy of prayers addressed to these saints of the popular religion.[7]

The lantern festival of the First lunar month, fifteenth day, (the first full moon of the New Year festival), is thought to be a propitious time to determine the sex of the child in the womb. Pregnant mothers burn incense on this evening before the ancestor shrine, and then step out into the busy street to listen for words which might indicate the sex of the unborn child. If words concerning flowers, clothes, or feminine matters are heard, the child will be a girl. If phrases relating to lanterns, (*teng* in Taiwanese means lantern and male child), fighting, or sports are predominate, the child will most likely be a boy. A newly wed bride who carries a lantern on this evening (teng) is thought to increase her chances to bear a son (Amoy-Min dialect: teng; mandarin: ting 燈,丁).

The labor and birth process is filled with homeopathic ritual and customs for easing the labor pains. First, as the contractions shorten and the mother feels the birth is near, custom demands that the woman in labor bow before her mother-in-law and ask forgiveness for any offenses given within the clan. Such an act of obeisance insures the help of mother-in-law both spiritually and psychologically for a quick delivery. Next, the midwife is summoned, and a special birthing chair (mandarin: sheng-tzu yi 生子椅) is laid on the floor. Tradition of bygone days insisted that the child be born over the hard earthen floor of the farming home. Thus the newly born child, filled with yang and new life would first touch and be blest by the spirit and power of yin, earth. A mat was placed over the floor, and the gestating woman sat on the low stool squatting or sitting just above the earth. The midwife assisted the child's entry into the world by sitting directly in front of the mother, while the mother-in-law or even the wife's mother held her shoulders from behind.

To assist the mother in the last stages of labor, all of the drawers in every cabinet, the doors to closets, and water faucets are opened. Men of the family pound the earth outside, and if necessary, certain Chinese medicines can be taken to facilitate delivery. A soup made from a dried seahorse is thought to be especially helpful for quick deliveries. Men were traditionally not allowed to assist at birth. Even in the modern maternity hospital doctors trained in western medicine often allow a midwife to attend the mother. Women immediately take over the care of the mother once the child has been born. Members of the family stay at the maternity hospital and provide the meals for the new mother as long as she remains away from home.

The placenta, as in parts of Europe, is in some places thought to be useful for medical purposes. If the placenta is not to be used for medicine, one of three possible alternatives are taken to dispose of it. A strict taboo forbids trodding on the placenta, and therefore it is 1) put into a pot filled with lime and buried with respect; 2) buried in some corner of the family property where noone will step on it or dig it up; 3) thrown into a river. The placenta of a girl child is sometimes handled in the third manner, since the "throwing away" of a placenta symbolizes that no more female children are wanted. The umbilical cord is cut, and tied with a piece of hemp cloth. In many areas of China and Okinawa the umbilical cord is kept and given to a daughter to take with her at the time of marriage. Dried and powdered umbilical cords are also thought to have medicinal properties.

A child born hand first, or in transverse position was thought to bring bad luck. If a transverse child was a girl, the chances of being sold as a child-bride, given away, or disposed of immediately after birth were high. Japanese criminal records kept during the colonial period in Taiwan show that infanticide was practiced occasionally after transverse deliveries, and punished by law. Though many parts of Taiwan and China consider the birth of twin children to be propitious, certain customs of the Austronesian tribes and south China villages dictate that the later born twin be suffocated at birth. Deformed children are blamed on a family that had offended the T'ai-shen (womb-foetus) spirit. A still born child was disposed of immediately, by being thrown into a river or a drain. The household registers kept by the Japanese and by earlier Chinese authorities in Taiwan often did not record the still born in records of vital statistics, and therefore fertility counts are often not accurate for Chinese and Taiwanese household registers.

Immediately after birth the child was wiped with a towel and rubbed with sesame seed oil. For the first two days a mixture of Chinese herbal medicines, boiled honey, and water is fed to the newly born child, while the mother's milk is expressed separately into a rice bowl and thrown away "against a wall" or in some out of the way place. Wasting mother's milk was considered to be an offense against heaven, and thus heaven was not allowed to witness the act. Meanwhile, the newly born was usually given its first taste of milk from a neighboring wife who had just given birth to a child. This custom is due to the fact that the mother who has just delivered often has too much milk, or difficulty in expressing enough to feed the baby for the first day or so. Thus the baby becomes used to breast feeding from a mother whose milk flows freely, and on the third day begins to feed from its own mother. Children who had shared mother's milk were afterwards called "nursing brothers and sisters" for the rest of their lives. It was not considered improper for the mother of a boy to give her milk to a neighbor's newly born girl child, thus establishing a quasi-sibling relationship and close neighborly bond from childhood. If the mother produced too much milk, the left over (after baby's satiety) was given to the elderly or the weak, as an especially nourishing drink to restore health. The extra milk was expressed into a rice bowl and given to a less healthy recipient.

In order to restore the strength of the mother after partition, special dishes are prepared, in accord with local custom. Taiwanese usage prefers chicken, wine, and sesame oil, while Cantonese from Chung-shan, in Kwangtung, prepare a special pigs-knuckle and wine dish to feed to the recuperating mother. This "wine stew" and many other special dishes were used to indulge the needs of the new mother during the first month of postpartum recovery. Work was not permitted, and the meeting of friends, leaving of the home, and other strenuous exercise were not permitted until the first month was completed.

The first month of recuperation, called *tsuo-yüeh* "sitting the month" is almost universally observed in China. High protein foods along with the sesame-wine chicken not only improve the health of the mother, but provide a plentiful supply of milk as well. Too many vegetables, it was thought, produced a *ts'ai-nai* "vegetable milk," while plentiful meat, peanuts, and other high protein foods made *sao-nai*, rancid meat-smelling milk.

The acts ritually prescribed for the recuperating mother are the following:
1. Eating of high protein or "warm" (yang) foods .
2. Drinking of herbal medicines such as *hua-sheng-t'ang*, peanut soup with five kinds of restorative herbs, one for each of the five elements.
3. Plenty of rest inside the home, with in-laws as well as husband's family (clan) providing help in all household chores, changing baby's diapers, and so forth.
4. Keeping warm, out of drafts, in pleasant circumstances.

Acts ritually taboo during the month after birth are the following:
1. Eating of cold substances, too many fruits, foods which might cause diarrhea or a weakened condition.
2. Leaving the house to visit friends for any reason; the woman who "sits the month" is the therefore considered to be ritually impure, i.e., recuperating from loss of blood, waiting for the body to return to normal health after the strain and stress of delivery. Ritual impurity therefore is related to a return to good health.
3. Marital relations until bodily strength is restored.
4. Bathing or washing the hair in cold water, which could cause chills or fever. Even the youngest mother of the clan is therefor insured warm water for a bath.

Since the woman who sits the month is considered to be ritually impure, she is exempt from religious obligations such as visiting temples (carrying all of mother-in-law's food offerings), attending funerals, or civic functions during the month of recuperation. Ritual taboo is therefore seen as a protective device for the welfare of the recuperating woman, inhibiting the clan from encroaching on the rights of the wife to full health. The taboo symbols of "emptiness" (child delivered from the womb), "cold" (powers of yin to harm the mother or child), and loss of blood (blood spilled at childbirth fills the "bloody pool" of hell, from which suffering mothers are to be freed by the meritorious acts of their children), are semiotics found in birth and death ritual.[8]

If the negative elements of postpartum recovery are expressed in the taboo elements of birth ritual, positive health- bringing acts and their symbols are promoted with equal fervor. The semiotics of gift giving, indicating "fullness" (man-t'ou or steamed buns colored red, formed in a circular shape, eggs, round stones) as seen in the presents given mother and child , the symbols for yang such as heat, warmth, high protein foods, typify the positive ritual acts prescribed for the mother to perform or receive. Society keeps the mother at home to recuperate, by making any unnecessary contact with her a symbol of bad luck, but gifts for her welfare a sign of blessing.

During the month of recuperation the wine-and-sesame chicken, lavish fried rice, round steamed buns or man-t'ou shaped like a turtle (for longevity) are put on the family altar and at the ancestor shrine on the sixth, twelfth, eighteenth, and twenty-second days of enclosure. Four is a symbol of death, while six is the number of the demonic spirits which bring disaster to the unprotected. Defense against the evil *chia* spirits[9] and from other demonic influences are therefore important on the sixth day and its multiples after birth. The child is often given a deprecatory name such as "little animal," "naughty child," and so forth, to keep demonic forces from envy, and protect the child from harm. Thus it is taboo to boast of the beauty of one's child, or to say that it is "fat", "delectable," and other such endearing terms, trite reminders of the foolish words often used by delighted parents and grandparents at the birth of a first child, to the boredom of guests who come to visit.

Naming the child is an art in China, for which an expert or an elder member of the clan is often hired in order to insure blessing. Good fortune, it is thought, rests in the choice of a name. A male is given a total of seven names throughout life and death. Beginning with birth, the various names and titles are: 1) "nursing" name given at birth (nai-ming); 2) nick-name (t'u-ming) used in childhood; 3) school name (ts'e-ming) often given by the teacher to the pupil; 4) the title or adult name (tzu-ming) used after the sixteenth year and the capping ceremony; 5) the *Hao* or literary title given after literary recognition; 6) the official title (kuan-chang) used by publicly appointed officials and Taoist priests when composing and signing official or ritual documents; and 7) the posthumous title given by official court approval after death (shih-ming).

The name to be used throughout life, which ordinarily identifies the boy or girl in the clan records, even after marriage, is chosen by the name giving expert shortly after birth. This name can be decided in any of a number of ways. Two rules are generally used. First, boys and girls of a nuclear family, of the same generation, often share one character in their *ming-tzu* or given name, thus identifying them as belonging to the same clan generation. For instance, all of the boys in family *A* will be given the Chinese character chia 嘉 (to begin, start anew) as the first of two characters in their names. Then as more boys are born into the family, each child is given a different second character to be identified by: Chao-chia, Chao-hsin, Chao-ko, and so forth. All of the clan and the neighbors can then identify the members of *A* family of that generation.

More commonly, names are chosen according to the yin-yang principle, i.e., strong and forceful objects are used for boys and soft, pliant objects for girls. Thus boys are named after mountains, streams, rivers, dragon, tiger, or other symbols of strength, while girls are named after flowers, decorative trees, birds, and other precious objects such as jade. Ching-hua (embroidered flower), Phoenix, Jade Swallow, and other poetic terms lend great beauty to names given to girls. Nicknames on the other hand are often merciless, and must be born by the child throughout a lifetime. "Big head," "horse face," "fat thumbs,' and other teasing names are given by children while playing in the street. Foreigners too become objects of such playful humor, often to the consternation of missionary and scholar.

On the third day after birth the midwife is called in to bathe the baby in warm water, *kuei-hua hsin* 桂花心 (osmanthus fragrans), leaves from the tangerine tree, and small round stones (symbolizing full yang, completion). Offerings of wine-cooked chicken, fried rice, and red steamed buns (man-t'ou) are laid on the ancestor shrine, then lifted and offered towards the home of the bride, that is, towards the home where she was born, or where her parents now reside. Announcements are formally sent to the in-laws and neighbors that the child (with the newly determined name) is healthy and well. Pictures of the child are taken without a stitch of clothing on, proving without question whether a boy or girl was born.

When the first month is over, the baby's head is ritually shaven. A symbolic offering is made of uncooked rice, boiled duck eggs and chicken eggs, twelve coins, and round stones in a circular basket. Fullness of yang, health and blessing are represented by the eggs (beauty and health), the twelve coins, (completion of the cycle of maturation), round stones (fullness, pure yang), and the circular basket of pure white rice. The first month is ritually finished on the twenty-fourth day after birth, representing the twenty-four stories of filial piety, and the fulfillment of blessing from the thrice eight or twenty-four stages of the cosmos, commemorated in the annual liturgical cycle. Beauty, success, and fullness of years are asked for the child. The grandmother proudly carries the baby outside into the sunlight for the first time. Just as death in a family is thought to bring good luck afterwards (yin at nadir brings back yang and blessing) so the birth of a child is thought to bring bad luck (yang at zenith brings a lessening of blessing). But from the twenty-fourth day onward the child is thought to bring good luck, and the ritual enclosure of mother and child is ended.

The in-laws, that is to say, the bride's family must supply a complete set of clothes for the newly born child on the first month, fourth month, and first year celebrations. The in-laws continue to play an important ritual role in the life of the child and mother. Monetary gifts are also given, to be laid away against the child's college education. To all those relatives and friends who sent gifts to the newly born child, rice cakes, fried rice, uncooked white rice and black beans are sent as signs of gratitude. Finally, the mother's month of seclusion is officially ended. She is now allowed to visit friends, and go out of the home at will. The duties of cleaning and cooking are gradually resumed, but mother-in-law, i.e., the wife's own mother may stay on to help out as long as the young mother feels the need for assistance. Even in the modern industrial age, the mother-in-law often comes to stay with the young mother who has just given birth to a child, living in the tiny apartments of industrial complexes and sharing the difficult duties of feeding, washing, and changing diapers.

When the child is four months old, a special ritual to the ancestors and the spirits of the family shrine is offered, thanking heaven for the continuing health of the child and commemorating the day when the child should "cease dropping saliva," that is, begin taking solid foods. Peach shaped steamed buns, colored pink, red, and white for artistic effect, are laid on the family altar. The wife's family once again

131

bring a complete set of baby clothes, called "head-to-foot presents," for the child, and add their own red and pink peach cakes to the altar . To every friend and relative who brings a present on this day the peach shaped cakes are given in gratitude. Red candy bean paste is put inside the peach cakes, and older children vie to receive these delicacies from their parents. A string of twenty-four cookies is hung around the neck of the four-month old child, and a single cookie put in its mouth, to "end the drooling of saliva." The baby is then carried around to neighbors and friends' houses, and made much of in the local community.

On the first birthday, the parents celebrate the child's safely passing through a year of healthy living. A banquet is given for the neighborhood, and a ritual performed to determine what the child will become in adulthood. A tray is prepared on which are laid twelve items: 1) a book, so the child will read well; 2) a brush, to write well; 3) rubbing ink, to be a scholar; 4) thigh of a chicken, to eat well and be healthy; 5) roast pork meat, also to eat well and be healthy; 6) an abacus, to be a wealthy merchant; 7) a small scale, also to enter business; 8) silver coins, to be a banker; 9) kindling wood, to burn brightly and be intelligent; 10) an onion, (ts'ung) for intelligence; 11) a clod of dirt, to work hard in the fields; 12) a Pao-tzu (Cantonese: cha-siu-bao) or steamed dumpling with meat inside, signifying that the child is now to eat regular food. After the child takes a bite, the dumpling is fed to a dog, and in its place the child is given a sweet rice cake (t'ien), to turn its mind from lowly to heavenly or high things.

Before birth the spirits who assist in delivery such as Chu-sheng Niang-niang are made patrons of mother and unborn child. After birth until the sixteenth year and the capping ceremony the "mother spirit of the bed," (ch'uang-mu 床母) is thought to be the patron saint of growing children. When the child cries at night a special ritual to ch'uang-mu is offered. A bowl of cooked rice with a red salted plum on top is put in the middle of the child's bed, with chopsticks inserted (as in the offerings for the dead). Incense is lit, and the chopsticks are immediately withdrawn. "Come here and take care of the child," the mother prays, symbolically showing that the bed mother and the real mother have no time to eat, so busy are they with caring for the newborn child.

The first year is indeed a difficult time for parents of all ages and civilizations. The Chinese manner of caring for mother and child avoids much of the post-natal depression and fatigue by sharing the motherly duties with members of the clan and the wife's own mother.

132

The child is indeed spoiled, carried around by older siblings, dry nursed even on the bosom of an aging grandparent. Until schooling, the life of the Chinese child is almost without discipline.

II. Rites of Initiation

The traditional ceremony of capping (kuan) for a boy and hairdo or coiffure for a girl (Chi-yi) are no longer observed as puberty rituals for young adults in modern China. In some parts of the diaspora of maritime China the capping and the coiffure ceremonies can still be seen as minor parts of the wedding ceremony, but otherwise the six-teenth year of the boy and the first hair-do for the girl are minor events celebrated rather quietly at home. In the case of a boy, the Fukienese of Taiwan and southeast Asia often celebrate by cooking a young rooster for the sixteenth birthday of a son, signifying the maturity of yang (rooster, especially a white rooster with a red comb, is a symbol of yang). Since capping was traditionally associated with graduation from the private confucian school of the village, the graduation ceremonies from upper middle school and from univer-sity, among other changes, did much to alter the need for a separate rite of maturation.

Kindergarten, through college or middle school, as the case may be, is a time of intense pressure and discipline for the Chinese child. Strict training in the Chinese written character, science, math, and the practical arts have superseded the former emphasis on a literary education. Middle schools and high schools of Maritime China, including Taiwan, Hongkong and some parts of southeast Asia, still require the study of the classics, T'ang and Sung poetry, and the Neo-confucian philosophers through middle and high school. But the major emphasis of the Chinese educational system is now geared to science, technology, and industrial progress. Only those boys and girls who do not do well in the sciences pursue literary studies in the Chinese universities, except for the rare exception of the truly gifted scholar. Literary genius and scholarly pursuits in the traditional dis-ciplines of China are often given employment and high salaries in western and Japanese universities.

Such was not true in traditional China, of course, nor in those families which are experiencing a rebirth of Chinese literary and traditional studies. In such cases the six year old child is made to present himself to the literary scholar who will be his mentor, and follow a strict regimen of learning and discipline in the classics. The young scholar brings to his teacher in the *shu-fang* school of the literary arts, the three traditional presents of the Confucian tradition: 1) an egg (for completion of studies); 2) an onion which is a homonym for intelligence (ts'ung for onion sounds like ts'ung for intelligent); and 3) Chinese parsley (Ch'in, which sounds like ch'in for diligence). The traditional Chinese education is extremely demanding, relying on the memorization of the classical texts, the reading of all the major commentaries, and the ability to compose essays in the classical style. Such scholars are rare in modern times, but are still to be found in the Chinese University of Hongkong, and are often given positions in the major universities of the west.

The rites of post-puberty maturation, like the Yom Kippur ceremony of Judaism or confirmation in the Christian tradition, make sense in the light of scholarly initiation. All three traditions demand a certain period of scholarly training for the recipient, and the fulfill-ment of certain moral and spiritual qualifications. When these qualifications have been tested and fulfilled, the boy or girl may present themselves to their family for the rite of maturation. The manual of Lin Po-t'ung will be used to describe the kuan ritual for a boy and the *chi* ritual for a young lady, as practiced in Kwangtung province at the beginning of the Nineteenth century. The commen-taries of Chu Hsi and Szu-ma Kuang are used by the elderly Lin in the form of glosses, thereby intending to make the ritual in its bare es-sence valid as a structural norm of initiation for all of China.

The master of ceremonies (MC) for the kuan capping ceremony can be either the father of the boy to undergo the ritual, the elder brother who is household head, or the grandfather if that person has not yet reached seventy years of age. The person performing the ceremony must be a leader in the clan or the immediate family . On the third day before the Kuan ritual is to be performed, the MC an-nounces the rite at the family ancestor shrine. For most of the urban families of mainland and maritime China, the ancestor shrine is kept of course in the main room on the family altar. But if the family main-tains a Szu-t'ang or separate ancestor hall, the capping rite is per-formed there. The ritual is as follows:
1. The MC lights incense, candles, and kneels before the ancestor shrine.
2. He reads from a prepared document the following words:

134

With sincerity of heart (ch'eng-shin 誠心)
On the_____day of_____(month)_____(year)
Master_____(boy's name)
Will receive his cap in the kuan crowning ceremony.
We hereby announce it respectfully to the ancestors.
3. Wine is poured out to the ancestors, and all bow three times.

After the announcement to the ancestors is made, guests are invited, including immediate family members, and a scholar or mandarin who has been successful in the pursuit of studies, as a form of blessing. Meanwhile the ancestral hall or front room is prepared for the rite, and a huge banquet ordered to dine the guests. In an ordinary family one hat or "crown" is prepared for the son, while in a wealthy mandarin family three hats are used, one for heaven, earth, and watery underworld (spring, summer-autumn, and winter).

On the day of the ceremony, all arise before dawn, and take their places in the main hall just at sunrise, or as early as possible after the day begins. The coming of day, the birth of yang and maturation are symbolically represented in the beginning of the capping festivities. The elderly sit in the west, and the youth sit in the east, for the ceremony. The table with the hat(s) is placed in the center of the room, and the boy to be crowned enters in full dress, but of course without a hat, for the ceremony. Confucian ritual always decreed that ceremonial hats be worn for liturgy. Only in the case of the kuan rite was the recipient allowed to enter the shrine without a headpiece. The rite is as follows:
1. The MC enters and stands in the center of the room, facing south, with the table and crown behind him to the north; (recall that the altar is always to the ritual north. Thus the MC begins with his back to the altar, facing outward, to the south. The symbolic meaning is that the boy to be crowned is at first "outside" the hall, then welcomed in and made to face north for the crowning).
2. On the altar are laid the sacrificial items, according to local custom and material culture. These usually include the three meats (chicken, pork, and fish, standing for heaven, earth, and water), five vegetable dishes, five fruits, five sweets, and so forth. Candles and incense are lit. Five cups of wine, five cups of tea and five bowls of rice are placed with the offerings.

3. The recipient enters dressed in ritual robes, but without a hat. He stands in the east, directly in front of the younger members of the family, facing west. The MC takes the hat from the table, and all stand.

4. The MC intones "Let the boy to be crowned come forward," (kuan-che chin ch'ien!). The recipient goes to the front of the table, facing north, and receives the crown. (If three crowns are used, he puts on one at a time, retaining the crown appropriate to the season).

5. The recipient and the MC then go to the offerings at the table and perform the rite called *chiao* 醮 (offering incense and wine) after which Taoist liturgy is named. The recipient receives a cup of wine from the MC, lifts it above his head in respect to the ancestors and spirits, and then pours it out into a receptacle placed under the altar. The offering is done twice, (once each for yin and yang). They then kneel, bow deeply twice, and arise, repeating the bows in front of the boy's parents, the elders, the guests, and the youth of the family.

6. The ritual document, called *tz'u* 詞 is now read. Since the local expert at writing the tz'u is often a Taoist, or a man trained in classical composition, the person employed to write the tz'u is most often called on to read it in the official, legal manner. The guest of honor also performs this public role. When the document has been read, the recipient thanks the guest of honor, and bows twice.

7. The guest of honor or the MC announce that the ritual is over. All are led out to enjoy the banquet. Each guest receives a present for having attended the ceremony, and leaves behind a hung-pao or li-shi (red envelope with monetary gift inside) for the boy who has been capped.

Lin Po-t'ung quotes the Sung dynasty scholar Szu-ma Kuang, stating that the kuan ceremony should not be put off until the wedding, as is done in many parts of China. The capping ceremony is truly a rite of maturation, "ch'eng-jen chih Tao," a way helping the recipient become an adult. The father, from what he is within himself must teach the son to assume the responsibilities of an adult. The rite is useless unless the boy has already learned to be selfless, concerned with the good of other family members, and filled with li 禮 respect for others. He should also be a scholar, filled with knowledge of the classics, filial piety, and knowledgeable in household as well as public ritual. Above all, the person who receives the crown should be temperate and restrained, self-controlled, and observant of other's needs. To be ma-

136

ture means to be strict on the self and benevolent to others. He must particularly have respect for the common man, the laborer, and the peasant.

With these simple rules, the work of Lin Po-t'ung turns to the coiffure ceremony for a fifteen year old girl. The refined family, Lin notes, gives equal care for the upbringing of the girl. Even though many peasant families neglect this rite (there is no coiffure rite listed for a peasant-commoner in Lin's book), it is recommended that the girl too be trained like the boy to observe the rules of propriety, learn the Confucian classics, and be filled with wisdom and learning. Lin's daughters aided in compiling and editing their father's book, proving the importance of educating daughters as well as sons in the traditional Chinese family.

The coiffure ceremony for a girl parallels the capping ceremony for a boy, except that the performers, guests, and officiants are all women. On a propitious day before the ceremony, guests are invited by a written invitation. The mistress of ceremonies is chosen, either the mother of the girl, the grandmother, or the wife of a favorite older brother within the clan. The same preparations for the altar, the main room of the house, and banquet are made as for the boy. But instead of the crown, the table in the center of the room holds a tray on which are laid the combs, brushes, hair ornaments, and other jewelry to be given to the young lady of the household.

The guests come early in the morning of the day appointed for the ritual, and are welcomed by the lady of the house and the MC. They take up their places in the main room as above, the elder women in the west, the younger in the east. In wealthy families, a special main room is kept in the lady's quarters but in the modern or the urban family, the main room of the home in front of the family altar and ancestor shrine is used. The ritual is as follows:

1. The recipient enters the main room quietly and alone, from an inner room where she has been waiting.
2. The lady guests arise, greet her, and lead her to the table in the center of the room where the combs, ornaments, and so forth have been laid out.

3. The ladies of the family and the guests arrange the girl's hair in the adult fashion for the first time, using ornaments, jewelry, or whatever strikes the young lady's fancy. The recipient then retires to her quarters, while the sacrificial offerings (as in the capping ceremony) are laid on the altar.

4. The recipient is called back to the main room, and the chiao 醮 sacrifice is performed, paralleling the rite of the boy receiving the crown, above. The recipient offers wine to the ancestors and spirits, holding the cup in her right hand and holding back the long sleeve of her dress with the left. Bows are made to the guest of honor who will read the tz'u, the other guests, her family, and siblings.

5. The MC then leads the recipient to offer incense and wine in the clan ancestral hall, if there is a separate shrine to the ancestors. The recipient must bows again to all present, in the following order: i. she bows to her mother and father; ii. she bows to the guest of honor, who reads the document; iii. she pays her respects to her grandmother, aunties, and all of the invited ladies; iv. she greets her older brothers wives; v. finally, she greets her younger sisters.

6. The grand banquet, presided over by the lady of the house, is then served to the guests and the entire family. Presents and red envelopes (hung-pao or lishi) are given to the family and the girl being honored.

There is no doubt in the mind of western scholars and of the Chinese themselves that the woman was treated in an inferior manner to the man in Chinese society. The power of a woman was limited to her role as head of the inner family. Though there are many cases of women investing their dowery money independently, and becoming wealthy inspite of the superior attitude of the males, the lot of the woman was often made and kept subordinate to that of the man. In external matters, roles traditionally taken by men, such as politics, women were and are kept either outside of, or in inferior positions. Yet there are eloquent exceptions to the general rule, as seen in the strong women in modern Chinese politics, the several women empresses of Chinese history, the role of the Buddhist nun, and the strong women of the Chinese novel and fiction tradition.

An excellent body of literature in English exists for the reader to explore the role of the woman in Chinese daily life. Only in Taoism, perhaps, is the place of woman made equal to and sometimes superior to man. Religion in its folk expression has always been the vehicle for the downtrodden, the oppressed, and the individual to find self-revelation and communication. The growth of Buddhism, Taoism, and other religious movements inside the People's Republic of China today reflects the role of religion in Chinese society to both preserve culture and protect the right of the individual, women and men alike, to free and open expression. The pursuit of ascetic goals, such as meditation in the Buddhist caves of Chiu Hua Shan, ch'i-kung in the Taoist hills of Wutang Shan and Ch'ing-ch'eng shan, are places where women equal and excel the role of men.

NOTES

1. See Qian Xinzhong, *Renkou Xinpian*, Chengdu: 1989, A New Look into Population Problems, pp. 310-11, for PRC farming families with more than one child.
2. Sources for Birthing Customs are: Suzuki Seichiro, *Taiwan Kyukan, Kan, Kon, So, Sai, to Ichinen Gyoji*, (Customs of Old Taiwan), Taipei: 1934, pp. 89-123; Ikeda Toshio, *Taiwan no Katei Seikatsu*, (Taiwan Family Life), Taipei, 1944.
3. See Saso, M., *The Chinese Family*, (in press, 1990) for changes in Chinese family structure between 1870-1970.
4. See Wolf, A., and Huang C.S., *Marriage and Adoption in China*, (Stanford:1980) and Wolf, margery, *The House of Lim* for classic studies of the Chinese family.
5. Wolf, Margery, *Woman and Family in Rural Taiwan*, Stanford: 1972, pp. 205-14.
6. *Shen-hua* myth and *Tsung-chiao* religion are clearly distinguished in China. There is no necessary relationship between religious festival and myth.
7. Shrines of Italy, Spain, and the Philippines follow similar customs.
8. De Groot, J.J.M., "Masses for the Dead at Amoy," *Acts of the VIth International Congress of Orientalists*, Leiden, 1883.
9. Described in Saso, M., TOTMC, (New Haven:1978) Ch. 4.

6. BURIAL AND ANCESTOR RITES

Rites of burial and ancestor memorial are intimately connected to the theory of soul discussed in Chapter One and Chapter Three. Death and dying for the Chinese is a process whereby the shen-spirit separates from the body, and hovers about the home until properly buried. The seven p'o spirits, i.e., the emotional *yin* powers of the body, accompany the body to the grave, and are buried with it. (See Chapter One, fig. 9). Two of the three hun aspects of the soul are dissipated at death, that is, the ch'i life breath and the ching intuitive essence. The shen-spirit alone is thought to be immortal. All care is taken by means of funeral and ancestor ritual to insure that the shen is properly cared for. Its journey through the purifying alchemy of the *yin* underworld to a blissful afterlife is hastened by Taoist and Buddhist ritual, and by the meritorious works of the living.

Even those members of the community who are highly educated agnostics, or disassociated from religion for political reasons, perform burial rites and sponsor Buddhist or Taoist memorials for the dead. Burial and ancestral ritual are public signs of family respect and self-esteem. To be absent from a funeral is to separate oneself from family, friends, and village community. To sponsor memorial services is to raise credibility within the community. Personal trustworthiness, filiality, reciprocity, benevolence, the whole range of socially accepted virtues are affirmed by the rites associated with death, burial, and memorial services. The data presented in chapter seven shows the importance still attached to these rituals in modern China.

Recalling the notions presented in chapters one and three, the ch'i primordial breath/intellect which rules from the head, the power of will and love residing in the heart, and the intuitive forces stored in the belly are dissipated by running after glory, fame, wealth, and selfish desires. All of the selfish deeds done by humans during life, good and bad, have macrocosmic effects. When the soul-spirit separates from the body at death, the normal course of events require that it sinks downward into the world of yin, where the fires of cosmic alchemy purify it from impediments to a happy existence after death. All social transgressions, cosmic unbalances, and debts must be paid off in the hot and cold punishments of Buddhist-Taoist hell.

The illustrations at the end of found Chapter Three displayed in the temple, funeral hall, or the temporary altar erected outside the home during the burial ceremonies. The scrolls depict ten or more stages of hell, where specific misdemeanors, felonies, and sins are given appropriate punishments. Shamans travel into hell to see how the soul-spirit is faring. Mediums who are possessed by the soul of the deceased blame the sickness of a child or the failure of a business on the soul-spirit of an ancestor, or a *kuei*, i.e., a spirit without descendants to pray it out of hell's punishments. Popular Buddhism, Taoism, and manuals such as the *Kan-ying P'ien* teach that good works bring blessing to the living by hastening the progress of the dead through hell's punishments.

The role of the shaman-medium throughout Asia provides a complement to the Buddhist and Taoist rites of burial, affirming human virtue as a means to hasten the release of the soul from the punishments of the underworld. Modern newspapers decry the money wasted on such trance and medium possessions, yet the care for, or fear of the soul-spirit in the afterlife still motivates many such folk-ritual practices surrounding burial and ancestral memorial in modern China. Inspite modern secular attempts to belittle such folk practices, the burial rite itself, and the care for the ancestor in the afterlife has a far deeper significance than simple fear of the unknown. The observance of funeral ritual, care for the grave, and maintenance of an ancestral shrine affirm the very structure of the Chinese social and cultural system.

Families or individuals who have received a share of the inheritance from the deceased must by customary law observe the rites of burial and ancestral memorial. Disciples, students, and successors of a great teacher must likewise burn incense before a shrine erected in their home to the master's memory. Some shrines and family altars in maritime and mainland China observe this practice today, a sign of the social and economic overtones of the rites associated with death and ancestral memorial. The descriptions of the rituals found below are drawn from Lin Po-t'ung's *Kuan, Hun, Sang, Chi*, Rites of Passage, the *Chia-li Ta-ch'eng* (Complete Home Rituale), and the detailed descriptions of Suzuki Seiichiro observed in north Taiwan.[1]

I. The Rites of Burial

The death-and-dying process, the most traumatic experience of the human condition, is carefully planned, in the Chinese tradition, as a rite to alleviate the stress and sorrow of the bereaved family. As the moment of death approaches, a Taoist and/or Buddhist is hired, to care for the burial details, and a Master of Ceremonies (MC) selected from within the family or clan elders to organize the family's affairs while mourning. Particular details of the burial, as in the life rituals, are determined by local material culture and family custom. The structural outline of the ritual, however, follows a standard pattern:

> 1. Care for the dying, and certain preparations for burial are attended to. Purchase of a coffin and a family burial site are provided for long before death.
> 2. Washing the body, encoffining, and sealing of the coffin.
> 3. Mourning for the deceased at home or in the mortuary.
> 4. The funeral procession and burial.
> 5. The ancestor tablet, shrine, and post-funerary services.

1. *Care for the Dying and Funeral Preparations*

The selection of a coffin for an elderly person is often made by the six-tieth birthday, or well enough in advance of death so that the choice of wood, size, and decoration may be approved beforehand. The gravesite was often chosen generations before the death of a family member occurs. In the case of a pioneer territory such as Hsinchu, Taiwan, the choice of a mainland family gravesite was made by the Ch'ing dynasty forebearers. The family tombs on the mainland in southeast Fukien are carefully recorded in the family *chia-p'u* 家譜 burial records.[2] To satisfy the principles of geomancy (*Ti-li Feng-shui* 地理風水) the grave usually must face the sea, have proper drainage, and be protected by mountains and forests behind the tumulus.[3] The family and the dying person faced death with these preliminary duties well in hand. The gravesite was known to the family members, and cleaned annually during the Ch'ing-ming festival.[4]

As the illness worsened, and death approached, the dying person was removed from the bedroom to a pallet next to the ancestral tablets in the main hall. The dying person was sometimes laid on a mat on the floor, so as to be close to the earth and the yin underworld at the moment of death. The sick man was placed in front of the ancestor tablet to the south (yang) while the woman was placed to the left (yin). In homes without an ancestor shrine, the pallet of the dying person was simply placed on the floor. When death was imminent, the expression of family grief and wailing began.

Men were required to remove all state and official clothing. Women took off all hair ornaments and jewelry, and let their hair run straight down the back. The immediate family encircled the failing parent, accompanying the dying person until the last breath. Men were required to stand to the east (yang) and women to the west (yin). Closer relatives stood to the front, and more distant affines to the rear. Literary families asked the aging parent to write or dictate a last testament in the classical literary style, sometime before death. This document was to be read aloud as the final moment approached.

At the moment of death grieving and mourning are allowed full expression. The younger children are permitted to leave the room, and the first preparations for burial are begun. A master of ceremonies (MC) is formally chosen, to care for all the details and take the leadership of the family into his own hands during the rite of passage. The first duty was to prepare a death notice called *fu* 訃 which is sent to all the relatives and friends of the deceased. The edges of the document are traditionally burned with a candle, the fire-darkened edges being a reminder of the sorrow of the entire clan at the life of a beloved member extinguished. The last testament read at the moment of death was included in the *fu* death notice for all to see.

2. *Washing the Corpse and Encoffining*

The washing and dressing of the corpse after death are described in careful detail in the burial manuals. Unless cared for by the hospital or some other method, the rite is as follows:

a. The body is taken up from the floor and placed on a special bed or table.

b. To the east of the bed on a table are laid out the utensils for washing, i.e., a white cloth, a pan of water, a comb, and a towel. On a second table are arranged the burial clothes.

c. The wailing ceases, and the head of the corpse is placed to the south, symbolizing yang, fire, and purification. The body is washed ritually, and the hair is combed.[5]

d. The clothes to be put on the corpse are first tried on by one of the sons of the family. This rite recalls the ancient custom of using a living person to represent the deceased (shih 尸) during the funeral rite, before encoffining. The clothes put on the corpse must be an uneven or yang number. After being put on the *shih* living representative, they are then put on the corpse.

e. The corpse is transferred from the washing table to a special bed used just before encoffining. The comb is broken, and is buried along with the washing implements.

The traditional rules of the classical burial text are open to local interpretation. The increase, modification, and adaptation of the text varies with local and family custom. The household in which a death occurred (the nadir of misfortune), would soon be blessed with good fortune, just as the family in which a birth occurred was avoided.[6] Local customs and myths surrounding death assure blessing for those who assist the family during the funeral ritual, just as it makes the mother who has just given birth to a child exempt from trying work and bothersome visits. Burial ritual, on the other hand, must be well attended, and all help possible extended to the bereaved family, to insure that every detail of the burial customs be observed.

Local custom through much of southeast China dictates that the water used to wash the corpse be drawn from the middle of a flowing stream, symbolizing the carrying of the soul-spirit quickly through the underworld into the peaceful western heavens. After washing the corpse, the first duty of the bereaved family is to call the relatives of the wife's side, if the deceased is a married woman. The woman's relatives examine the corpse, and assure the community that the wife and mother of the family had not been mistreated by her husband's family. The entire family goes out to meet the relatives (affines) of the deceased woman, explain the cause of death, and show their affection for their deceased mother. In some areas the wife's relatives bring a stick to the corpse-washing, to symbolically "beat" the husband's family for any sign of mistreatment during the woman's life.

Taoists who specialize in funerals (called *O-thau* in the Min dialect of southern Fukien) are often hired to take care of the ritual details of the encoffining. Drums and sona (double read flute) are played during the washing, and special cymbals are used to purify the interior of the coffin. Children are exempt from watching this process, lest they be upset from continually viewing the corpse. Lamps are lit, and the interior of the house is kept continually bright to assist the soul-spirit of the deceased find its way to the yang realms of light.

With the corpse still on the bed, facing the south, the coffin is now prepared to receive the body. A special table covered with a white cloth is prepared in the front room, next to where the coffin is to be placed. Over the table is suspended a white *hun-p'o* cloth scroll, usually

144

made of silk, with characters written on the surface to represent the soul-spirit of the deceased. Brass bowls to hold food offerings, a change of clothes, and an incense burner are put on the altar. Offerings are made here, and a change of clothes provided twice a day for the deceased. The center of the burial altar also displays a picture of the deceased, two lamps kept lit day and night, and a series of elevated platforms with more brass vases, bowls, and other ritual paraphernalia to honor the tablet and picture of the deceased. The coffin is usually placed to the east (yang) of the temporary altar, facing south.

The family altar and all of its decorations are covered and hidden with white cloth throughout the burial rite. Thus the ritual for the deceased supersedes all other activities within the household. Marriages, New Year celebrations, and other festivals are not permitted while the coffin is in the home, and the family is in mourning. The color white for death, the west, and final rest is used to cover the walls, and all other paraphernalia in the front room of the house where the burial altar and the coffin are displayed. With these preparations made, the coffin is now brought into the main room of the house, and the body is prepared for the encoffining ritual.[7]

The entire family meets the coffin as it is carried into the residence of the deceased, and accompany it with much wailing into the front room. The coffin is placed next to the bed where the corpse is resting, and a special board with the seven stars of Ursa Major (The Big Dipper) placed near the headboard inside the coffin. The pot of the dipper always points to the north, while the tail points to the "gate of life." By placing the stars of the Big Dipper into the coffin, the semiotic sign of eternal rest with the Transcendent Tao (Wu-wei chih Tao) and the pointing of the soul towards the gate of life, is symbolically applied to the soul-spirit of the deceased.

Children are called upon to put the favorite things of the deceased into the coffin, such as cigarette lighters, rings, jade bracelets, other jewelry, fur coats, and so forth. Adults, who are less objective in such matters, tend to lay aside objects that the living might want to utilize, while children are inclined to remember what parents or grandparents liked best.[8] The costly items put into the coffin are used when the body is exhumed to help cover the cost of a columbarium or geomantic shrine burial. Urns for the washed bones of prior ancestors often decorate the elaborate mountain tomb sites of southeast China, financed by the jewelry put in the coffin at burial.

Pots containing favorite foods, five kinds of dried fruit (for the five elements), rice, wine, and other edibles to be used during the long journey through hell, are also placed in the coffin. Local custom sometimes follows the imperial practice of placing pearls in the mouth, eyes, ears, and nostrils, as a sign of rebirth in the Taoist heavens. The pearl is a semiotic sign of the drop of yang in the depths of yin (death's) ocean, that brings about rebirth or renewal in the Buddhist/Taoist heavens.

Before putting the corpse into the coffin, a quantity of ground limestone and straw is put on the floorboards. This action insures that the bones are completely whitened when the coffin is opened five or so years later, and the bones are washed before storage in a burial urn. The custom of bone-washing and urn burial is found throughout Southeast China. On top of the straw is placed a favorite blanket of the deceased, with the ends left draped over the side of the coffin. The body is placed on the blanket, and the ends are folded over the clothed corpse, so that the upper part of the chest, throat, and head are visible.

A Taoist may be hired to officiate at this part of the ceremony, according to the will of the MC and the grieving family. White paper talismans perforated with a myriad of patterned holes are laid over the corpse, as the family members approach the coffin, and placed the deceased person's favorite things, the food, flowers, and other things inside.[9] The talismans remind the living to avoid close contact with the corpse, any diseases, "evil spirits," or unrequited wishes that the deceased may have left behind. Customs such as the scattering of lead powder and covering the body with layer-after-layer of white talismans served to separate the world of the living from the dead.[10]

Once the coffin has been prepared, and the body comfortably placed inside, the coffin lid is closed and sealed. The seating arrangement of immediate family and relatives during the encoffining, whether at home or in a a funeral parlor, strictly follows the yin-yang rules enunciated in Chapter One. The MC and all of the male relatives sit to the east of the coffin, facing west. The wife, concubines, female relatives, and children sit to the west, facing east. The men assigned to perform the ritual stand by the northeast wall, the "gate of demon" (Gate of Hell) to send off the soul on its long stygian journey. The head of the coffin faces south, i.e., the deceased has already assumed the place of a spirit, while the living, the MC, and the Taoist or Buddhist priest officiating at the burial rite face north when they pray or chant sutras for the deceased.

While the Taoists chant the rites seeing the soul through hell's bureaucratic hallways, the white talismanic papers placed over the body are continuously removed, burned, and replaced. Once the coffin has been sealed, the encoffining process is officially over, and the family of the deceased must serve all guests a banquet. The food is usually catered, and always includes bowls of long noodles, that are eaten whole, without cutting the long strings into shorter lengths. The long noodles symbolize long life, and are eaten to insure the living the blessing of old age and health, as well as to win merit for the deceased, to quickly attain eternal life as a Taoist immortal or in the Buddhist western paradise.

The rituals for preparing the corpse for burial and encoffining are filled with a myriad details governed by local practice and custom. It may seem impossible at first sight to find any universal order in the rituals that are used to bury the dead throughout China. The officially approved manuals in fact allow for this diversity and openness to variation. The bare structural details of encoffining found throughout China are classified as follows:

a. Washing or purifying the corpse: *mu-yü* 沐浴 .

b. Dressing the corpse in burial clothes: *hsiao-lien* 小殮 .

c. Putting the corpse in the coffin: *ta-lien* 大殮 .

Whether in the modern funeral parlor or the traditional home, these three structural elements are generally found in funeral ritual throughout China, while the details within each segment are determined by local custom, the manuals tell us.

3. *The Mourning Period Before Burial*

Once encoffined, the traditional "Confucian" rules demanded that the mandarin and gentry family mourn anywhere from six months to a year before the formal funeral cortege and burial could be held. Ch'ing dynasty law forbade the peasant class from mourning for more than a month, in order to keep the farmers working in the fields. The choice of a burial day was worked out after consulting a Taoist or *T'ung-shu* almanac specialist. Burial days are carefully worked out by mathematical calculation, depending on the year, month, day, and hour of birth of the deceased. In general, the moment of burial was chosen according to the direction in which the tail of the Big Dipper pointed at the moment of birth. Just as the first life breath of a child was drawn at the moment of birth, so the moment of the soul-spirit's return to eternity through earthly burial should ideally be when the tail of the Big Dipper pointed in the same direction. The soul returned to the bosom of the Tao, in the Taoist spiritual tradition, from the same direction in which life began.[11]

The exigencies of modern life make long mourning periods impractical, even impossible. A minimum of three to five days of mourning are preferred in modern maritime and mainland China, equivalent to the mourning period allowed in the west. No matter how long or short the period, custom requires that breakfast, tea, incense, and a new set of clothes be laid out each morning by the coffin during the mourning period. Likewise, meat dishes, incense, wine, and pajamas are laid out at night. The morning offerings are called *ch'u-chi* 初祭 in the Confucian manuals, while the night offerings are named *ta-chi* 大祭. The food offerings are determined by local custom. A bowl of rice, tea, wine, and incense with chopsticks laid to the left side are left on the altar during the day. Incense is lit and wailing intoned when guests come to pay their respects, and leave a small money offering to help cover the expenses of the funeral.

The morning and evening food offering is performed as follows:
a. The MC or the mother of the household lays out the food offerings in sets of three, one each for heaven, earth, and underworld realms that the soul must travel through.
b. Incense is lit, while wine and tea are poured into the empty cups. Chopsticks are placed to the left of each set of offerings.
c. Each of the food offerings is lifted by the MC, raised above his head, and offered to the memory of the deceased while praying that the soul-spirit may quickly attain eternal rest. The MC bows twice after each offering.
d. Each family member present then approaches, offers a stick of burning incense, prays, bows twice, and retires. Visitors who come during the day to offer their condolences follow this segment of the ritual only.[12]
e. A set of business or working clothes are laid out in the morning, and pajamas are brought out at night, after the food offerings are completed. The soul of the deceased is treated as if present, until the funeral cortege and coffin leave the house.

The rules for mourning during the period that the coffin is kept in the home or the mortuary suggest that vocal wailing is better than shedding copious tears. The burial rite is a lengthy and trying process. Too many tears can injure the eyes, the manuals tell us. The *T'ung-shu* daily almanac is again consulted for the best time to begin the funeral procession. The grave is readied, and arrangements for the funeral procession itself are planned. At this point Taoist, Buddhist, Christian, or Islamic experts are called in to perform the burial rite according to religious belief or custom.

4. *The Funeral Procession*

All consanguinal relatives on the father's side to the sixth degree, and mother's relatives (affines) to the third degree are required by customary law to attend the funeral procession. Sickness or birth of a child (sitting the month) may excuse a relative from attending the funeral. Otherwise non-attendance indicates that a public offense has occurred between the family of the deceased and the relative who does not attend the funeral.[13] Each family and friend of the deceased provides a large funeral wreath of white flowers, (paper or real) in the center of which is written the character *yi* 奠 for mourning. Either a coolie is hired to carry the wreath, or it is placed in one of the many open bedded trucks which accompany the procession.

The funeral procession must be as long and as lavish as the family can afford. No expenses are spared to make the funeral a grand public event, showing the love of the immediate family for the deceased, and at the same time the respect of the entire community for the clan and its members. Though lavish funerals were forbidden during the period of the Cultural Revolution in the People's Republic, and discouraged by legal prescriptions in Taiwan and parts of overseas Chinese communities, the funeral procession is still one of the most expensive and colorful parts of the Burial Rite. Common elements found throughout mainland and maritime Chinese communities include the following:

a. Banners and procession leaders, sometimes blowing trumpets several meters in length, to announce the cortege.

b. Burial wreaths carried by coolies, or trucks.

c. Foreign bands playing "Auld lang syne," and Chinese troops playing official funeral music called *pei-kuan* 北官 respectively.

d. Public notices of mourning, scrolls, and banners prepared by friends and officials for the funeral.

e. The "spirit cart" bearing the *hun-p'o* silk banner from the burial altar, a picture of the deceased, and a willow branch, with a lantern attached to it.[14]

149

f. The coffin, suspended from a large wooden frame carried by coolies, or in modern days transported on an open truck.

g. The immediate family of the deceased, dressed in mourning clothes according to degree of relationship to the deceased. A long hemp rope is sometimes attached to the coffin, and held onto by the mourning relatives, as if trying to prevent the coffin from being taken to the grave.

h. The more distant relatives and friends of the family. This part of the funeral entourage usually does not go on to the graveyard, but returns at the city gates to the home of the deceased, where a funeral banquet is served.

The laws governing funeral ritual and mourning decree that first degree relatives wear rough burlap, second degree light burlap, and third degree white muslim, for the burial procession. A mourning cap and veil made of burlap cover the face, and the character yin 引 (to lead the coffin to the grave) is affixed to the veil. Relatives from the fourth to the sixth degree wear a patch of colored cloth on the sleeve, indicating the degree of relationship. The immediate family must wear a burlap band around the arm for an entire three month mourning period after burial, and observe the first and third year anniversaries of death with Taoist, Buddhist, Christian, Islamic, or other ritual.

The procession can be expanded to a grand display of wealth and public entertainment. The twenty-four scenes of filfial piety are sometimes depicted in twenty-four hand propelled or motorized floats. Children dressed as "jade lassies and golden lads" ($y\ddot{u}$-$n\ddot{u}$ $chin$-$t'ung$), the Taoist immortals who lead the soul to the Taoist heavens, Ksittigharba, Kuanyin, and other Buddhist figures adorn the procession. A strange custom of providing scantily-clad singing women from local bars and night clubs to entertain the demonic spirits, (ku-hun and $kuei$) has become popular in recent years in Taiwan.[15] Only demons and unseemly elements of society are supposedly entertained by these segments of the funeral procession, thus avoiding contamination of the purer elements of society who attend the funeral.

Taoists, Buddhists, Christian, or Islamic ministers who attend the funeral usually walk in front of the coffin, and attend the final burial rites at the grave. In traditional China the women of finer families were allowed to be in the procession only if an ovular screen was carried in the procession, allowing them to walk or ride protected from view of the inside. Custom forbade that unmarried younger

150

women and recently married younger wives of refined families appear in public except at stated times such as the Ch'ing-ming festival or the Festival of Lights.[16] In modern times the entire funeral procession is often motorized, and proceeds slowly through the city streets, providing several hours of entertainment, songs, and pious scenes of filiality.

5. *Burial Rites at the Grave*

The size of the grave, shape of the tombstone and inscriptions on the epitaph were once strictly controlled by national law. Thus the decorative elements, length and height of retaining walls, square base (earth) and circular tumulus (heaven) were regulated according to the rank of the mandarin family.[17] The long mourning period during traditional times usually allowed the gravestone to be prepared and decorated in the officially approved manner before burial. In modern times the government no longer controls or is concerned with the decorative elements on the tombstone and burial site; wealth alone determines the size and decoration of the gravesite.[18]

When the burial procession arrives at the grave, the party divides into two groups. Men are on the right, or east side of the grave, while women stand to the left or yin-west. A table has been set up under a tent, to receive the picture and the willow branch-with-lantern that stands for the soul-spirit of the deceased. A temporary white ancestor tablet made of paper, decorated in silver, green, and purple, with the deceased name and the title *shen-wei* 神位 is sometimes placed on the table. The title *shen-wei* 神位 seat or location of the soul-spirit is always written on the wooden ancestral tablet at home. This paper tablet will be placed on the home altar, and left there usually for the first year of mourning, or until a Taoist priest is hired to install the temporary tablet inside the permanent ancestor memorial on the family altar.[19]

Wine is poured to the west (yin) side of the grave by the MC, and then at the foot of the grave in honor of the spirit of the soil (hou-t'u 后土 , Marquis of the Soil). This spirit whose duty it is to keep the world of yin separated from the visible yang world of mankind, is found by the side of almost all Chinese gravesites.[20] He is honored at the Ch'ing-ming grave cleaning festival of spring, as well as at the burial ceremony. Five nails, representing the complete fulfillment of blessing from the five elements, are driven into the coffin lid by the MC, or by a Taoist hired for the occasion. The last nail is just barely pressed into the wood, then drawn out again with the teeth. It is brought home with the temporary paper ancestor tablet, willow branch, and lantern; here it is placed in the incense burner, where it gradually rusts away and mingles with the ashes. This small reminder of the burial rite is thus kept within the clan. When a son and his family move away, ashes are taken from the incense burner (fen-hsiang 分 香) to start a new household shrine.

The Taoists or Buddhists who are hired to assist at the funeral perform a parallel set of rituals and chant texts that complement the bare structure of the traditional state approved manuals. Thus at each of the above five stages, and sometimes after the burial, chants of merit and repentance, dramatic rituals to see the soul-spirit through the trials of hell, and other liturgies based on the semiotics of the yin-yang cosmos are enacted.[21] The Taoists mime the process of the soul through the nine bureaucratic stages of hell, buy off corrupt public officials, lure demons into traps, invoke Buddhist Kuanyin, and dance the steps of the Big Dipper that lead the soul through the gateway of life whence it first entered existence, to union with the Transcendent Tao.[22]

All of these rituals, Buddhist, Taoist, Confucian, and trance-medium, are meant to assist the living through the difficult stages of burial. Scholars suggest that the burning of paper money, chanting of Buddhist sutras, performing of Taoist alchemy ritual are a kind of *fang-pien* (upaya), convenient skillful means to elicit a Buddhist act of faith in Amida, or a Taoist insight to the close relation between micro and macrocosm. The devout Buddhist and the elite Taoist do in fact accept the reality of the soul, the spirit world, and the yin-yang five element cosmos. It is important to see that the semiotic aspects of this all-encompassing system effect the structure of the temple, the cycles of life and nature ritual, and regulate the categorizing of experience in an unconscious way.

The men and women who attend the rites know where to stand, what items to offer, how many cups wine, and sticks of incense of burn, without asking why. The fact that a Buddhist or Taoist expert can be called upon to give a reason is irrelevant to the practical use of ritual custom. Any reason, myth, or legend suffices to explain why a local or household custom is observed. The common element in the Rites of passage is the temporal-spatial structure, the semiotic signs that are obvious in meaning. Night and day, woman and man, left and right, west and east, earth (where the feet stand) and heaven (where the head rests), water and fire are real constants. Whether they are good or bad, what items they are offered in a given ritual, are open elements to be decided by local usage.

II. Ancestor Rites

The Ancestor Rite is the semiotic sign of the continuity and centrality of family in the Chinese system. It can be performed in three places/occasions: 1) in the special ancestral temple of a wealthy gentry or literatus family; 2) before the ancestral tablets of a merchant or farming home; or 3) as a simple memorial for one's parents before a festive meal, such as at the Chinese New year, or the Ch'ing-ming festival.[23] The directions for performing the rite are simple. It may be followed in any religious or secular context, the intent of the rite being respect (dulia) rather than worship (latria), in the technical or theological sense of those words.

The two basic offerings in Chinese ritual are wine and incense. The burning of incense and pouring out of a wine libation in respect is called *chiao* 醮 , the same word used for the Taoist rite of renewal. Wine and incense are placed before the ancestral shrine (whether a separate ancestral hall, or on the family altar) twice a day, i.e., in the morning and evening. The placing of the wine and incense is accompanied by a prayer in memory of the ancestor, often reporting on the day's activities, or asking blessing for a coming event. On special occasions, however, such as at the Winter Soltice, the New Year banquet, a memorial day for a deceased member of the family, and so forth, a grand scale ancestor rite is offered for the deceased.

If the family maintains an ancestral temple, the altar is already set up for the ritual, If not, four placards or tablets must be erected, one for each generation of grandparents to the fourth degree of ascendancy. The altar is arranged as follows:

candle	flowers	incense	flowers	candle
ni 禰	**tsu** 祖	**tseng** 曾	**kao** 高	
(4th)	(1st)	(2nd)	(3rd) ascendant	

tsu: 祖 the grandparents generation.
tseng: 曾 the great-grandparents generation.
kao: 高 the great-great-grandparents generation.
ni: 禰 the great-great-great grandparents generation.

The incense burner in the center of the altar, the flower vases and the two candles to either side of center constitute the standard Chinese altar. All altars are arranged in such fashion; wealthy families and temples use pewter vessels, while the farming and working class use ceramic or metal for the vases, candle holders, and incense burner. The central position directly behind the incense burner sometimes displays a small glass box inside of which is a statue bearing the likeness of the clan's earliest remembered ancestor.[24] Ordinary families maintain a simple ancestral memorial tablet to the left side of the altar, as in Fig. 6, Chapter One.

The following foods are laid on the altar in sets of four, two sets or bowls for each tablet (male and female grandparent):
1. Chopped and cooked meats, including chicken, and pork.
2. Two bowls of cooked legumes (e.g., beansprouts).
3. Two bowls of fresh fruit.
4. Two dishes of dried fruit.
5. Two bowls of soup.
6. Two plates of cookies or cakes.
7. Two bowls of rice with a dried red plum on top of each.
8. Two cups of tea.
9. Two cups of wine.

A pair of chopsticks are laid to the left of each set of offerings, thus inviting the spirit of the ancestors to be present and witness the proceedings. If a recent death has occurred in the family, a fifth place is set in honor of the newly deceased.[25] When the food offerings are in place, the head of the family, or a Master of Ceremonies chosen for the occasion comes before the altar, bows, and stands to the east (yang) side of the altar. All of the men of the clan then stand to the east, while the women stand to the west. The MC lights incense, and bows to the altar three times, *k'ou-t'ou*, by bowing down on hands and knees and pressing his forehead to the floor. The sticks of incense are then placed in the central incense burner, and the ancestors are invited to be present.

All of the family members present follow the lead of the MC, and bow from their places, while standing. As stated above, the bowing or offering food does not constitute an act of *latria* or worship, but is a sign of respect such as shown to the emperor or a person of high standing. Similar bows to statues in temples, such as the Buddhas, Boddhisattvas, and popular heroes do not bear the connotation of worship, but

154

rather represent an attitude of suppliant petition or request. Thus, by bowing before a mandarin or public official, one hopes to thereby win approval of the request. So in bowing before the ancestors, nature's continued blessing for the world of the living is sought. The oneness of micro and macrocosm, past, present, and future time, and the continuity of family through space and time are symbolized in the rite of ancestor respect.

The MC then walks to the front of the ancestor shrine, and offers the gifts there to the ancestors, beginning with the eldest (ni). He pours out one cup of wine into a bucket (placed there beforehand, under the altar), whereupon the cup is refilled by an attendant. He then lifts up one dish slightly above his eyes, and lays this again on the altar. The offering is repeated three more times, one for each of the four tablets. The relatives of any recently deceased member of the clan also approach the altar and offer a fifth cup of wine and dish of food in honor of the recently deceased.

The official ritual document called shu-wen 疏文 i.e, the rescript is then read. The rescript is composed by a scholar member of the family or by a Taoist, both being the most literate and able members of the community to compose documents in the official court style.[26] Models for writing the document used at the Ancestor Rite can be found in the book of Lin Po-t'ung, and in the Chia-li Ta-ch'eng. The document contains the date and place of the ritual, the petitions of the family members for blessing, and the names of all those present, or all those who contributed to the ritual and banquet that follows.

The conclusion of public and private ritual is always as follows:
1. The ritual document once read is laid on the altar, and the MC again offers an assortment of the foods on the table a total of three times, once each for the heavens, earth, and underworld. While holding up the offerings the words "Ch'u-hsien" for first offering, "tsai-hsien" for second offering, and "san-hsien" for the third offering are intoned.
2. The document is then burned in a special incinerator, or in a clean receptacle laid outside the doorway of the household, accompanied by quantities of folded paper money, and firecrackers.
3. If a new ancestral tablet is to be installed on the altar, the tablets are opened and the ancestor's name is entered at this time.
4. Finally, all present are invited to bow three times, while the MC chants "t'ou chü-kung," (bow once), "tsai chü-kung," and "san chü-kung."

5. All then retire for the family banquet. The food offerings laid on the altar are consumed at this time, along with a sumptuous feast. The number of dishes served may include as many as twenty-four selections, one for each of the (3 x 8) divisions of the cosmos (see figures 2 and 3 in chapter one).

III. Local Variations

As in all of the rites of passage, local custom and household taboo are allowed free expression in the variations permitted for the burial ancestor rites. The list of such customs literally fills volume after volume of local gazetteers, *t'ung-shu* almanacs, and ritual manuals published through private presses and temple bookshops. The following customs are found throughout Taiwan and the Min dialect areas of Fukien and Kwangtung province:

1. The breaking of a rice bowl at the time of death.
2. Replace the pillow of the deceased with a large rock, to signify the primordial source of *ch'i* life, hun-t'un 混沌.
3. Put away the family incense burner dedicated to the heavenly (yang) spirits, and in its place use a ceramic or other special incense burner dedicated to the realm of yin.
4. Cover the altar in the main room, with its statues, candelabra, and scrolls with a white cloth, as a symbol of mourning.
5. Cover the mouth of the deceased with a cooked goose egg, duck egg, or stone, in place of the pearl used by wealthy families.
6. Offer a bowl of cooked rice to the deceased immediately after death, with the chopsticks inserted in the rice, and two duck eggs (yang) holding them upright. A bowl of rice with chopsticks inserted in it thus represents the food of the dead. One must never leave chopsticks inserted upright in a bowl of rice except for the dead, throughout the Min dialect area.

Death by drowning is especially feared along the coastal areas of China. The soul of the drowned person is thought to remain in the ocean, after the body has been recovered. Local shamans or mediums are employed to find the whereabouts of the soul-spirit, and recover it by means of trance possession. The proverb *lu pien niao, hai pien yü* "The roadside bird, the shoreline fish" means precisely that the souls of those killed in roadside car accidents inhabit birds, while the spirit of the drowned person may be in a fish caught by the shore. The following medium-possession rite is commonly seen in Taiwan, to recover the soul-spirit lost at sea.

A circular wheel of life with six spokes on it, one for each of the six Buddhist paths of re-incarnation (deva, human, animal, preta, asura, demon) is erected near the shoreline where the person drowned. A medium (*tang-ki*童乩) or shaman (*kuan-luo-yin*觀落陰) is hired to find the soul lost at sea. When in rhythm induced trance, a long bamboo pole is given to the shaman, who enters the water and flails the pole left and right, inviting the soul to enter the hollow interior. As the trance deepens, the pole suddenly begins to shake violently. A dozen or so young men are needed to control the medium and the flailing stick. Running wildly from one side of the road to another, the pole is brought to the deceased person's home, and made to strike the ancestor tablet. Once the pole has touched the tablet, the shaking stops, and the soul of the drowned person is thought to be localized in the family ancestor shrine.

Buddhists nuns are often hired to find and pacify the soul of a person killed by a roadside accident. The Ullambhana ritual is performed by the roadside, with a large *t'an*壇 or outdoor altar set up dedicated to Ksittigharba (Ti-tsang Wang地藏王). The ever popular Kuanyin (Avalokitesvara), Amida, Mañjusri (riding on a lion) and other scrolls representing Bodhisattva are hung from the walls of the temporary altar. The ceremony requires an entire day and part of the night. It is climaxed by the rite for breaking open the gates of hell and freeing the soul of the deceased lost there with no place for ancestral ritual. The soul-spirit without an ancestral tablet, where prayers for its delivery from hell can be offered, is thought to wander perpetually as an "orphan spirit," (gu-hun孤魂). The ancestral tablet for such a person who died young, or by accident is therefore taken to the Buddhist nunnery, and commemorated in a special *T'a* pagoda erected just for that purpose.

The soul of a girl who dies before marriage is thought to be especially dangerous, since there are no provisions within the family ancestral system to care for such a person. Three possible solutions can be chosen to care for an unmarried girl's spirit: 1) her tablet can be taken to a Buddhist nunnery, where she is commemorated as a Buddhist devotee in the afterlife; 2) a picture of the girl can be preserved in

157

the space between the kitchen and dining room, and a special rite in her memory performed at the New Year banquet, Ch'ing-ming, and All Soul's day, 7/15; 3) she can be married after death to a poor man's son, who agrees to take her ancestor tablet to his own family altar, and burn incense in her memory. A mock marriage ceremony is performed in this last case, and the poor young man is richly remunerated.[27]

Those who die away from home must be brought back to the family cemetery for a final burial. The overseas Chinese, officials on public service, and women from gentry or noble families are returned to their own family's burial sites, often years after death and first burial. The burial site is cleaned annually at the Ch'ing-ming festival, 105 days after the Winter Solstice. The science of Geomancy always chooses a spot for burial which preserves the watershed forests, and helps the alluvial soil of rainy southeast China.[28]

The mourning period for the deceased continues after burial. The first three months are called the Greater Mourning period, the second three months the Lesser Mourning period. Rituals in memory of the deceased are held on both these occasions, as at the first and third year anniversary of death. Buddhist, Taoist, Christian, and Islamic rites follow this prescription throughout China. The mourning family is not supposed to take rich or luxurious foods at the New Year banquet, and do not observe the fifth month fifth day, or the seventh month seventh day celebrations for children and teenagers, described in the next chapter. They are permitted, however, to celebrate these festivals at the home of a friend or neighbor, away from the family ancestor tablets.

All of the above local customs confirm the importance the Chinese give to family, and the rites of passage associated with its support. Everyone, even the deceased, have a right to receive the rites of passage. The multiplication of family and local customs in fact re-affirm the centrality of the Chinese family, and the underlying yin-yang structure of rituals that sustain the popularity and importance given to the festive system. The lasting quality of Chinese family oriented festival, and the stability of Chinese religious and cultural life have withstood the upheavals and changes of the modern capitalist and socialist period. These questions are re-addressed in chapter eight.

NOTES

1. See Bibliography for more titles on Chinese burial. Suzuki, op. cit., pp. 212-224, and Lin Po-t'ung, op. cit., *sang* are used here.

2. The *Chia-p'u* family records often list family gravesites from mainland origins; cf. *Wu-shih Chia-p'u* Hsinchu: Cheng-i Ssu-t'an, 1865.

3. See Thompson, Laurence, *Chinese Religion in Western Languages*, Tucson: University of Arizona Press, 1985, pp. 73-74, for studies of Geomancy; see also Feuchtwang, Stephan, *An Anthropological Analysis of Chinese Geomancy*, (Leiden:1910).

4. See Chapter 7, the Ch'ing-ming Festival.

5. Taoists of the Cheng-i Ssu-t'an tradition, north Taiwan, use a white cloth (yin) with a red line drawn over it (yang) to wash the corpse.

6. See Chapter 4, "Sitting the Month," above.

7. The MC or a son of the deceased wear the burial clothes for a brief time, while standing on a stool, to signify that the deceased when wearing the clothes in the coffin has already ascended into the heavens.

8. Shoes are never put on the corpse, "lest the sound of walking" be heard should the ghost return to visit the family.

9. Evil spirits must pass through each hole in the talisman before reaching the world of the living.

10. Guests at a funeral tuck juniper or pine needles wrapped in a pomelo leaf into a pocket or seam, as protection against *yin* spirits.

11. See Saso, M., TOTMC, (New Haven: 1978) Ch. 6, pp. 246-50.

12. Non relatives and affines turn up a corner of the table cloth, to show the color "red," signifying that ritual impurity from contact with the dead is avoided.

13. See Lin Po-t'ung, Vol. III, *Sang*, The Funeral Procession. The coffin cannot be moved until family quarrels have been settled.

14. The willow branch, a symbol of the *hun* soul, is carried back to the ancestor shrine from the gravesite.

15. Immoral entertainment, striptease acts, and rock singers are carried on floats in the procession, to attract evil spirits away from the living

16. See Chapter 7, the Ch'ing-ming, and the 1/15 day festivals.

17. Lin Po-t'ung, Vol. III, *sang* lists the various decorations allowed on the grave for the nine *p'in* ranks of mandarin.

18. Grand *Feng-shui* oriented tombs are being rebuilt in the free economic zones of Fukien and Kwangtung (1987-89) as part of the religious restoration in The People's Republic of China.

19. The family ancestor shrine keeps a record each generation on a separate wooden slip inside the tablet, for easy comparison with the *Chia-p'u* manual.

20. The Hou-t'u shrine is found to the left or the rite of the grave.

21. Saso, M., *Chuang-lin Hsü Tao-tsang*, (Taipei: 1975), Vol. 13-16.

22. Saso, M., TOTMC, (New Haven: 1978), pg. 247.

23. Emily Ahern-Martin, *The Cult of the Dead in a Chinese Village*, (Stanford: 1973), pp. 91-116.

24. Likeness of the original ancestor are found in many shrines; e.g., the Lum Sai Ho Tong on River street in Honolulu keep a statue of the first Lum (Lin) clan head from Chung Shan county in Kwangtung.

25. When a family head dies, each ancestor moves up one slot, and the *Ni* tablet memorial is put with ascendants in a box under the altar.

26. See Schipper, R., "The Written Memorial in Taoist Ceremonies," A. Wolf, ed., *Religion and Ritual in Chinese Society*, (Stanford: 1974), pp. 309-24, the *piao* memorial and *shu-wen* rescript.

27. Custom requires that the young man sleep with the girl's ancestor tablet by his side for one night. Wet dreams are a sign of placation.

28. The washing of the bones and re-interment in an urn occur up to the fifth year after burial, in many parts of southeast China. The teeth are removed from the skull and interred separately.

7. THE ANNUAL CYCLE OF FESTIVALS

The annual festivals celebrated in the cities, villages, and households of China, follow the yin-yang model of the cycling changes in nature. The role of Buddhist, Taoist, and Confucian expert is subordinate to family needs and local custom. Unlike the Rites of Passage, for which a large body of written directives exists, the celebration of the annual cycle of festivals depends almost wholly on a local oral tradition, rather than the written word. Nevertheless, the yin-yang model is still evident in ritual observance, as is seen in the seventh chapter. Taoists, Buddhists, Confucian scholars, Christians, socialists, and capitalists, all celebrate the annual customs without necessarily ascribing to any religious belief system by so doing.

The festivals of China have been described in a variety of English sources, and are readily available to the interested reader.[1] Each district and province of China prides itself in the local customs and rites surrounding the annual cycle of festivals. It is almost impossible to propose general norms for the celebration of New Year's day, the Dragon Dance and Lantern Parade, the cleaning of the graves and other events celebrated universally throughout China. So many are the variations between villages in the same district and even within the branches of a clan family that the expert pretending to draw up rules for the whole of China would indeed be hard put to find a consensus. A massive literature exists in Chinese describing the legends, customs, and performance of local festivals. Records can be found in local gazetteers, historical archives, and district records concerning the local celebration of national festival.

From this bountiful source of local data it is possible to examine the role of Yin-yang theory in the annual festivals, and test the theory as a normative guide to the spatial and temporal celebration of nature's annual cycle. As in the rites of passage, the annual festivals are clearly governed at the structural level by the rules of yin-yang and the five elements. Recalling the theoretical charts of the first chapter, the festivals of China follow the changes of nature peculiar to the temperate zones of the northern hemisphere, with certain regular changes allowed for the more tropical weather of south China. As in the rites of passage, household directives, local customs, and semiotic meanings depend upon material culture and the local dialect for interpretation.

By distinguishing spatial and temporal structure from local custom, it is possible to construct the chart below, modeled upon the yin-
yang theory explained in the first chapter, which adequately defines the
festival system of China.

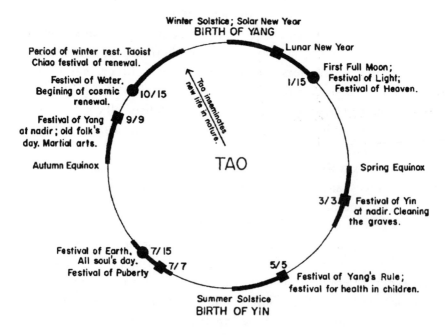

Figure 1. The Annual Cycle of Festivals

Even though the chart is limited to a two dimensional figure on
paper, the time-space symbols expressed in this diagram, typical of illustrations found in Chinese prognostication, almanac, and internal
meditation books, is in fact three and four dimensional. The circular
figures representing the festivals of heaven, earth, and watery underworld symbolize the three dimensional aspect (head, chest, belly;
heaven, earth, underworld) of the Chinese cosmos. The rectangular
marks for the 1/1, 3/3, 5/5, 7/7, and 9/9 festivals represent the fourth
dimension of time, and a fifth dimension marking the renewal of nature
by the ingestation of the eternal transcendent Tao at the Winter
Solstice.[2]

The workings of the five elements in nature are external replicas
of the gestation process conceived within the eternal Tao.[3] Thus the
Ling-pao Five True Writs (Ling-pao Wu Chen-wen) "planted" (an 安)

by the Taoist in the cosmos during the Chiao renewal rites at the Winter Solstice represent a process relating the Transcendent Tao to the working of the four seasons and five elements in nature. The cycle of festivals are therefore a semiotic system describing the workings of the Tao in nature. The following list arranges the festivals in their order of occurrence as village and community celebrations:

a. The Winter Solstice; beginning of rebirth in the cosmos. 冬至

b. 12/15: the last festival for the spirit of the soil. Bonuses are given to all employees to help celebrate the new year. 尾月, 拜土地公

c. 12/24 (or thereabouts) cleaning of the house and preparations for the new year festival. Lion dances exorcise the old year. 送灶神

d. 12/30,(12/29): celebration of the new year eve festival. 過年

e. 1/1 New Year's day. Family visits to temples and relatives. Lion dances for blessing. Beginning of spring. 春節 元旦

f. 1/15: first full moon of the new year. Lantern parade and dragon dance. Festival of heaven, primordial breath. 上元節

g. 2/2: first offering to the spirit of the soil for new year. 頭月拜土地公

h. 3/3 until 105 days after the winter solstice: festival of yin at nadir; cleaning the graves, called *ch'ing-ming* or *pai-shan*. The Girl's day festival in Japan is an adaptation of the Chinese custom. 清明拜山

i. 5/5: Ascendancy of yang. Festival for preserving summer health in children. Dragon boat race. Taoists perform the *Wen Shen* rite to expel the demons of pestilence. It is celebrated as Boy's festival in Japan, children's day in China. 端午送瘟神

j. 6/6 (or thereabouts): the Summer Solstice; birth of yin. Ritual celebrations are taboo. Day for airing out bedding and cleaning the house. Birthday of Kuan Kung (Martial Arts). 夏至

k. 7/7: celebration of puberty; girls use make-up, and search for a husband. Mediums or shaman retell the spinning girl and cowherd boy tale. *Tanabata* or youth day in Japan. 織女牛郎

l. 7/15: the festival of earth. All souls day in China and Japan. *Yü-lan P'en* (Obon) ritual for freeing all souls from hell. 中元節

m. 8/15: harvest moon. Moon cakes and poetry reading. 中秋節

n. 9/9: yang at nadir; old folks day. Celebration of the Pole Star and Big Dipper; practice of martial arts in the lowlands, while women and children hold a picnic in the hills. Village warfare is overcome by blessing from the Big Dipper. 重陽節, 拜斗

o. 10/15: festival of the watery underworld. Beginning of the annual renewal in nature. From this day until the Winter Solstice, Taoist Chiao festivals of cosmic renewal occur with the greatest frequency. The cosmos is mystically renewed by the power of the transcendent Tao. Primordial breath is reborn as a bright red pearl in the depths of the ocean. 下元節. 道師建醮

A renewal of Chinese festivals in the People's Republic, as well as the communities of overseas Chinese in America and southeast Asia has become a phenomenon in the post modern world of the past decade. The streets of Chinatown, San Francisco, the shops of the Chinese section of Honolulu, and other cultural centers for Chinese woven into the fabric of American life boast lion and dragon dances, dragon boat races, full scale All Soul's day festivals, and the celebration of the Taoist Chiao rites of renewal. Pilgrims flock to the traditional festivals and sacred shrines of China, including Taoist, Buddhist, and Christian sacred places. Modernization in both the socialist and capitalist environment has not dampened the joy of the Chinese community in celebrating the annual household and community festivals.

The fact that much of the heritage of China, with that of Japan and other southeast Asian cultures, has become a part of the architectural, artistic, culinary, and spiritual life of the western world points to the festive-spiritual rather than a dogmatic or doctrinal focus to Asian religion. Festivals are a tapestry of interwoven threads, binding together the material and spiritual elements of Chinese family and social culture. The seasonal changes of yin-yang, celebrated in art, rhythm, and music, become an integral part of the cultural-festive system. The celebration of the Chinese cycle of festivals, therefore, does not require a religious belief system to follow. Wherever found, the Chinese festivals elicit open community participation, and are compatible with socialist and capitalist goals.

Highlights of selected festivals are given in the following pages. The bare outline of the rituals described here can be used in any context, whether Christian, Buddhist, capitalist, or modern socialist state. The rubrical details are meant to be mere guidelines for usage. In all cases, it must be remembered, local custom and household taboo take precedence over the directions given by scholars or self-appointed local critics. In the barest structural description, each Chinese festival is only what it claims to be in the spatial and temporal perspective; a marking

of the changes of yin and yang in the cosmos. The celebration of the
annual festivals is a household and community affair. Buddhist, Taoist,
or other expert may be called upon to with various rituals for each festival, but the planning of the festival and preparation of the banquet are
the prerogative of the laity.

a. *The Winter Solstice; Beginning of Rebirth in the Cosmos* 冬至
The celebration of Chinese new year extends from the period following
the tenth month fifteenth day's festival of water through the Dragon
Dance and Lantern Parade of the first lunar month, fifteenth day. The
period preceding the lunar new year is a time for paying debts, house
cleaning, marriage, and worker's annual bonuses.[4] The actual day for
celebrating the New Year festival has varied from ancient China until
the present. The Winter Solstice, i.e., the solar new year, is technically
speaking the true cosmic new year, while the first day of the first lunar
month is a celebration of the beginning of spring. The rituals of the
Winter Solstice festival are therefore properly associated with the birth
of yang in the cosmos, that day when the sun sets earliest and the night
is longest. After the winter solstice (except in some parts of the tropics)
the days begin to lengthen, even though the weather continues cold
through the twelfth and first lunar months.

There are three basic rituals celebrated at the Winter Solstice.
The first is the offering of round glutinous rice balls, with red bean
paste in the center, to symbolize the rebirth of yang in the cosmos.
These round rice balls, called mochi cakes in Japanese, are pasted or
placed around the household in the various places where blessing has
accrued to the family. Sweet rice cakes or rounded balls (with the con-
sistency of thick marshmallow) are put on the lintels, the altar of the
main room, the kitchen, the well or water faucet, the parent's bedroom,
and the toilet (n.b., night soil is used as fertilizer). In modern times the
rice cakes are also placed on the television set, to give thanks for the
entertainment provided the family on the electronic screen. In some
parts of China and in Japan at the New Year festival, the branch of a
tree is placed in the main room by the altar, and decorated (rather like
a Christmas tree in the west) with various symbols of blessing. Paper
money, rice balls and ornaments, paper flowers, and so forth, symbolize
blessings sought for the new year.

165

The second part of the feast consists in a ritual sacrifice offered to the ancestors. The rite described in the previous chapter for ancestor memorial can be used at this time. The rounded rice cakes, in pink and white colors, are made into a sweet soup (a sugar flavored syrup, warmed, with pink and white rice balls) and placed on the ancestor altar as an offering. The round rice cakes symbolize the rebirth of yang, seen as a bright pearl found in the depths of the ocean, where life is annually regenerated by the powers of the Tao in nature. The rice cakes are first offered to the ancestors and the household spirits, then eaten by the living members of the family at the banquet.

The third stage of the festival is the banquet. The table set for the banquet is often pushed up against the ancestor shrine, to show that the deceased members of the family are also present. (Note that the ritual north, that is, the seat which is placed directly in front of the family altar, back to north and face to south, is the seat of honor at a Chinese banquet). The rice balls are served in the sweetened soup as a part of the banquet. The Winter Solstice is a family festival, and is not usually celebrated in public. The rituals prescribed for the emperor and the imperial court on the Winter Solstice are of course no longer observed.

b. 12/15: *The Last Festival of the Guardian Spirit of the Soil* 尾月
The Duke or Marquis of the Soil, T'u-ti Kung, is one of the most popular patron spirits of China. Folk legends abound concerning his origins, and shrines dedicated to him and sometimes his wife (T'u-ti Ma) are found on every street and in every household in China. Local Cantonese and other dialects may change the name, but the function of this sometimes benign and sometimes angry soil spirit are analogous. Temples and households of China, whether Buddhist, Taoist, or folk religion oriented offer sacrifice to the soil spirit on the first and fifteenth day of each month. Temples always offer special services on these days, and many trades such as barbers and butchers take the day off.

The last day of the lunar year on which the Marquis of the Soil is fêted is the twelfth month, fifteenth day. Custom decrees that on this day employers give a banquet for all of their employees, and present a bonus to each worker, from the lowest kitchen help to the vice-president of the company. Foreigners residing in China who do not give a bonus on this day will be bothered later by occult compensation in the

form of servants or cooks stealing from the kitchen and household sup-
plies. Work does not go well in companies which do not provide the
twelfth month bonus. The custom is also observed in Japan in the form
of the *Bo-nen-kai* (end of the year party) where the giving of a bonus
is strictly observed. 往年會 (望年會)

From the end-of-the-year party until the new year festival, all
families prepare for the rituals and banquets of new year. Fancy foods,
new clothes, and a renewed life express the changes soon to be
celebrated in nature. (Chinese New Year, it must be remembered, falls
at the end of January or the beginning of February in the western solar
calendar). Lion dance teams begin to practice for the lion dances to be
performed in the market places and merchant districts at New Year.
The route of each lion dance team or kung-fu club must be determined
ahead of time. Competition between teams for the"best" (wealthiest)
stores which give the largest stipend in the red envelope (li-hsi or
hung-pao) is keen between the lion dance clubs. To avoid street battles
and bad feelings in the community, the lion dance teams and their
kung-fu club sponsors agree amicably among themselves to trade off
streets and shops each year, so as to share the profits. Sometime immediately preceding the New Year festival in Canton, or immediately
following the festival in Fukien and other parts of China, the lion dancers perform in front of each store and pray for blessing. A stipend is
hidden in each shop, and a puzzle given to the lion to solve, before
receiving the money.

c. 12/24: *House-Cleaning day. The Patron Spirits of the House
are Sent Off to Heaven* 送灶神

The day for cleaning the home and sending off the household spirits
varies throughout China, Japan, Korea, Okinawa, and those nations influenced by Chinese culture. The entire house must be cleaned from
top to bottom, windows washed, bedding aired out, and dust
scrupulously swept away. The family altar especially must be cleaned,
the brass incense burner and candle holders polished, and the ritual
utensils made to shine anew. In many parts of China the custom still exists to send off the spirit of the hearth, *Tsao-shen* (灶神), to report to
the heavens on the good and bad bad deeds of the family during the past
year. The spirit of the hearth is the *szu-ming*, (司命) the spirit official
who controls fate in the mandarinate of the heavenly rulers. Since the
entire family tend to gossip in the kitchen, the hearth spirit hears and

167

and records all of the good and bad deeds of the village community. A paper effigy of the spirit is put atop a small paper horse, and (in some areas) sweet glutinous rice or honey smeared across the lips, so that he can only say "sweet" things when he reports to the Emperor of the heavens. The effigy is then burned, thus "sending off" the hearth spirit to the heavens by fire and wind.

With the hearth spirit go all of the household guardians, to spend the new year holiday in the heavens. Since the spirits are away and cannot object to any changes made in the family, the best time to marry a bride is said to be between 12/24 and 1/4, when the spirits return to take up their household duties. The practicality of such a custom is obvious. The huge wedding banquet can be combined with the new year celebration. The buying of new furniture for the family, painting the rooms of the house, and other changes necessary at the time of marriage fit in well with the spirit of the new year and home improvements. Myth and ritual confirm the practicality of the Chinese farmer and merchant.[5]

d. 12/31: *The New Year Eve Banquet* 過年

Since cooking, cleaning, and other chores are forbidden for the first three days of the new year, the entire new year eve is spent preparing food, setting out new clothes, and performing ritual duties at the family altar. The stores in Chinatown of Honolulu, San Francisco, and the other communities of the diaspora are especially busy during the last few days before the New Year. *Tui-lien* scrolls must be purchased to hang on either side of the door, *nien-kao* sweet rice cake must be prepared for the New Year feast, and *hung-pao* or *li-hsi* red envelopes with money gifts inside presented to every member of the family. The various events and duties of new year's eve are listed as follows:

1. Buying and preparing the foods for the new year banquet.

In bygone days the rice grains (glutinous rice) were pounded by hand or ground by a foot-powered machine, whereas nowadays glutinous rice powder is found in supermarkets throughout Hongkong, Taiwan, Honolulu, and the mainland United States. The *nien-kao* glutinous rice cake is made of rice flower, brown sugar, and sometimes coconut juice, poured into a *ti* (liliaceaous plant) or banana leaf, and steamed until cooked. When cooled and hardened, a piece of the *nien-kao* is sliced off the large cake, and deep fried or steamed to softness, before eating. Puffed glutinous rice is also deep-fried into a sweet round ball, called jin-dui in Cantonese, by mixing with sugar and water syrup, peanuts, and sesame seeds. Boxes of sweet puffed-rice rice cakes are given to close friends and relatives (Mandarin: t'ung-mi; Cantonese: tung-mai). Candied fruit peels, winter squash, lotus roots, and other delicacies are prepared in sets of five (for the five elements) to present to guests who come after new year's day to visit. Since material culture decides what foods are to be prepared and eaten at the new year eve banquet and for the first three days of the new year, it is impossible to describe the abundant variety of good dishes prepared for the banquets. Kwangtung province, especially in the Chung-shan and T'ai-shan area, eat only chai (齋) or vegetarian food for the new year banquet; Taiwan, Fukien, and most of north China eat the five meats (pork, chicken, goat, duck, fish, but never beef, since the water buffalo helps plough the fields, and so is taboo as a dinner food at New year banquets) along with the abundant variety of vegetables, legumes, bean-curds, and sweets.

2. *Tui-lien*: hanging paired scrolls with felicitous Chinese characters to bring good fortune.

One of the most important ritual duties of the new year is the hanging of good fortune scrolls on either side of the main door, and in propitious places around the home. In scholarly families the father of the household usually composes his own scrolls, from a great variety of felicitous phrases. In modern China, Taiwan, Honolulu, and southeast Asia the scrolls are found in supermarkets, temples, and even youth clubs as money raising projects for charitable organizations. Each family have their own favorites, which might include:

> *Kung-hsi fa-ts'ai*: Blessing and wealth for the new year.恭喜發財
> *Yang ch'un chieh fu*: Welcome spring and have blessing.迎春接福
> *Szu-chi p'ing-an*: Peace, blessing for the four seasons. 四季平安
> *Wu-fu lin men*: May the five blessings enter these doors.五福臨門
> *Hsin ch'un ta-chi*: The new spring brings great blessing.新春大吉

In some areas of China the hanging of a character for blessing upside down over the door post is a sign of blessing. The word for upside down (tao) is a homonym for "arrived!" (tao-le).

3. New clothes, hair ornaments, and flowers.

Children are given new clothes, and must bathe in herbs on new year's eve. Young girls and elderly women wear flowers in their hair, since flower (hua) sounds like change (hua) for blessing and good fortune. Since it is not allowed to sweep on the new year, comb the hair, or do

anything such as bathe (wash away) which might sweep out or wash away the new blessing, all care is given to personal and household cleanliness on new year's eve. Brooms are put away after the final cleaning, lest the taboo be broken by a forgetful person new year's day.
4. The New Year Eve meal.

The last meal of the old year is a very important and moving occasion, celebrated by the entire family and a few chosen friends. To be invited to a Chinese new year eve banquet is indeed a rare and fortuitous honor . No evil or scolding word can be spoken on this evening, and all must dress in their newest and prettiest clothes. A small fire pot (hibachi) is put under the main banquet table,(or a fire pot with red paper inside, symbolically representing fire, if the banquet takes place in a warm climate) to represent the new fire of yang enkindled by the transcendent Tao in the center of the cosmos. Before the banquet begins, a sampling of each dish is presented to the ancestors on a special table laid out before the main altar. The dishes are laid out in sevens, i.e., with seven rice bowls, wine cups, and chopsticks. After the incense is lit, and a few minutes of quiet prayer spent by the ancestor shrine, the dishes are laid on the banquet table and the celebration begins.[6]

In many parts of China the doors of the houschold are sealed or closed at this time, until the new year opens. In other parts, the doors are left open, and the banquet begins with family members and friends coming in throughout the evening. Toasts are made to each member of the family. Foreigners are warned to sip at each toast (sui-i) and not drain the cup (kan-pei). Riotous and boisterous talk would destroy the rapport of the new year banquet; if one drains the cup (kan-pei) to one member of the family, it is necessary to "bottoms up" with each adult male member. Discretion at Chinese banquets is the better part of valor. At least 24 dishes are served; a sweet dish, often mistaken for dessert, is presented half way through the evening. The more enjoyment during the banquet, the greater the blessings won for the coming year.
5. Items offered on the family altar.

Even though material culture determines for each part of China what foods are to be offered at new year's on the family altar, there are certain rules and items observed almost universally throughout China. Fruit, especially oranges stacked in sets of five (five elements, five blessings) must be on the new year altar. The orange is sweet (t'ien 甜),

a homonym for heaven (t'ien). So too the candied fruits and peels are sweetened, as is the new year cake (nien-kao) and the various cookies and candies. Sweets and fruits are laid out on plates in sets of five, on the family altar. Also de rigeur are cakes made of baking powder or yeast, which have swollen out and broken open at the top. The swelling cake (fa-kao) symbolizes abundant good fortune and blessing. Into each cake is inserted a paper flower made of red and gold cut-outs. On the flower is pasted in gold the Chinese character for spring (ch'un 春), which is a homonym for ts'un (增) abundance. Sweet, pure foods are offered to the heavens. Cooked and chopped foods are offered to earth spirits and to the living. Raw foods (never seen at new year banquets) are for the dead, and for exorcism.

A special offering is made at new year's for those members of the family who may have died young, who are not commemorated in an ancestor tablet, and for the original owners of the land on which the household is constructed. This lesser sacrifice is called the offering to the spirit of the foundations, and the orphan souls. In Hawaii on such occasions poi (pounded taro root) and Primo (local) beer are often laid out for the Hawaiians of long ago. Paper money with silver trim is offered to these spirits, while paper money with gold decoration is offered to the heavenly spirits and the ancestors at new year's.

6. Computing the beginning of the new year.

Some families still observe the old Taoist custom of computing the exact beginning of the new year. Fire crackers must be burned at the moment the new year begins, the doors and windows opened, and sometimes a model ship hung over the front door to symbolically represent the coming of the new year and heaven's blessing. The new year is computed by watching the tail of the Big Dipper (Ursa Major, 北斗) in the heavens. When the tail of the dipper points to the east (the cyclical character mao 卯), the new year's blessing is thought to arrive. It is at this moment that firecrackers are exploded. People who hate the sound of firecrackers are said to be demonic, while those not frightened will receive blessing. Firecrackers exorcise evil and welcome good, telling the entire neighborhood of the festive ritual.

e. *New Year's day*: 1/1, *Ch'un-chieh* 春節 .

On the first day of the new year the family arises early, and begins to visit local temples, relatives, and friends. The li-hsi or hung-pao with money gifts are given to the children of the family at this time. Red (black) tea with sugar can be served to guests, with dishes of five kinds of candy, fruit, and cookies. Food offerings are placed on the family altar, incense burned, and guests served a bowl of *chai* 齋 , a gourmet vegetarian dish prepared on the first day of the new year.

Chai is made of the most luxurious vegetarian ingredients. These can include a variety of bean curds made to look like meat, the so called "long rice" or "spring rain" noodles, a translucent pasta made from bean flour, rice flour, or sweet potato starch. "Cracked seed," dried red plums (salted), ginko nuts, a variety of dried mushrooms, fresh mushrooms, water chestnuts, bamboo shoots, and so forth, are used in these exquisitely prepared dishes. Children bow before their parents and grandparents, and receive presents from visitors.

The second day after new years, called *k'ai-nien* (year is open)閉年 allows the family to eat meat again, and continue the holiday festivities. No work is allowed until the fourth day after new year, when the patron spirits "come down" and resume their duties in the household. If a wedding took place during the new year period, the young bride is allowed to return home for her first visit only on the fifth day after new year, that is, after the three days of rest, and the fourth day when the household spirits return from their vacation in heaven.

Other festivals occur during the week or so immediately following the new year, according to local custom and provincial norms. In old China the seventh day after new year is thought to be the occasion on which one year is added to each person's age; thus no matter on what day the birthday is celebrated, each person in the family is counted a year older on the occasion of the new year celebration. The ninth day after new year is the festival of the Jade Emperor, *Yü-huang Ta-ti*, the heavenly emperor who controls the spirits of the cosmos much as the visible emperor acts as head of the Chinese state. The Jade Emperor's festival is celebrated by raising a banquet table off the ground on stilts, offering sugar Cane (t'ien for sugar is homonym for t'ien, heaven), and burning large sheets of gold coated paper money. The sheets of paper money are rolled into large cylindrical tubes, standing for *ting*, the male organ, and fertility in bearing children. It is taboo to carry washing through the room in which the Jade Emperor is being honored. Menstruating women, or mothers "sitting the month" after birth are also forbidden to take part in this ceremony.

f. 1/15: *Dragon Dance and Lantern Parade; Shang-yüan Chieh* 工元節
The first full moon of the first lunar month is called *Shang-Yüan Chieh*,
the festival of the principle of heaven. Technically, the first full moon of
the new year is seen as a sign of the strengthening power of yang, and
the working of primordial breath (yüan-ch'i) in the cosmos. Like a
bright red pearl flaming with the power of new life, the transcendent
Tao has implanted a new charge of primordial breath in the center of
the cosmos. This charge of pure yang or primordial breath is seen atop
the Chinese temple as a bright red ball of flames, and atop the Taoist
priest's crown as a *hua-yang* flame pin representing the presence of the
Tao within the center of the microcosmic body.

The festival of 1/15, *Shang-yüan chieh* celebrates the awareness
of this principle of life-breath within the macro and microcosm. Two
customs are observed almost universally throughout China to celebrate
new light. The first is the dragon dance, in which young men (and
sometimes women) dance through the streets carrying a huge 150 foot
long dragon, sewn in elaborate embroidered cloth. The dragon attempts to catch a bright red ball of flame carried by another youth,
which symbolizes the "primordial breath" (yüan-ch'i) principle of new
life. The second custom, called *Hua-teng Chieh* or lantern festival, calls
for the carrying of ornate lanterns around the city, and hanging more
elaborate artistic lanterns in temples, to celebrate the renewed
presence of the immanent Tao in nature. 花燈節

The dragon dance is a strenuous and entertaining event. Youths
from the kung-fu martial arts clubs usually carry the dragon, and perform a series of intricate dances, twists, and patterned drills while
moving the 150 long effigy in graceful swirls. In front of the procession
is carried the lighted circular lantern, shaped like the round ball of
flames seen atop temples or atop the Taoist's ceremonial crown. The
dragon chases the red ball through the streets until finally the ball is
caught and swallowed. Then sitting contentedly in the middle of the city
plaza, the dragon allows the people of the village or urban community
to pass in and out under the Tao-laden belly. Humans who pass under
the belly of the dragon which has swallowed the Tao (the alchemical
pill of longevity) are filled with blessings.

While the dragon dance is proceeding through the streets, and
throughout the evening of 1/15, children and adults carry lighted
lanterns in procession, representing the rebirth of Yang and the

presence of the Tao in nature. Children especially love to walk in the lantern parade, and are warned to keep their colorful lamp lit no matter how strong the wind. If the lantern goes out, it is immediately lighted by an observant adult. To lose the light of renewal through the winds of ill-fortune or slander is considered a sign of bad luck. Fortune therefore smiles on those who keep their lanterns lit, i.e., always aware of the workings of the transcendent Tao in nature.

The awareness of the Tao as present in the center of the microcosm is of course one of the first principles of Taoist spirituality. The penetration of the ideas of religious Taoism into the very core of Chinese ritual and festival life is clearly seen in the festivals surrounding the new year. It is especially evident in the festival of heaven. Taoist spirits are honored on this day, especially Primordial Heavenly Worthy, *Yüan-shih T'ien-tsun*, and his heavenly analogue *T'ien-huang* ruler of the heavens. The structure of festival cycle follows the threefold division of the cosmos into heaven, earth, and watery underworld, and head, chest, and belly in man. The families who celebrate the festivals and the temples who hire Taoists to perform the rituals on these days do not necessarily relate to the practice of internal alchemy, i.e., the interior circulation of breath, or centering meditation on the Tao's presence in the Yellow Court. Practitioners of T'ai-chi, Kung-fu, and other meditative exercise often do understand the Taoist meaning of the festival. All celebrate the festival in its external meaning, i.e., joining family and village life with the cycling process of nature.

Time	Taoist Spirit	Taoist term	spirit in macrocosm	folk spirit	folk festival	place in microcosm
1/15	Primal Worthy	breath gestate	Heavenly Emperor	Heaven officer	dragon dance	head
7/15	Ling-pao Worthy	spirit mediate	Earthly Emperor	Earth officer	All Soul's day	chest
10/15	Tao-te Worthy	intuit indwell	Water Emperor	Water officer	water festival	belly

The significance of the 7/15 and 10/15 festivals will be explained below, as they occur in the cycle of festivals. It must be pointed out here, however, that the name and identity of the various heaven, earth, and water spirits varies greatly throughout China. The Heavenly Ruler *T'ien Kuan* has a specific name within the esoteric teachings of orthodox classical Taoism. But amongst the believers in the popular religion throughout China the names given to heavenly, earthly, and watery underworld rulers differ according to locale and proximity to Buddhist, Taoist, or popular folk religious centers. The Three Rulers (san-kuan) are sometimes named after the three mythical rulers of ancient China, Yao, Shun and Yü. The first of the Taoist trinity, *Yüan-shih T'ien-tsun* is identified in popular redhead Taoist texts and folk tales with Yü-huang Ta-ti, the Jade Emperor who is in charge of the spiritual bureaucracy of the cosmos. The Three Emperors (San-huang) are called Lord of Heaven, Lord of Earth, and Lord of Man, while the three officials are called Ruler of Heaven, Earth, and Water.

Without careful application of the yin-yang structural rules, it becomes almost impossible to interpret the semiotic meaning of the various titles assigned to the Chinese hierarchy of spirits. The varying third title "water" for "man" can be interpreted in the same structural context to refer to the place of man in the invisible afterlife, or to the watery underworld itself. We know that the legend of the Three Emperors (San Huang) which uses the title Emperor of Man, comes from an earlier Taoist and fang-shih source, while the title *San-kuan* for the Three Officials comes from the later Celestial Master tradition of the Later Han dynasty and liturgical Taoism.

In the strict classical Taoist sense, the Three Emperors (San-huang) are distinct from the Three Rulers (San-kuan). The Jade Emperor (Yü-huang) is not the same as the Primordial Heavenly Worthy. Each of these spirits is given a separate scroll and structural position during classical Taoist ritual. But all of these subtleties are ignored by the common folk, who simply enjoy the dragon dance and lantern parade on the 1/15 festival, and explain the identity of the spirits according to local myths and legends.[7]

g. 2/2: *The First Ritual to the Guardian Spirit of the Soil* 頭月拜土地公
On the second and sixteenth days of the lunar month, or in some places the first and fifteenth day, a special offering is made to the ubiquitous T'u-ti Kung, Marquis of the Soil, throughout mainland and maritime China. Each street and each family altar commemorates this spirit of the earth who watches over the blessings coming to the community from earth. The 2/2 festival is a particularly grand celebration for the

portly, bearded, smiling figure of T'u-ti Kung, who wears the hat of a feudal marquis and protects the world of humans from the powers of underworld Yin. It must be noted that spirits such as T'u-ti Kung are not identified with a specific human being, but are more like a feudal office which can be filled by any benign human spirit enfoeffed to such a duty after death, by the Jade Emperor. Food offerings to T'u-ti Kung, and other patron spirits and saints of the Chinese temple, the social and spiritual guides of the community, are alike. The five meats, five vegetable dishes, five bowls of rice, wine, tea, and sweets, are offered with incense and paper money. After laying the foods on the altar, reading an oracle, and praying, the paper money is burned and the foods taken home to eat.

h. 3/3: *The Lustration Festival* 禊祓節: 清明拜山

The rituals of 3/3 vary greatly throughout China, in rubrical detail and in temporal extent. The lustration or cleaning festival in fact lasts from the third day of the third lunar month until the 105th day after the winter solstice on the solar calendar, sometime in the month of April. During this time the graves must be cleaned, the waning of yin in the cosmos noted, and young girls honored with a picnic or party of some sort. Often all three events are observed on the same day, that is, on the *Ch'ing-ming* 清明 or "bright and clear day," 105 days after the winter solstice, graves are cleaned, the family goes on a picnic, and the girl of the family may point out or look at the young man of her fancy whom she intends to marry.

In feudal times, we know from Confucian commentaries, the shamans and mediums of south China sacrificed a young girl to the spirits of the river on the 3/3 festival. But a wise king ordered that only the children of shamans be thrown into the river, and so the custom came to an end. In Japan to this day the 3/3 festival honors girls. Fancy dolls as heirlooms are presented to daughters of the family, and a special sweet wine given to children for health and beauty. The Chinese observe the honoring of girls at the time of the grave cleaning-picnic, when the young ladies of the family were allowed to go to the hillsides, eat a banquet in public, and perhaps spot a young man suitable for engagement and marriage.[8]

Today the Ch'ing-ming festival or *Pai-shan* 拜山 (offering at the mountain-grave) is performed during the fourth lunar month, usually on a Sunday or holiday, due to the exigencies of modern industrial society and time-clock salary. On the day before Pai-shan or Ch'ing-ming, cold food is eaten in honor of the Chou dynasty official Ch'ieh-tzu-t'ui who "cut meat from his leg" to feed to his starving parents.The taboo on lighting fires and cooking food on the day preceding Ch'ing-ming is an ancient custom described in the fourth century CE *Ching-ch'u Sui-shih Chi*, a "Record of Festivals observed in the Ch'u Kingdom" ca. 4th century CE, that is useful for explaining customs observed today.[9]

Material culture decides what objects are to be offered at the gravesite, and then eaten at the hillside picnic, (or brought home for later consumption). In south China the three meats, namely: 1) a slice of roast pork (for earth), or a whole roast pig if the entire clan is present; 2) a salted and baked red fish (for water) such as a bream; and 3) a whole boiled chicken (bird, for heaven), plucked but with the head left intact are usually prepared on this occasion. Local dialect determines the foods chosen according to homonymic meaning. Thus bean curd (tou-fu) means blessing (Tuo-fu), bean sprouts mean new life, noodles mean longevity, fried rice with shrimp mean blessing and abundance, and so forth. The entire family or clan assemble at the grave, clean the area, and lay yellow and red talismanic charms on top of the gravestone as "new roofing" for the soul's home in the underworld. The foods are laid out in front of the grave, with the Tou-fu bean curd usually at the end of the line of offerings. Incense is lit, all bow three times, a document-prayer read, paper money and firecrackers burned, and the simple ceremony is over. A special offering of wine, incense, and food is laid to the left side of the grave for the Marquis of the Soil, under the title of *Hou-t'u*, symbolizing that his duty is to keep the world of the dead (yin) away from the living (yang).[10] The family then goes to a nearby hillside and holds a picnic.

i. 5/5: *Tuan-wu* 端午; *The Dominance of Yang During Summer*
The 5/5 festival is called *Tuan-wu*,literally, the beginning of summer. Just as 3/3 was dedicated to the health and well-being of girls, so the 5/5 festival pays close attention to boys in particular, and the well-being of children in general. Summer is a time for colds, diarrhea in children, flu, and serious epidemics such as typhoid fever and cholera. The 5/5 festival therefore prays for health in children, and exorcises the demonic spirits and baleful influences which cause illness. The ritual and festive activities of the day can be divided into five categories:

1. The bathing of all family members in preventative herbs and bath salts, according to local and material culture in China. Herbs can include sword grass, peach leaves and bark, artemisia, sulfur powder, and so forth.

2. The making of glutinous rice cakes wrapped and steamed in the leaves of the ti plant, or a banana leaf. Called *tseng-tzu*, the rice cakes are steamed in any of a variety of sweet or salty flavors, and given to friends and family members for health and blessing. The *tseng-tzu* are also thrown as an offering into the water in memory of the feudal hero Ch'ü Yüan who cast himself into the river and drowned in protest against an unjust ruler.

3. The dragon boat race in a river or ocean, trying the skills and strength of young men of the community as a sign of yang's blessing.

4. The making of charms to protect against the "five venomous animals," i.e., the viper, centipede, scorpion, toad, and spider. Small cloth or grass images of the five venomous creatures are made and hung around the neck of children, to ward off sickness.

5. The celebration of the Taoist Chiao ritual called "expelling the boat of sickness," anytime from the 5/5 festival until after the summer solstice. The extent of the ritual for expelling pestilence goes far beyond the borders of China. Similar rituals can be found in Okinawa, Vietnam, and Japan, where the Gion Matsuri of Kyoto (now celebrated in July) structurally resembles the Taoist rite for expelling pestilence spirits in boats or carriages. The western coast of Mindanao in the Philippines, from Cagayan de Oro to Iligan often places St. Peter's statue in a boat and pushes it out to sea when children are plagued by flu or cholera.

The Taoist festival *Ta Wang Ch'uan* (Exorcising the Demon King's boat) or *Ta Wen-shen* (Exorcising the Spirits of Pestilence) is a magnificent ritual seen along the coast of southeast China. The ritual in its most common form derives from the popular redhead style of liturgy known as Lü-shan and/or Shen-hsiao reform ritual of the Sung dynasty. After performing a classical Chiao ceremony (as described in Saso: 1972; and 1978),[11] the Taoists change vestments, wrap a red cloth around their heads, and exorcise the Demon-kings of pestilence. Effigies of the 3, 12, or 41 (even 360) Wen-shen who cause pestilence are placed in a waiting paper-maché boat or carriage. Often twelve or fifteen feet in length, the boats can be made of wood and have masts with canvas sails. The demons of pestilence are depicted as gaudily painted bulging-eyed mandarins who died unjustly or by suicide when in official employment.

Villages along the coast of southeast China and Taiwan celebrate the Wang-Yeh or Demon Kings of Pestilence festival regularly. The pestilence boats are either burned or pushed out to sea, where they float on the tides and often return to shore. The cult has thus spread up and down the coast of Taiwan, and is found among Chinese communities of southeast Asia. Rituals such as the Gion Matsuri celebrated in Kyoto on July 16-17, and the Okinawan festival for expelling bugs and rats on rafts in spring, are examples of analogous rituals celebrated by nations bordering on the China coast line.

j. 6/6: *The Summer Solstice* 夏至

The *hsia-chih* or summer solstice in many parts of China is not observed as a festive occasion. Throughout most of the subtropical area of south China, bedding is aired on this day and the house cleaned, in between the monsoon showers which precede the planting of the second rice crop. The summer solstice is sometimes called *k'ai-t'ien-men,* i.e., the day when heaven's gate is opened, and yin is conceived in the cosmos. The days begin to shorten after the solstice, and the humid weather of the sixth and seventh months (solar July and August) are still to come. In most of southeast China the birthday of Kuan Kung, patron of merchants and the martial arts is celebrated in the sixth month. In Kwangtung province and Honolulu, the 6/16 is Kuan Kung's and other kung-fu clubs' martial arts festival. 開天門

k. 7/7: *Spinning Girl and Cowherd Boy; Festival of Initiation*

The seventh month seventh day festival is celebrated throughout the Chinese influenced countries of east and southeast Asia. The myth of the spinning girl and the cowherd boy is retold by medium-shamans on this day, and thus 7/7 is also a shaman's festival. The Seven Spinning sisters of the Pleiades constellation came down to earth and bathed in an idyllic river. The cowherd boy, an ordinary mortal, fell in love with the seventh sister and married her, preventing her from returning to heaven. Enraged, the Jade Emperor of the heavens condemned both to be imprisoned eternally in the spinning girl star and the cowherd boy star *ch'ien niu,* separated by the heavenly river (T'ien-ho, the milky way). once a year the lovers are allowed to unite, on the evening of 7/7.

Throughout southeast China, Hongkong, and Honolulu the story is acted out by seven women mediums and one male, who become entranced and retell this lovely tale. Seven sets of clothes and small shoes are laid out on the altar, and a box of rice seedlings just sprouted are placed on the table as a homeopathic offering asking for a fertile marriage. Girls come to the temple where the performance is being held, and offer cosmetics to the mediums depicting the seven sisters. Fortunes can be read in tea leaves on this night, and the girl who can thread a needle by moonlight, a fertility symbol, will surely find a good husband.

The seventh sister, sometimes identified with Ho Hsien-ku, one of the Eight Immortals, is the patron saint of mediums-shamans in south China. As servant to The Queen Mother of the Western Heavens (Hsi Wang Mu), two stories of the spinning girl are commonly told on this evening. Hsi Wang Mu and the spinning girl are invoked for giving birth to a child. Two puppet shows are performed for 7/7. The first depicts Hsi Wang Mu with the spinning girl bringing the peach of longevity and the *Ho-t'u* (the Taoist talisman which gives heaven's mandate to the emperor to rule) to Han Wu-ti, the martial emperor of the early Han dynasty. A second puppet show shows the spinning girl coming with her sisters to Liu Hsin, who restored the Han throne after the Wang Mang usurpation in 23 CE. Liu Hsin's wife bears a child when the spinning girl visits from heaven. The Wen-wu Miao temple in Palolo valley, Honolulu, continues this custom until the present.

The 7/7 festival is also the day on which a woman can propose to a man. In traditional China women climbed atop a tower in the evening and threw an embroidered ball to the man they loved. Four days in the lunar calendar are dedicated to the role of woman in Chinese society. The 7/7 festival is the most obvious of these days, when the teenage girl is made aware for the first time of her dignity, and right to choose. The other days are: 1/15 for fertility, 3/3 for "looking over" the young men of the village, and 8/15 for celebrating the harvest.

l. 7/15: *Festival of Earth; Yü-lan P'en, All Soul's Day* 中元節.盂蘭盆會
The 7/15 is, after the Chinese New Year, one of the most important festivals celebrated by the Chinese family. For this reason both Buddhists and Taoists make much of the day, and offer grand rites of amnesty for freeing all souls from *Ti-yü* the hell-purgatory found deep under the earth's soil. The summer harvest is soon to begin, and the earth,

like the fertile womb of a mother, is about to yield its blessings for human life. Therefore those who are lodged in the depths of the earth and under the waters are released and sent off to the heavens, lest any offenses and forgotten misdeeds of the past hinder the harvesting of nature's bounty. All members of the family return home for this festival, to pray for the deceased, and seek release for all souls from the sufferings of the afterlife. Hell indeed is life without friends and family. The 7/15 banquet is offered by the entire community. Temples hire Buddhists or Taoists to perform salvation ritual, and feed all villagers, strangers, and hungry souls who come to the festival.

The Taoist *P'u-tu* 普度 ritual is structurally similar to the Buddhist *Yü-lan P'en* (Sanskrit: Ullambhana). Buddhists and Taoists (physically or mentally) create a "magic square," i.e., a nine squared grid or set of scrolls, depicting Ti-yü a series of tortures for the deceased. Small mounds of rice are arranged in nine piles on a pewter plate, and flicked away with the fingers, symbolizing that the gates of hell are broken open. Food and drink are then offered to the spirits, and lanterns floated in the rivers to guide the souls on their trip to the heavens. Lengthy canons of merit and repentance are chanted by Buddhists and Taoists, while the laity return home to enjoy the family banquet. The Obon festival in Japan is the equivalent of the Chinese Yü-lan P'en, with the addition of drumming and folk dancing to entertain the returning spirits.

The Yü-lan P'en ritual is performed from the 7/15 festival until the end of the seventh month. Taoists more frequently perform the rite on 7/15, while Buddhist temples sometimes wait until 7/30, the feast of Ksittigharba (Ti-tsang Wang), the Boddhisattva who saves the lost from hell. Ksittigharba is patron of souls freed from the earth, as well as children freed in gestation from the womb of the mother. The Gates of Hell open at the beginning of the seventh month, and close on the 7/30 festival. The whole month is therefore a time of special prayer preceding the harvest. Souls freed from hell, children delivered from the womb of the mother, and crops harvested from the bosom of earth are the objects of prayer on this family festival.

m. 8/15: *Festival of the Autumn Harvest Moon*　中秋節
The festival of 8/15 is a family celebration. Taoist priests or Buddhist monks may be hired to chant prayers in the home for blessing, but the ritual duties of the evening are done by the women of the family. A

sumptuous banquet is served in the backyard of the family residence to the light of the full harvest moon. Special delicacies of the harvest season, freshly picked fruits, oranges, pomelo, persimmons, and nuts are offered on the altar. A special moon cake (yüeh-ping) made of bean paste, lima bean candy, seeds, nuts, candied fruit peel, and so forth are universally made throughout China to celebrate the round, full, autumn moon. Lanterns are hung in the garden, and poetry read during the moonlit evening. The rituals offered to the spirits on this day are usually performed by women.

n. 8/28 (or thereabouts): *The Official Festival of Confucius* 祭孔 Larger cities with a Confucian temple, or the official plaza in the Chinese village sometimes offer the traditional rite to Confucius on this day. This is the only occasion that an ox is sacrificed as an official offering, according to the prescriptions of pre-Han dynasty China (the T'ai-lao offering). Boys dressed as mandarins perform a stately classic dance while holding long pheasant tail-feathers. Official Confucian music is played with flutes, bells, and gongs. A slow procession of local officials escort the memorial tablet of Confucius to the altar, pausing every fifth step (in honor of the five elements). Wine, incense, and sacrificial meats are offered in honor of Confucius and his 72 disciples.

o. 9/9: *Chung-yang* 重陽 *festival; Yang at Nadir, Yin at Zenith* The festival of 9/9 was originally dedicated to the Big Dipper, the pole star constellation, and its patron saint the Dark Emperor of the North (Hsüan-t'ien Shang-ti) who protects the martial arts. In traditional China the martial arts and kung-fu clubs often competed on this day, or even initiated warfare between villages. Women and children went on picnics to the hills, as did the poets and the literati scholars whose poetry celebrating the chung-yang festival are still memorized by high school students. A special Taoist ritual to the Pole Star, the Big Dipper, and the Taoist Thunder spirits is offered on this day. Boys celebrate by flying kites in the brisk winds of autumn.

p. 10/15: *Hsia-yüan Chieh* 下元節 ; *the Festival of Water* The festival of 10/15 celebrates the principle of water, the source of life and the principle of intuitive essence within the belly of man. The days immediately preceding 10/15 are especially important to Taoists. Beginning from 9/9 when the spirits of the Pole Star are feted until 10/15 when the annual renewal of nature begins with winter's cosmic rest, Taoists begin to prepare for the grand Chiao festival of renewal.

10/1 begins a period of fast, penitence, mediation, and purification before celebrating the renewal of the cosmos. Taoists and laity who will be participating in the Chiao liturgy observe celibacy, refrain from eating meat, and practice *nei-tan* or "internal alchemy" meditation during the tenth month. From this day until the 12/8 *La-pa* festival, the old *la* festival on which feudal China celebrated the new year, the Taoists are busy performing rites of renewal. The La ritual is observed today by eating a porridge made of the five grains.[12]

q. *Rites of Renewal. The Taoist Communal Chiao* 醮 *Festival*

The annual cycle of festivals has now completed a full cycle, and the Winter Solstice is again at hand. Throughout the cities and villages of north Taiwan, Fukien, and Kwangtung the people celebrate the community festival of nature's renewal called Chiao. Let us analyze the Chiao festival, to see how this basically Taoist ritual influences Chinese popular religion and folk belief. The Chiao is commonly celebrated throughout Taiwan, Fukien, and northern Kwangtung province. It is possible to see one of these ancient rites especially at the time of the Winter Solstice, when the changes in the seasons indicate that nature too is about to renew herself. The festival is organized by community leaders, elected by the village temple members. The entire village takes part in the celebration, by contributing money donations, abstaining from meat for a week before the rites begin, and attending the colorful temple rituals.

Since the Chiao is a summation of the Chinese popular religion, we give a list of the rituals most commonly seen in Taiwan, Fukien Province, and the great monastic centers of China during the three day village celebration. The structural process from the many to the one, i.e., from the multiplicity of nature to union with the Transcendent Tao, is a "return to the origin, restoral of roots" (hui-yüan fan-gen 回元返根) Under the ritual leadership of the Taoist High Priest, Master of Exalted merit (Kao-kung Fa-shih 高功法師), all of the spirits of the 36 divisions of heaven and the 72 sacred places of earth (108, the entire cosmos) are invited to be present. Over the nine halls of the magic square (lo-shu 洛書 earth), the five bushels (tou 斗) of the magic circle (ho-t'u a symbol of heaven) are planted. The people are invited to three audiences with the Tao of nature, and to the final rite of union with the Transcendent Tao. The souls of ancestors are released from hell in a rite of general amnesty, and the spirits are thanked and sent back.

183

I. The First day. Heaven, Purification, Gestation

1. Announcing the Chiao, *Fa-piao*, 發表 .

2. Inviting the spirits to attend, *Ch'ing-shen* 請神. The spirits of the 36 heavens and 72 sacred areas of earth are invited to attend the Chiao festival.

3. Purifying the community temple, *Chin-t'an* 禁壇. During this rite the Taoist establishes the *Lo-shu*, the Magic Square of Nine halls, envisioning a sacred area within the village temple filled with Taoist spirits. He/she closes the "Gate of Hell," i.e., the access of the demonic, impure, and selfish to the hearts of the participants, the ritual northeast. The "Gate of Heaven," the northwest is then ritually opened, to bring Tao's blessing.

4. Raising the lamps and standards on bamboo poles, to announce the spirits of the three worlds, heaven, earth, and underworld, that a Chiao is to begin.

5. The *Su-ch'i* 宿啟 rite for renewing the five elements. The Taoist builds a Ho-t'u magic circle within the sacred area, and makes a treaty with the spirits of the five elements-directions, to renew and regenerate the four seasons and the human contact with nature.

6. The *Fen-teng* 分燈 rite, a reading of the Forty-second chapter of Lao-tzu, accompanied by the lighting of a new fire for renewal. "The Tao gives birth to the One, ...two, ...three, the myriad creatures."

7. Chanting of the Canons of merit and repentance, the canons to the Pole Star and the Big Dipper, to win blessing for the community.

8. Offering of foods, folk opera, puppet shows, and kung-fu demonstrations for the spirits and the people who attend the festival.

II. The Second Day. Earth, Mediation

1. The morning audience with the Tao as gestating, *Tsao-ch'ao*. 早朝

2. The noon audience with the Tao as mediating, *Wu-ch'ao.* 午朝

3. The night audience with the Tao as indwelling, *Wan-ch'ao.* 晚朝

4. Sending off the people's petitions to heaven, *Sung-piao.* 送表

5. A continual reading of the Canons of Merit and Repentance.[13]

6. Floating lanterns in a river, to summon and free all souls.

III. The Third Day. Water, Union, Liberation

1. Audience with the Tao of Transcendence, *Tao-ch'ang Cheng-chiao.* The purpose of this rite is union with the Transcendent Tao; *yü Tao ho-i* 於道合一. The Taoist High Priest receives a rescript back from the heavens, granting nature's blessing and eternal life to the community.

184

The five elements planted during the *Su-ch'i* rite on the first day are harvested (*shou chen-wen* 收真文) and stored within the microcosm, i.e., the villagers interior, to bless the new year.

2. The *P'u-tu* 普度 rite for freeing all souls from the underworld, similar to the Buddhist Yü-lan P'en ritual.

3. Ritual thanking and seeing off the spirits, *sung-shen.* 送(謝)神.

4. Public opera, puppet show performances, and kung-fu demonstrations in the public plaza.

5. Communal banquet.

The underlying theme of the chiao festival of renewal is the oneness of man and nature. The head, chest, and belly of man correspond to the heavens, earth, and underworld of the macrocosm. What happens inside man is reflected in the totality of nature. The village temple becomes the structural symbol for the process of renewal. The north wall of the temple is heaven, the head of man. The central part of the temple is earth, the chest of man. The lower part of the shrine is the realm of water, man's intuitive powers of the belly. The first, seconds, and third day of the Chiao festival celebrate these relationships. Just as breath is circulated from the nose down through the body, bringing with it renewal of life, so Tao's primordial breath circulates through the entire cosmos, bringing renewal of the five elements, crops, children, and total blessing. These eternal truths of the Chinese yin-yang system are taught through the public ritual of the Chiao festival of renewal, a summation of the annual cycle of festivals.

The announcing and inviting rituals of the first day address the three stages of the cosmos, heaven (head), earth (chest) and underworld (belly) in song, dance, and a publicly read document called *piao*, a memorial sent to the heavens. The people act out the drama with the Taoists. The temple is purified and made into a sacred area by using the nine sections of the *Lo-shu*, magic square. The *Ho-t'u*, a magic circle representing the five elements, is established by planting the "Ling-pao Five True Writs" in five bushels of rice. The forty-second chapter of Lao-tzu is acted out as drama, showing the Tao giving birth to the "one," primordial breath, the two-yang, and the three-yin. The people are made one with the Tao's gestating process. All of the community is brought together for a banquet, after the living have been forgiven and the dead freed from sorrowful memories of the underworld.

A different kind of Chiao ceremony is seen in Hongkong, Kwangtung Province, and communities of Overseas Chinese who come from these areas. In this reformed style Chiao festival, the five rites of inner alchemy and union with the Tao, i.e., the Su-ch'i, Morning, Noon, Night Audiences, and Tao-ch'ang are not performed. Only the "A" popular and "B" merit liturgies, (described in Chapter Two) are used, reflecting the influence of the reformed Ch'uan-chen Taoist movement of the Sung dynasty and thereafter. The voluminous work of Tanaka Issei, *Chugoku Goson Saiki Kenkyu* (A Study of Village Festivals in China, (Tokyo: Tokyo University Press, 1989, 1232 pp.) describes Chiao village festivals of this popular, reformation style.

The Chiao ritual, we can now see, is similar in structure to the annual festivals celebrated throughout the Chinese liturgical year. Its elements are Confucian, Buddhist, and Taoist, showing the unity and holistic structure of the Chinese world view. The three teachings are in fact united into a single system, by the structuring principles of the yin-yang five element cosmology, which unifies Confucian intellect and virtue, Buddhist "heart," i.e., care of the afterlife, and Taoist "belly," intuitive oneness with nature's cycle. Note that belly (Yellow Court) is the place where the prayer of union with the Tao is experienced. The Taoist ascesis of emptying is made a part of the Chinese religious system, by ritual and festival process. The virtues of the Confucian system, the chanting of Buddhist canons for merit and Taoist meditations of giving-emptying, are governed by nature's yin-yang cycle. The role of Taoist, Buddhist, and Confucian, are subordinate to this structured system.

With these statements of the Chinese religious festival system, the work of Blue Dragon White Tiger comes to an end for another cycle of life and nature's passage. Recalling the words of the *Li Chi* in the introduction, we must look at the variegated and colorful rites of local Chinese religious practice from the family, the village, and the national-cultural aspects, to see their unicity (t'ung-i hsing 同一性). Village custom and family taboo are everywhere different. Only the national norms, such as found in the perennial ritual prompt books, and the yin-yang five element system, are everywhere the same. If at first we cannot see the structure for the fire and smoke of the pyrotechnics, or hear the melody in the singing and drumming of the musicians, we are assured by the grandmothers, geomancers, Taoists, and masters-of ceremony that indeed yin-yang and the five elements are there. We see them in the phoenices on temple roof tops, the play of blue dragon and white tiger in art and in human relationships, the red glow of incense and the light shed by candles, the sounding of the wood fish and brass bell, all signs that yin and yang work everywhere in the Chinese ritual cosmos.

By studying the chart of festivals in figure one, and the list which follows it, the structural role of yin-yang and the five elements can be clearly seen. Spring and summer, the time for ploughing, planting, and attending the growing crops in the farming cycle, celebrate the renewal of nature by the inseminating power of yang. The New Year (1/1) solemnizes the annual rebirth of Yang in the cosmos. Girl's day (3/3) and Ch'ing-ming (105 days after the solar solstice) celebrate female Yin by cleaning of the grave, earth's womb, from the fresh growth of grass in spring, and allowing the right of the girl to choose or approve a future mate. The beginning of summer (5/5) commemorates the cycling of yang, strength and health of boys, and prays for the good health of children in the hot summer months.

Autumn and winter solemnize the working of yin in nature. Yin's birth is called "opening heaven's gate" (k'ai t'ien-men) refering to the meditative as well as the harvesting and birthing role of the female principle of nature. Teenagers and courtship are commemorated on 7/7, while the elders of the family and long life are honored on 9/9. These five festivals, the most ancient in the Chinese system, clearly solemnize the human life cycle through the semiotic nature of the five elements. That is, birth in winter (1/1), the spring of life seen in the maturing of girls (yin, 3/3) and boys (yang, 5/5), the ripening of family in fall's preparation for marriage (7/7), and the honoring of the elderly and ancestors in winter (9/9) are annual reminders of the structural similarity between life and nature's cycles.

A second series of festivals, observed on the fifteenth day of the first, seventh, and tenth months, celebrate the relationship between macro and microcosm. The festival of lights on 1/15 honors the resurgence of Yang in the heavens. Lanterns are carried through the city and decorate the temples. A huge dragon, 150-200 feet long, dances through the streets in chase of a bright red ball which represents the rebirth of Tao in the cosmos. When the dragon swallows the ball, (end of the procession) the people of the village try to walk under the dragon, to be blessed by Tao present in the belly. The same dragons stand rampant on temple roof tops, waiting to devour the flaming red pearl, a sign of Tao's presence in the village temple.

7/15, the festival earth, blesses the earth before the crops are harvested. The souls of the departed who are imprisoned under the earth are freed from punishments on this day, before the crops are freed from earth's womb, the soil. The gates of hell are opened (k'ai kuei-men 開鬼門) on this day, and all souls granted an amnesty. 10/15, the festival of water, begins the lengthy celebration of Tao's annual restoration of nature. The Chiao festival, which has been described in chapter three and here again in chapter seven is a recap of this entire cyclical process. It is interesting to note, as will be seen again in chapter eight, that the Chiao festival continues to be so popular in Taiwan, and is being restored with much vigor and care for authenticity in Fukien and Kwangtung communities. The festival, as seen above, encapsulates the entire structure of the Chinese religious system, in a three or five day village retreat. Head, chest, and belly in the microcosm are related to heaven, earth, and water in the celebration of this Taoist ritual-alchemy system. The Tao's gestating presence, the focus of Taoist meditation, becomes the theme of the village festival of renewal.

A third set of festivities are observed during the Chinese liturgical year that do not follow the strict structure of the yin-yang system. These are the so-called birthdays or ascent days of the *shen-ming* 神明 folk heroes, "saints," and Boddhisattvas. The observance of these commemorative days differs for the various provinces and districts of China. No universally applicable schedule of feast days for the spirits and heroes of the folk religion can be given that will be valid for all China. Some of the more popular spirits are listed below. Each area, sacred place, and village temple has its own schedule for celebrating the festivals of these popular spirits.

Kuan Kung, the red-faced black bearded general of the Three Kingdoms period (221-264 CE) is patron of merchants and martial arts. His statue is found in almost all of the shops and offices of Kwangtung, Fukien, Taiwan, Hongkong, and other areas where the people of southeast China do business. A shrine in his honor is also found in the meeting places of most Tang and Hui Chinese societies, and martial arts clubs. The popular novel *San Kuo Yen-i* (The Romance of the Three Kingdoms) tells the legend of how Kuan Kung kept accounts of pay received from Ts'ao Ts'ao, ruler of the northern kingdom. When returning to the service of his own ruler Liu Pei in the western kingdom of Shu, Kuan Kung returned every last coin to Ts'ao Ts'ao, with an accurate record of the time, place, and amount of money received from the rival Wei kingdom. Because of his legendary loyalty and honesty, he is revered as patron of merchants and warriors. The story of Kuan Kung rescuing the kidnaped wives of Liu Pei, keeping accounts of Ts'ao Ts'ao's money, and other tales of loyalty are commemorated in opera, puppet shows, and festival throughout China.

Matsu or T'ien-hou 天后 (Cantonese: Tin-hau) is revered by almost all fishing, farming, and merchant families of southeast China, and overseas Chinese communities. Daughter of a fishing family from central Fukien Province, named Lin, Matsu died before marriage. Her cult soon spread throughout southeast China. Farmers and fishermen who invoked her efficacious aid when in trouble set up shrines in her honor when prayers were answered. The officials who memorialized the throne about the cult extolled the filial aspects of this maiden who served her family in quiet fulfillment of social duty and *li* respect. Rescripts from the Ming dynasty emperors gave her the official title *T'ien Hou* 天后, i.e., the imperial concubine of the heavenly Jade Emperor. Her statue is therefore crowned with the headdress of an empress. Processions in her honor show her riding an imperial palanquin, with her courtiers including "See a thousand miles" and "hear with the wind," two demons converted to her service. These fearful effigies whose statues appear in many T'ien-hou temples are thought to carry the prayers of the faithful to Matsu for fulfillment.

The Bodhisattva Kuanyin (Avalokitesvara) is popular throughout mainland and maritime China. Buddhists and Taoists alike pay respect to this idealization of the virtue of compassion. A statue of Kuanyin that is popular in family shrines shows a woman dressed in white robes holding a vase of dew in one hand, and a lotus stalk in the other. An even more popular statue in temples displays Kuanyin with 11 faces and 1,000 arms. Legend says that Kuanyin must have a face to reflect every human emotion and a hand to come to the aid of the thousands of people addressing prayers addressed to her. Some versions of the statue show an eye in the center of each palm, giving Kuanyin the power to see the needs and come to the aid of suffering humanity.

Other popular statues found in temples and family altars include *Hsüan-t'ien Shang-ti*, dark spirit of the North Pole, the Eight Immortals, the Boddhisattva P'u-hsien riding an elephant and Manjusri riding a lion, the Buddha Amida with Kuanyin to the left and Chih-shih (Mahasthama) to the right, the guardian deities of Buddhist and Taoist shrines (Wan-ling Shen-chu), and a host of local heroes and their cults. All cities with an official *yamen* government mandarin's office built a temple to honor the Ch'eng-huang spirit, governor of the world of yin-punishments directly beneath the city. On his festival day the entire court of hell found in the Ch'eng-huang temple comes out to parade around the city.

The effigies of the spirits carried in procession include the short dark-faced general Fan, and the tall white faced General Hsieh. Fan, symbol of the Confucian virtue Yi, reciprocity and loyalty to friends, drowned while waiting for his friend general Hsieh. Hsieh, symbol of filial duty to parents, hanged himself in sorrow for Fan's death. These two figures are said to bring the souls of the recently deceased to hell for judgment immediately after death. Ghost stories told to children at night claim that Fan and Hsieh come to punish the disobedient who do not study. During temple processions the two effigies are seen to chase after children, who tease them as they march through the streets.

Also included in the procession are the spirits who administer punishment in hell for social misdeeds, such as horse face, ox head, and other terrifying figures who symbolize the system of retribution for socially unacceptable deeds. The Confucian value system is thus confirmed by the prophylaxis of popular Buddhist and Taoist hell imagery. Children watching the procession are encouraged to practice virtue and avoid the punishments administered by the Ch'eng-huang's courtiers.

Traditional Chinese cities often constructed a temple dedicated to T'ai-shan and the Emperor of the East, *Tung-yüeh Kung* in the eastern quarter of the city. The temple of the East traditionally honored Fu Hsi, Shen-nung the patron of agriculture, and Ssu-ming, the keeper of destiny.[14] The *Wang-yeh* spirits of Pestilence, the Spirit of the Soil, popular pioneer mandarin heroes who founded a village or district, are all commemorated in the festival system. Just as the festivals in honor of the popular spirits are celebrated at times determined by local myth and custom, rather than by the principles of yin-yang five element cosmology, so to the stories told by the local puppet shows, operas, and professional storytellers may differ in many details.

The text of the storyteller and the time for celebrating the tale's hero are always open to interpretation and local variation. There are at least three popular versions of the folk legends and myths of the saints and heroes of folk religion. The first is that told by the puppeteer and opera singer on the stage of the local temple. The second is that of the medium who is possessed by the spirits, and speaks in their voices, a profession pursued in private homes and small temples. The third source is the printed word, that of the Taoist Canon, local printing presses, and novels about immortals, spirits, and ghost tales. These rich sources provide the stuff of folk tales, children's stories, and drama celebrated at the time of the annual cycle of festivals.

In this openness to creative expression and change lies the strength of the Chinese religious system. The ultimate deferral of meaning, the non-closure of text, and the adaptation to political and social change, are hallmarks of the Chinese culture. Religious festivals have survived the secularizing influence of the socialist and capitalist state, because of this openness. As will be seen in the last chapter, the ability of Chinese rites of passage and festivals to exist in the context of the socialist as well as the secular capitalist state gives promise of festive celebration well into the coming centuries.

NOTES

1. Cf. Laurence G. Thompson, *Chinese Religion in Western Languages*, (Tucson: 1985), pp. 117-125, for studies of Chinese Festivals. Also see Eberhard, Wolfram, *Chinese Festivals*, (New York: 1952), and Bodde, Derk, *Festivals in Classical China* (Princeton: 1975), and *Annual Festivals and Customs in Peking* (Peking: 1936).
2. The Transcendent Tao (Wu-wei chih Tao) breathes *ch'i* primordial breath to renew the cosmos at the time of the Winter Solstice.
3. Saso, M., TROCR, (Pullman: 1990), pg. 10.
4. Marriage is celebrated in winter, the time of cosmic rebirth, rather than at the summer solstice, the time of ripening and harvest.
5. Sacrifice to the Heart Spirit is the duty of women. Note that in Okinawa only women may perform this and other priestly duties.
6. See Chap. 1, Fig. 6, for the family altar and the wooden moon blocks.

7. See Saso, M., *Chuang-lin Hsü Tao-tsang*, (Taipei: 1975) Vol. 1-13 for examples of these ritual documents.

8. See Bodde, D., *Festivals in Classical China*, pp. 273-288.

9. *Ching-ch'u Sui-shih Chi*, Ssu-Pu Pei-yao edition, (Taipei: 1961).

10. See Chapter 5, Burial Rite, Hou-t'u graveside ritual.

11. Ofuchi, Ninji, *Chugokujin no Shukyo Girei* (Chinese Religious Rituals), (Tokyo: 1983) presents a collection of Taoist rites from the Tainan area, south Taiwan. See *Chuang-lin Hsü Tao-tsang* (note 7, above), Vol. 24, *Sung Ch'uan K'o* the Wang Yeh ritual.

12. For detailed descriptions of the internal meditations used with the Chiao ritual, see Saso, M., TROCR (Pullman: 1990) and TOTMC (New Haven: 1978).

13. See *Chuang-Lin Hsü Tao-tsang* (Taipei: 1975) Vol. 2-4.

14. See Day, Clarence, *Chinese Peasant Cults*, (Shanghai: 1940) and Baity, Philip, *Religion in a Chinese Town*, (Taipei: 1975).

8. RELIGION IN CHINA TODAY

The first seven chapters of *Blue Dragon White Tiger* provide an overview of the rites and festivals of Chinese religion as they are structured by the Yin-yang Five Element system, an ancient cosmology found in late archaic sources. This system was proven to be at the core of Taoist philosophy, meditation, and ritual, as well as the basic structuring principle for Chinese festivals from ancient times until the recent past. In this final chapter we shall examine how Chinese Religion has fared in the modern socialist environment of the People's Republic of China, i.e., how Marxism has effected the practice of the Rites of Passage and the Annual festivals. We shall take special note of the changes of the momentuous past ten years, from 1980-1990.

    The history of the People's Republic of China, from its founding in 1949 until today, bears witness to profound change and transformation. During this period China grew from a war ravaged colonially oppressed third world nation into an industrially developing front rank economic power. Changes wrought over the past forty years were cataclysmic and unforseeable. Early attempts were made to build a socialist society and farming collectives, (1949-1957). The rapid leap into communes and a radical communist society (1958-1965) evoked natural and man made calamities. The Great Cultural Revolution, (1966-1978) which set out to destroy the remnants of past culture, wrought havoc in the economy, harmed public morality, and negated the very structure of society. Real economic growth and the progress of China into the modern industrial world began after 1979.

    The economic and cultural reforms begun by Deng Qiaoping in 1979 have turned the energies of China's one billion and more people to bettering the way of life of the nation by developing public and private enterprise. Socialist China has opened free economic zones for foreign investment. Free markets encourage the buying and selling of farm produce. Modern department stores are filled with consumer items. Factories produce TV sets, radios, refrigerators, air-conditioners, bicycles, cars and trucks, for internal as well as overseas consumption. Small business enterprises spring up everywhere, like phoenixes from the ashes of China's cultural revolution. In the words of a university intellectual, China has produced one billion emperors, striving for the good things of capitalist economic life under a socialist political system.

For the past ten years, coinciding with the end of the cultural revolution and the new policy of economic growth and expansion, China has opened itself to a limited form of religious freedom. This new and enlightened policy differs from and is more open in many ways than the policies of other Marxist-socialist nations of East Europe. Some modern thinkers in China compare these reforms with the intellectual trends of Marxism in western Europe, a practical contrast to South America's radical liberation theology. Religion, in this new way of thinking, is no longer an "opiate of the people," but a positive factor in production, education, economic growth, and morality. The goals of the communist party for the immediate bettering of the quality of life are not inconsistent with religious belief.

Buddhist, Christian (Catholic and Protestant), Islamic, and Taoist practitioners are allowed to restore buildings destroyed or closed during the cultural revolution (1966-1978). Believers may establish seminaries, hold religious ceremonies, and raise funds for self support. Even more to the credit of the communist leadership of China, much of the restoration is being done with government support. Many religious leaders are paid salaries. Select seminaries and training institutes are partially financed with state funds. Practices forbidden for thirty years are tolerated and studied, as a part of the present needs and desires of China's people for bettering the quality of daily life.

The restoration and growth of religious practice in China was begun in 1979, when the religious freedom clause was promulgated along with directives for new economic growth. The reforms were, however, carefully controlled by Party and State directives. Religious renewal was to be watched over and monitored by three government sponsored bodies: 1)the United Front Association, 2) the Religious Affairs Bureau, and 3) a special body of state approved specialists from within each religious organization. The United Front Association is the official organ of the communist party, and consists of communist party officials appointed by the party to safeguard the principles of religious freedom under guidelines approved and promulgated in party directives. The Religious Affairs Bureau consists of officials appointed by the state or local government, not necessarily party members or affiliates, to give official status and sanction to approved local religious practices. The approval of the Religious Affairs Bureau for the repair of buildings, the restoration of religious practices and celebration of customary festivals, is crucial in the process of religious restoration.

The last body of officials in the series of buffers between the central government and local religious practice is chosen from within the ranks of each religious organization. These semiofficial guardians of religious practice from within the system are given different titles in each religious tradition. The Protestant "Three Self" movement, the Catholic "Patriotic Association" *Aiguohui* (ai-kuo hui),[1] the Buddhist, Taoist, and Islamic "Religious Studies" Associations, have more or less analogous roles in controlling religious practice. Liturgical expression, festivals, and manner of worship are not wholly determined by the state, but depend frequently on the enlightened or conservative attitude of individuals (sometimes self appointed) from within the belief system. These lay leaders assume the role of guiding rank and file believers towards state approved forms of worship, and away from "superstitious" or "out-of-the-ordinary" forms of religious expression.

A broad range of devout, semi-devout, and downright bureaucratic members of the "patriotic" and "study" associations are found throughout China. Visitors to Buddhist monasteries, Taoist mountain retreats, Protestant communities and Catholic seminaries have found widely divergent roles assumed by these semiofficial custodians. They can be extremely devout, and overly meddlesome. Some provide economic assistance and manage state funds, using political influence with state and party to win more religious freedom. Others, according to Chinese laity who visit shrines, temples, and churches in every part of China, are said to interfere with religious practice.

Regardless of obstacles put in the way of reform and renewal by bureaucratic elements within the state and local systems, the Chinese themselves seek an authentic renewal of cultural as well as religious practices. The goals of modernization, scholars and cadres insist, and the moral stability of the state are in fact not different from religious renewal in China. Religion as we shall see below, must continue in China for the "next fifty years," according to conservative guidelines within the party, and for "the next 200 years," in the words of Premier Chou Enlai before his death in 1976.[2]

Where there is religion, surveys show, morality is foremost, production is high, loyalty to the state is assured, and the Chinese family is strong. These goals are not opposed to the goals of the communist party for a better China. Though Deng Qiaoping once identified religion with the "flies and mosquitoes" brought into the room when the window of economic reform was opened, more than 50% of the party approve of the religious reforms as bettering the quality of life in China. This is partially due to the special place of ritual and festival in traditional Chinese society, i.e., birth, puberty, marriage, healing, burial, and the annual cycle of festivals, are still an essential part of Chinese cultural life. They do not fall under the Marxian epithet "opiate of the people," a term coined in nineteenth century Europe to condemn religion as a tool of the oppressive capitalist class. But China is a classless society, note modern communist thinkers, and religion in the classless socialist state need not be an opiate of the oppressed.

The role of religion in the modern Chinese state, as in the traditional past, is legally and socially defined by its service to the people, and its role in providing rites of passage. But beyond these needs, religion also functions on its own terms, in accord with the spiritual teachings of each of the religious traditions. The training of priest, monk, nun, minister, and mullah in state recognized seminaries, the practice of monastic asceticism and prayer on sacred mountain tops, and the pilgrimages of tourists as well as devout believers are also permitted under the new laws of religious freedom. Such practices are allowed, among other reasons, to maintain the integrity of the individual religious systems.

Recent party directives have classified all religious activities according to the following criteria: 1) normal, 2) abnormal, and 3) superstitious and/or illegal.[3] Normal religious activities, as determined by the religious Affairs Bureau and the Study-Patriotic Associations, are permitted without special approval. Abnormal activity, such as parades, processions, or large scale festivals such as the Taoist Chiao, require special permission from the authorities. Superstitious practices, a term not clearly defined, and underground or hidden activities, are considered illegal and reprehensible. The Religious Affairs Bureau and the various patriotic or study associations are given the difficult task of defining what is abnormal and superstitious-illegal. Local authorities often decide the meaning of such terms without recourse to learned or expert definitions.

The definition of normal, abnormal, and superstitious practice, recent directives have insisted, must be based on the teachings of each religious tradition, rather than on the whims of untrained local cadres. A number of religious studies institutes have been established in universities to observe the religious phenomena of socialist China, and assist in providing objective guidelines for implementing the directives for authentic religious practice.[4]

It is difficult for non-Asians to understand the continuing role of religion in modern China and other East Asian nations, without a clear understanding of the role that rituals and festivals described in *Blue Dragon White Tiger* play. It would be impossible, for instance, for a westerner to claim adherence to the tenets of Christianity, Islam, and Judaism at one and the same time. Yet most Chinese who are not strict Marxist-socialists consider Confucian ethics, Buddhist burial, and Taoist feelings towards nature to be a part of the warp and woof of the Chinese cultural fabric. "Confucian head, Buddhist heart, Taoist belly," still define the ordinary Chinese attitude toward religious custom.[5]

Perhaps no more than six percent of the Han (Chinese) population, state statistics show, openly claim adherence to a religious system. Another six percent is counted by the State as being members of the communist party, with faith in Marxism. A majority of the population of Chinese Turkestan may be nominally Islamic (though fewer attend the mosque), and a majority of the Tibetan minority people are Buddhist (including those in Hsikang and Szechuan, as well as Tibet). But the majority of the Han Chinese race claim no specific religion, even though the rites of passage and some or many of the annual festivals, Buddhist or Taoist burial, may be observed in the home. Socialist China, like most of the secular western world, is primarily interested in material possession, economic advancement, and profit. Material wealth, not Marxist or other ideology, is the *de facto* faith system of the majority in modern socialist China.

To understand the place of religion in modern China, we surveyed specific places known for their popularity and historical relevance. Taoist priests on mountaintops, Buddhist monks in temples, Christian seminaries and Catholic churches can now be freely visited and studied. A wide range of attitudes and responses to the question of religious practice are found throughout China, determined as in traditional times by local and provincial practice. We shall now turn to examine some of these places and the responses of local experts to our survey. It was surprising to find, for instance that many more people attend Catholic and Protestant services in China on a Sunday, than in Taiwan, or Japan. The need for rites of passage, role models, and cultural archetypes is strong in the socialist milieu.

I. The Official Party Response and State Policy

The political and economic reforms initiated by Deng Xiaoping in 1979 have been followed by an implementation of the constitutional religious freedom clause, allowing liberty of believers to practice their faith within the context of China's new realistic approach to progress in the socialist state. The subsequent restoration of religious structures and traditional festive practices associated with them, some at state expense, has received some attention from the Chinese press, and has been the focus of much intellectual discussion. Official response to the policy of freedom of religious belief has polarized the party along the same lines as the political and economic reforms, i.e., the conservative "leftist" Marxist view based on the dictum of Marx that religion is still the "opiate of the people," and the "seek truth from facts" school that considers China to be a special case within the wider boundaries of Socialism adapted to the modern condition.

A. Two Official Party Views of Religion

The conservative leftist wing, echoed in *Red Flag,* holds to the view that the continuance of religion in the PRC is but a remnant of backward thinking, a left over from a defunct class conscious society.[6] The presence of religious practice in China can only be tolerated until such a time as sufficient education and correct socialist thought have eliminated blind faith, i.e., beliefs not based on reason or scientific analysis. Religion can, however, be tolerated inasmuch as it does not go against Party directives, or a law passed by a Party Congress.

The opposite view, expressed in the December 7, 1984 *People's Daily* holds that:[7]

"Marx has been dead for 100 years. His works are also over 100 years old. Some were tentative ideas for those times. Later conditions underwent changes. Some theories were also not necessarily correct. Marx and Engels had no experience about many matters; neither did Lenin. They did not come into contact with many (Chinese) conditions. Therefore we cannot require Marx and Lenin's works of those days to solve problems today.... We cannot have a dogmatic attitude towards Marxism."

B. Some Scholarly Responses

The fact of the existence of religion in the modern socialist state, in this realistic view, can no longer be ascribed to reasons asserted by Engels or Marx. A recent publication in English entitled *Papers of the*

198

Shanghai Academy of Social Sciences, gives three reasons (among many others) why the policy of freedom of religious belief must be allowed to continue indefinitely China:[8]

1. Concrete evidence shows that the existence of religion in China today does not stem from the reasons brought by Marx against forms of western religion, i.e., a blind faith of the oppressed proletarian masses, whose suffering was brought on by an oppressive capitalist class. In today's classless socialist society, religion exists as a source of festival, rites of passage, and joyful celebration, not as a tool of a capitalist class that no longer exists in China.

2. Virtues such as love, selflessness, social responsibility, education, hard work, and honesty, which are fostered by the five traditional religions of China (Taoism, Buddhism, Protestant and Catholic Christianity, and Islam) are certainly in line with state policies, and foster patriotism and production.

3. With the extinction of the exploiting system, the *class basis* for the existence of religion has also disappeared. The key to this fundamental change of attitude in the socialist state with regard to the exercise of religious freedom is found in the interpretation of the above dictum. That is to say, "with correct handling and proper guidance, religion can be compatible with the new socialist society." The author of the SASS article strengthens the argument by quoting Zhou Enlai, affirming that in the new socialist society of China, religion is an "ideological issue within the ranks of the people, not a political issue."[9]

C. *Statistical Surveys and Reports on Religious Renewal*

The survey of the Shanghai Academy of Social sciences provides important guidelines through statistical studies for the instruction of local and provincial officials. The policy of "seeking truth from facts" has provided the following information, published by the SASS.[10]

1. "Workers, peasants, and intellectuals who believe in religion are engaged in developing industrial and agricultural production, raising scientific and technological levels and doing their utmost to open up new prospects for the socialist modernization program. Statistical data gathered from religions where farmers and fishermen who believe in religion are concentrated show that the production output quality of products, per capita income, and quota of grain distribution, do not lag behind regions where non-believers live." Whenever religious faith or

feelings are respected, the report shows, and normal religious activities are protected, production is high, and the modernization program as well as cooperation between all levels of society is implemented.

2. Higher levels of education in medicine and science are achieved, on an average, in communities with a Christian educational background. The guidance of patriotic religious leaders is seen to be an important element in such cases, "to implement the policies of equal importance to devotion to the motherland and devotion to the church," as well as "adding splendor to the land of our country and giving service to fellow beings." Religious ideals and beliefs are therefore seen to play a positive role in socialist construction.[11]

3. Where religious morals and teachings are practiced, there is a statistically lower crime rate, traditional family virtues are preserved, and concern for the common good is high:

"Our survey of rural areas indicates that quite a number of families of believers (who are) bound by religious moral obligations, can better handle the problems between mother-in-law and daughter-in-law, between husbands and wives, and between sisters-in-law, and often win titles of 'model family.' The concern which believers have for one another can to a certain extent unite people to overcome difficulties. The survey points out that such good deeds on the part of believers do not belong to the category of communist morality. As long as religious morality encourages people to do good deeds, we must affirm its positive social function, in a realistic way."[12] The problem, the report concludes, is to communicate these findings to the RAB and Study organizations, through training, education, and an enlightened state policy.

D. *Re-evaluation*

The new policy of freedom of religious practice has brought about a revival of Buddhist, Taoist, Christian, and Islamic studies at the university level, fulfilling a need for educational programs aimed at the RAB, and the Study-Patriotic Associations. These newly formed intellectual groups are found mainly in university-sponsored research programs. Gao Zhennong (Kao Chen-nung 高振農) *Buddhist Studies and Modern Philosophy in China*, summarizes the revival of interest in Buddhist Studies as follows:[13]

1. The importance of Buddhist Studies abroad, and the role of such Chinese scholars as Liang Qichao, Hu Shi (Hu Shih) and the two volume work of Feng Youlan (Feng Yu-lan) show the influence of Buddhism on Chinese philosophy.

2. Modern Buddhism influences countries other than China, i.e., the worldwide acceptance of Buddhist religious practice throughout Asia and the West.

3. Scholars have made achievements in Buddhist studies inside modern socialist China. For example, the Jinling Buddhist Scripture Engraving project, in Nanjing, where the Chinese version of the complete Buddhist scripture is being printed, the theory of *Hetuvidya* categories of Buddhist logic, and Xiong Shili's transformation of the Buddhist theory of *Vijnapti-Matrasiddhi-sastra* through the use of ideas "inherent in Chinese thinking," stressing that even if matter is called "false" it cannot be said to be non-existent, are cited as examples of the importance of Chinese contributions to modern Buddhist philosophical studies.

Taoist Studies are also being promoted as a part of the state-sponsored education program for young Taoists at the Baiyun Monastery (白雲觀) in Beijing, and at such research centers as the Shanghai Academy of Social Sciences, the new Religious Studies department of Sichuan (Szechuan) University, and the Center for the Study of World religions in the Academy of Social Sciences, Beijing. The Shanghai Academy of Musicology has published a videotape of Taoist ritual in the Shanghai area, and four audiotapes of Taoist Music of Shanghai, Wudang Shan, Mao Shan, and Suzhou. Under the auspices of the Bureau of Ethnomusicology of Hupei province, a 246 page study of the Taoist music of Wudang Shan has been published with musical annotations of the complete *Chiao* repertory. The Taoist Association of Beijing produces a monthly periodical, two articles of which are devoted to strict scholarly studies, while the remainder of the materials are of the nature of local gazetteers.[14]

II. Truth from Facts: Religious Practice in the PRC

The reality of religious practice has been the subject of a second Chinese language study published by the Shanghai Academy of Social Sciences in April, 1987. The total first 8,000 copies of the study sold out within the first two months, and a second edition was soon in press. In this remarkably frank and open study can be found descriptions of various aspects of religious restoration and reconstruction that support the opinion that religion will indeed be a long-lasting phenomenon in the People's Republic of China. The following data is a part of the survey:[15]

A. *Buddhist temples that support themselves in Fujian Province*
Fujian, a province famous for its Buddhist and Taoist temples and centers of devotion, is one of the most religiously active areas of the modern PRC. The Buddhist temples of this economically progressive area have experienced a large enrollment of young men and women, seeking the life of prayer and contemplation along with work in the fields for self support and useful production. The young monks and nuns farm the temple lands, study Buddhist scriptures in a scholarly way, and perform traditional Buddhist chant and *Chan* (Zen) meditation. The reasons for choosing the Buddhist way of life was made a special point of the SASS study. Sincere religious vocation was the rule in the majority of cases.[16]

B. *A Taoist mountain near Chengdu (Ch'eng-tu), Sichuan*
The famous Qingcheng (Ch'ing-ch'eng 青城) monastery complex near Chengdu city, in west China, which escaped serious damage during the period of the Red Guards and the Cultural Revolution, is a flourishing center of pilgrimage and Taoist practice. Some dozen elderly Taoist masters teach over a hundred young men and women, who have come to the mountain to lead a life of celibacy, prayer, and vegetarian diet. Apart from the donations left by pilgrims to the various mountain temples and retreats, the younger Taoists and aspirants support the temple by farming, producing medicinal herbs, a fine mountain wine, tea, and mineral-soda water. The mountain has become famous for its vegetarian restaurants and hostels for pilgrims.[17]

C. *A Catholic Fishing Village near Shanghai*
The Sheshan (余山) fishing village near Shanghai has had a devout Catholic community since the earliest Jesuit Missions of the Qing (Ch'ing 清) dynasty. Some 10,000 members of the Sheshan church have maintained their faith through the years of the Great Leap and the Cultural Revolution, and were one of the first communities to restore the church and the practices of the past after the liberalization of 1979-1980. But the majority of the practitioners were in their forties-to-sixties, at the time of the restoration. Within the past three years, however, a great number of younger people have been entering the Church, drawn not so much by the "night prayers and home devotions"

202

of the elders (television is now popular in the family evenings) as by the festivals, pilgrimages, and liturgies of the Church.[18]

D. *The Nanjing Union Theological Seminary*

Under the enlightened and sometimes distant guidance of Bishop K.H. Ding, the Nanjing Union Theological Seminary, which re-opened its doors to students in 1981, now has some 200 young men and women studying for the ministry, in an interdenominational program that stresses scripture studies and an ecumenical theology in line with the needs of religious believers in the new socialist state. The equivalents of the B.Th. and the M.Div. degrees are given to the graduates, who return to work as pastors in the provinces and villages of origin. The seminary also runs lay training classes, correspondence courses, and a printing press for Christian materials. Funds coming from overseas, which cannot be used for direct support of propagation in line with the principles of the "Three Self" movement, are put into a special fund known as the "Amity Foundation," to support hospitals, social work, and the teaching of foreign languages in universities throughout China.[19]

E. *Islam in the People's Republic of China*

The Islamic faith of Chinese Turkestan, and the larger cities within China where mosques have traditionally been established, flourish in modern China. Along with the interest in ethnic minority studies and their religions, the academic study of Islam in China is growing in academic circles. The presence of Islamic mosques, restaurants, and minority peoples is everywhere in evidence.[20]

In spite of a sometimes negative and incorrect description of religion appearing in the press (e.g. the *China Daily* article for July 9, 1987, gives a rather pessimistic view of Taoism), it is clear that the prophetic words of Zhou Enlai described a reality that can only grow as China enters the modern world. Religion in the PRC will flourish for more than 200 years, in the view of most social scientists who study from within the PRC.

The continuing existence of religion in Marxist-socialist society has generated lively intellectual debate in Eastern bloc countries, the European West, and Latin America, paralleling the dialogue going on within the People's Republic of China. In the view of many social scientists, Marx had failed to account for the human and cultural elements in societies that did not conform to the nineteenth century European model. The Chinese contribution to this dialogue must be seen as an important new development, beyond the limitations of the western definitions of the nature of religious belief. In this sense, Chinese rites of passage and annual festivals, to which Buddhist, Confucian, and Taoist belief systems conform, are eminently adaptable to the socialist, as well as the capitalist cultural system.

III. A Survey of Religion in China

An actual survey of the various shrines, sacred places, and temples of China today reveals a strongly growing and flourishing religious awareness in socialist China. True to the cultural origin and function of religion in the past, the rites of passage and annual festivals are everywhere in evidence. Furthermore, all walks of society, communist cadres, peasant farmers, and religious devotees volunteer to talk about religion in the socialist context. With support of the National Science Foundation, and the Bureau of Education in Beijing, a survey of the condition of religious practice in China was conducted during 1987-1988, to complete the final chapter of *Blue Dragon White Tiger*. The survey was carried out under the auspices of the Religious Studies program at Nanjing University, and covered Taoist, Buddhist, Christian, and Islamic practices.

A. Religious Taoism

For various reasons, relating to the historical past of China and the largely unnoticed role of religious Taoism in the writings of scholars and bureaucrats, the fate of Taoism during the years of the cultural revolution and its restoration since 1979 have received little notice from the press and the least amount of state supported reconstruction. The great Taoist sites of the past, such as Mao Shan, Ch'ing-ch'eng Shan, Wu-tang Shan, Lung-hu Shan, and so forth, were rebuilt by pilgrims, devotees, and the enduring Taoist masters who continued their practices on the summit shrines. These last mentioned men and women continued their lives of ascetic celibacy, macrobiotics, and meditation throughout the entire period of cultural and economic crisis. The survey will begin with the restoration of Taoist practice.

1. Mao Shan Shang-ch'ing Taoism. 茅山

Mao Shan rises abruptly from the Chiangsu plains, a pine covered refuge 60 km to the southeast of the old capital city Nanjing. Its pine covered peaks are named after three brothers who practiced meditation and healing there in the early Han dynasty, ca. 160-140 BCE. Mao Shan flourished as a center of Taoist meditative arts during the North-south period, (280-581 CE). Ritual meditation, medicine, and the alchemical arts of Mao Shan influenced China throughout the Sui-T'ang dynasties (581-906 CE). More than a thousand shrines, temples, monuments, and monasteries were built by emperors, sages, and savants by the Sung dynasty (960-1281 CE).[21] All of these glories of the past were destroyed by the ravages of the Japanese army and the Red Guard, in a brief 32 year period, between 1938-1970.

My first trip to the sacred mountain, June of 1986, was made with scholars from Nanjing University. We procured a cab, and drove through the pleasant Chiangsu plains. The first rice harvest was in progress. The roads were covered with rice stubble. White geese, dyed bright pink, yellow and blue (for identification), ducks, goats, and pigs scurried from underneath the taxi wheels. The driver, Hsiao Wang, refused to drive over the rice stubble, placed in our way by the peasants, who used the road and passing vehicles for threshing. We stopped at the shrine of General Chen Yi for lunch. Leader of the Fourth Route communist army, this hero of the revolution chose the environs of Mao Shan to billet his guerrilla forces. In an act of savage vengeance, the brutal Japanese First Army (famed for the rape of Nanjing) killed the Taoists found on the mountain, and burned all the buildings, in retaliation for the guerrilla presence. The flames that consumed the mountain in Feb., 1938, burned a Sung dynasty Taoist Canon, and destroyed the original woodblocks, an irreplaceable loss, for which no reparations were made by Japan.

Those Taoists who escaped the flames and the killing tried to restore a portion of the buildings and the library after the Second World War. Visitors to the mountain in the late forties reported that a portion of the Taoist Canonical books had escaped destruction, and the monasteries atop Great Mao Shan were still functioning. What was so laboriously restored in the forties and fifties, however, was finally burned and eradicated by successive waves of red guard youth in the 60's and 70's.

Mao Shan, center of worship for centuries by peasants and emperors, was a first choice for restoration in the early 1980's. When the religious freedom clause was promulgated, peasant farmers began to ascend the mountain on festival days. Mao Shan again became a center for pilgrimage. Medicinal herbs were still found on the mountainside. New rows of pine trees, famed for the dew collected from needles in the cool mornings, (from which Mao Shan tea was brewed), again covered the hills. Taoists who had hidden for years in the villages at the

foot of the mountain ascended to the summit to rebuild the monasteries. Young men from the villages flocked to the mountain to be admitted as novices for Taoist meditation and ritual practice.

The visitors the summit are greeted by Yüan Chih-hung, and
Yang Shih-hua, Taoist scholars in their mid-thirties who work in the
Mao Shan Taoist Studies association. Yüan has been to the state sponsored Taoist seminary in Beijing, operated by the Ch'uan-chen Taoist
school, and is highly thought of in Taoist and government circles. He
has published widely, and is responsible for the new five volume Mao
Shan Gazetteer, and a series of articles in the Taoist Studies Periodical.
He does not, however, practice Taoist meditation or ritual, even though
he dresses in the robes of a Taoist master. Yüan and Yang's roles on
Mao Shan are that of director, historian, and accountant. They lecture
almost daily to visiting cadres, scholars, and visitors, and are responsible for the rebuilding and restoration of Mao Shan to its former
beauty. The 5th-6th century scholar T'ao Hung-ching, Yüan says, is his
model for Taoist research and preservation.

The summit of Great Mao Shan has been restored by the efforts
of such young Taoist scholars. Peasant farmers and pilgrims from the
lowlands who come to the highest of the three peaks in the thousands
on festival days, leave small contributions, averaging about $10 ren-
minbi (U.S. $3.70) each. The Wan-fu Kung temples, library building,
refectory, monastic rooms, *chang-t'ai* platform for addressing prayers
and sending ritual documents to the cosmos, and a guest house have
been reconstructed from the rubble left after the Japanese and Red
Guard destruction.

Looking down from the summit of Great Mao Shan, named
after the eldest of the three brother Taoists, one can see the Yin Kung
monastery and the hillside of Second Mao Shan, where some forty-five
monasteries once stood. Until 1989 the Sung dynasty structure of the
Yin Kung housed the Shang-ch'ing master Shih Tao-ch'ang, an eminent
and unassuming Taoist in his seventies, who trained some fifteen
novices in the music, drumming, and ritual meditations of the Mao
Shan Shang-ch'ing tradition.[22] The official Taoist title used by Shih
when signing the *Piao* memorials and *shu-wen* rescripts used during
Chiao ritual includes the registers and meditations of the Shang-ch'ing,
Ling-pao, Ch'ing-wei, and Pole Star traditions, linking Mao Shan with

the Taoist practices of Lung-hu Shan in Chianghsi, Wu-tang Shan in Hupei, and Hua Shan in Shensi (The Three Mountain Alliance: for which association, see below).

In all some sixty Taoists, novices, postulants, and workers reside on or near Mao Shan. Some of the younger Taoists have been to the state sponsored Taoist school in Baiyun Gwan (Pai-yun Kuan 白雲觀), Beijing. These state educated Taoists dress in the traditional garb of the Mao Shan sect, but are not taught the meditations or rituals of Mao Shan. In the words of Shih, they have not yet *ting-hsin*定心(quieted the heart-mind) and thus cannot be taught the secrets of the Yellow Court Canon, the meditations of interior alchemy, or the rituals of the Chiao. Mao Shan also welcomes Ch'uan-chen reformed Taoists to its monastic circles, and allows equal opportunity to practice the Ch'uan-chen or the Shang-ch'ing way of life.[23]

2. Wu-tang Shan: Pole Star and Ch'uan Chen Taoism. 武當山
Wu-tang Shan is a grueling three day journey by boat from Nanjing to Wuhan, a fifteen hour hard-seat train ride to Shih-yen on the Hupei-Shenhsi border, followed by a six hour ride into the Wu-tang Shan hills, and a three hour climb to the 4,600 ft. summit. Set in one of the most beautiful and out-of-the-way natural settings in China, 800-1,200 people a day come to Wu-tang Shan on tour or pilgrimage. The stately Tz'u-yun temple, funded by the Yung-lo Emperor in the early 15th century, still contains the original Ming dynasty statues, and a well preserved Taoist Canon.[24] Here some 90 Taoists, both monks and nuns, live by the strict monastic Ch'uan-chen rule. Celibacy, vegetarian diet, breath meditation, and care for the pilgrims who come to the mountain embody the life style of Wu-tang Shan Taoists.

The Taoist master La-pa (trumpet), noted as a musician and ritual expert, has trained an entourage of younger Taoists to perform the Chiao festival, in a combined Ch'uan-chen reformed and Cheng-i style rite. This reformed Chiao ritual has been recorded on videotape by the Hupei Bureau of ethnology and ethnomusicology with an audio-cassette available to the public. The musical score has also been published, and compares with the melodies used by the "Three Mountain Alliance" of the Taoist ritual tradition.[25] That is, the Taoism of Mao Shan, Lung-hu Shan, Ko-tso Shan (which has not yet been fully restored) and this beautiful mountain in Hupei are comparable. With the other great Taoist mountains, Wu-tang Shan is assured survival in the modern socialist system.

3. Lung-hu Shan, Celestial Master Taoism. 龍虎山

The T'ien-shih Fu in San-ch'ing village Chianghsi province, has been the headquarters of Celestial Master *Cheng-i Meng-wei* Taoism since the Sung dynasty. The village of San-ch'ing, named after a temple dedicated to the Taoist "Three Pure Ones," is on the main line from Ying-t'an industrial city in Chianghsi and the port of Hsia-men in Fukien Province. San-ch'ing is noted for its year-round fine weather, a lack of mosquitoes, and scenic beauty. The area from San-ch'ing to the nearby Lung-hu Shan lakes is called "little Kueilin," since it resembles the famous scenery of that noted tourist district on a lesser scale.

Celestial Master, or Cheng-i Meng-wei Taoism claimed this area to have been its legendary headquarters from the Han and the Three Kingdoms period onward. Chang Tao-ling, founder of Celestial master Taoism, was said to have moved here from Szechuan, and taught his Taoist methods from a villa by Lung-hu Shan lake. Taoists from Fukien, Kwangtung, Chianghsi, and Taiwan came to Lung-hu Shan, San-ch'ing village, for a state approved license to perform Taoist ritual, a law honored by Taoist masters from the Sung dynasty until the present.[26] Since Taoists ordained at Lung-hu Shan, Ko-tsao Shan, or Mao Shan received equivalent instructions in ritual, meditation, and literary sources, the three mountains formed an alliance called the *San Shan Ti-hsüeh P'ai*, the Three Mountain "Drop-of-blood" Alliance. A special manual of ordination was given to Taoists who came to one of these three mountains, listing the titles, ranks, and grades of license given by each mountain.[27]

The state approved law for licensing Taoists to practice ritual has not been restored by the modern socialist government. Taoists from Taiwan, and many overseas communities of Chinese, however, hope to be able to return soon to San-ch'ing village, Lung-hu Shan, as well as to Mao Shan, to renew their licenses as in the past. Eight elderly Taoists, headed by Wang Shao-lin, maintain the liturgical traditions of Cheng-i Meng-wei Taoism, and preserve the ordination manual with its traditional grades and titles at San Ch'ing village, Lung-hu Shan.[28] The Chianghsi province Ethnological Studies Association has videotaped the complete Chiao festival, but the audio-recordings have not yet been made public. Each of the eight Lung-hu Shan Taoist masters intends to pass on his ordination documents and ritual manuals to younger sons and disciples, thus preserving the legacy of this traditional source of classical Taoism.

4. Taoists of Fukien Province.

One of the traditional sources for Taoist ritual manuals and their scholarly preservation has always been the Taoist masters of Fukien Province. The various Sung dynasty Taoist Canons relied on Fukien Taoists for many of the liturgical materials included in printed woodblock editions.[29] The restoration of Taoism in the areas of Chang-chou, Ch'üan-chou, An-hsi, and other areas of southeast China has been the subject of a number of recent studies. Abbreviated versions of the Chiao ritual were observed and reported on in these districts, adjacent to or a part of the free economic zones of Fukien and Kwangtung.

The Taoists of these areas perform Chiao rituals with an analogous structure and content to the grand Chiao liturgies of Taiwan across the straits. The origin of the Taoists and the majority of the settlers of Taiwan was of course southeast Fukien and Mei county, Kwangtung. That is, Taoists who serve the Min dialect speaking Taiwanese, came originally from Ch'üan-chou, Chang-chou, T'ung-an, An-hsi, and environs, while Taoists who serve the Hakka speaking minority of Taiwan come from west Fukien and Mei county, Kwangtung. True to the principles enunciated in the first chapter of *Blue Dragon White Tiger*, the local variations in Taoist nomenclature and practice prove true today, in a comparative survey of Taiwan and southeast Fukien.

The terms "Redhead" and "Blackhead" used to distinguish the Taoists of Taiwan, are also used in southeast Fukien, in a more or less analogous way. The original meaning assigned to the terms by the Japanese ethnographers who studied Taiwan in the early twentieth century was derived from the titles given Taoists according to ritual. "Redhead" (ang-thau 紅頭) was used of Taoists who performed ritual for the living, while "Blackhead" (O-thau 黑頭) meant Taoists who also performed burial ritual.

In my earlier surveys of north Taiwan, it was evident that these two terms had a different meaning for the people who attended ritual, and the Taoists. The Blackhead Taoists of north Taiwan customarily held ordinations and licenses in the Cheng-i meng-wei tradition. The Redhead Taoists, on the other hand, were quite varied in their titles and licenses.[30] Though researchers and even the younger redhead Taoists did not make the distinction, the manuals and registers of the Redhead Taoists of north Taiwan included Shen-hsiao, Lü-shan,

Cheng-i, Ling-pao, and other popular local forms of Taoism from Fukien and Kwangtung. The two terms as used in Tainan, south Taiwan, had yet another meaning.[31]

One of the more surprising discoveries of the recent survey of religion conducted in southeast Fukien was the even broader use made of these two terms in mainland China. In the best sense of *différance*, i.e., deferral or non-closure of semiotic meaning, the term "Blackhead" as used in Chang-chou city, south Fukien, refers only to Taoists and other ritual experts who bury the dead. The term "redhead" is used of all Taoists who specialize in performing the Chiao festival of renewal, a broadening of the usage in north Taiwan. The orthodox Liu Taoist family of Chang-chou preserves the ritual manuals and the Chiao liturgies of the Cheng-i meng-wei Taoist tradition, but are known as "Redhead Taoists" throughout Chang-chou city.[32]

The renewal of folk religion in Ch'üan-chou city is even more progressive than in Chang-chou, due to the enlightened attitude of the Taoist Studies Association and the Religious Affairs Bureau of that city. The Kuan-kung temple next to the central market has been totally restored, and is open for public prayer and worship. A guest book is kept by Mr. Lin, the temple custodian, that records with pride the number of visiting scholars. The role of the university scholar is important in this regard, since the disposition of the Religious Affairs Bureau experts towards religious practice is visibly enhanced by the presence of an expert from outside the system. The function of the university scholar to affirm the authenticity of religious ritual, and give prestige to the fledgling renewal of traditional festival is essential, from the viewpoint of the Chang-chou and Ch'üan-chou Taoist Associations.

The Taoists of Ch'üan-chou city and environs have not yet found complete sets of the Chiao festival manuals, and are forced to substitute other manuals in the structural slots meant for the classical rites of renewal. The Ch'en family of the East Peak area of Ch'üan-chou, a traditional Blackhead group of Taoists who practice funeral ritual and classical Chiao liturgy, are attempting to restore the correct manuals from collections in other parts of Fukien. The Chiao festival is being revived throughout the two greater areas (Ch'üan-chou and Chang-chou districts) as more and more temples are rebuilt and dedicated.[33] The restoration of village temples for public worship, and the practice of Taoist ritual go hand-in-hand throughout southeast Fukien.

Taoism, perhaps the slowest of the religious traditions to be renewed under socialism, is growing apace with the religious reforms and restoration in China. The great Taoist centers of the past, such as Lao Shan in Shantung, Hua Shan, Ch'ing-ch'eng Shan in Ch'eng-tu (Chengdu), T'ien-shui in Kansu, the Taoist associations of Kwangtung, Shanghai, Suchow, and Pai-yun Kuan in Beijing are flourishing in a quiet and unassuming fashion.

The role and support of the scholar is crucial in this process of Taoist restoration, due to the low place always given religious Taoism in the official government view of popular religion and the Taoist role in village festival. As with the case of folk religion and popular festival, the will of the people for the continuation of the great customs of the past insures the continued existence of Taoism in China. Taoism's customs, such as pilgrimage to sacred places, herbal medicine, martial arts, ch'i or breath therapy, as well as the grand Chiao festival of renewal, are an essential part of China's traditional culture.

IV. Religion and Ritual in Modern China

Buddhism and its revival, as stated above, is the most visible and widespread phenomenon of the religious renewal in China. The T'ang dynasty Buddhist temples of Hsia-men, Ch'üan-chou and Chang-chou in Fukien, P-u-t'uo (Puto) Shan in Chekiang, Lo-fu Shan in Kwangtung, Le Shan in Sichuan (Szech'uan) and Hsi-hsia Shan near Nanjing, as all the other great Buddhist monuments and monasteries throughout China, are kept busy on a daily basis with ritual for the souls of the deceased. Ritual chanting of prayers for the deceased, the prayer of petition for blessing for the living, the burning of incense by tourist-pilgrims, must be seen as parts of a single process in the Chinese cultural-religious system.

The more profound aspects of this system, which extend far beyond the surface level of burning incense and paper money, speak to an innate sense within the Chinese of a holistic cosmos, where every human act has consequences far beyond the present moment. The past, and all its memories, energies, and relics, are everywhere visible in China. The home of Confucius, the tomb of Ch'in Shih-Huang (First Emperor of China, 221 BCE), the Buddhist Caves of Lung-men, Yun-kang, and Tun-huang, are but a train-ride away. The destruction of the books by Ch'in Shih-huang after 221 BCE only reconfirmed the Chinese

211

respect for the written word. The destruction of the architectural and artistic relics of the past by the Red Guard only reconfirmed the Chinese sense of past, present, and future as part of a single process.

Ritual is, for the Chinese, a part of the semiotic system that confirms this three dimensional process. Ritual summons the spirits of the past, in a grand eidetic (i.e., moving, creative, living) vision. The present hopes of the Chinese for the future are invoked in the presence of the spirits of the past. Whether seen as statue, scroll, or imaginary vision, the spirits of the past confirm the greatness of China as a perennial culture. The destruction of the Red Guard was a hopeless gesture, the frustration of adapting a way of thought foreign to the reality of China's triple vision. The socialist future of China must be built on the cultural-philosophical-religious past, just as branches, leaves, and fruit must grow on the roots of a tree deeply embedded in the soil of China.

The restoration of religion must therefore be seen as a renewal of the three dimensional Chinese sense of the relationship between past, present, and future. This unifying philosophy of the macrocrosm, in turn, is related to the microcosm of the human body. Mind and word are to the past, heart and will to the future, as belly and intuition to the present, in the Chinese ritual system. The rites of renewal, freeing the souls (memories) of the past and petitioning blessings for the future are predicated on a full belly and the necessary things of life in the present. The rites of passage and annual festivals are no more and no less than an affirmation of this basically sound and pragmatic philosophy of life. The restoration of religion in China must be seen as an confirmation of this basic Chinese philosophy, affirming the need to build a new socialist society on the ethical and cultural values of the past.

The Blue Dragon and White Tiger have thus brought China through a full historic-religious cycle, "spring, summer, autumn, winter," to renewal in the modern socialist present. Chinese Rites of Passage and Annual Festivals persist in the modern Chinese state. Blue Dragon White Tiger have survived all efforts of Confucian, Capitalist, and Socialist secularism to undermine their influence. We propose that the festivals of China will continue to flourish well beyond the next 200 years, in the lives of the people.

NOTES

1. Wade-Giles romanization used consistently through Chapters 1-7, is here substituted with the *pinyin* romanization wherever the printed materials or usage of the PRC seem appropriate.

2. Adapted from *China news Analysis*, Dec. 15, 1987, pp. 1-7.

3. Lei Zhenchang, *Guangming Daily*, May 9, 1988.

4. Beijing, Nanjing, Shanghai, Chengdu, Gueiyang, and Kunming have university level religious studies programs.

5. See Julian Baum, *The Christian Science Monitor*, Aug. 1988, six articles on religion in modern China.

6. *Red Flag*, 1986, No. 9, pp. 25-30.

7. *People's Daily*, National Edition, Dec. 7, 1984.

8. *Shanghai Academy of Social Sciences Papers*, (SASS Papers), Shanghai: Guoji Shudian, 1988, pp. 369-379.

9. SASS Papers, p. 380.

10. SASS Papers, pp. 387-8.

11. Ibid., p. 389.

12. Ibid., p. 392.

13. Ibid., pp. 352-368.

14. Shanghai Academy of Social Sciences, Hui-hai Ching-lu, 622-7.

15. *The Religious Question in the Socialist Era*, (Shanghai: 1987).

16. Op. cit., pp. 188-210.

17. Ibid., pp. 211-213.

18. Ibid., pp. 231-246.

19. Ibid., pp. 257-68.

20. Ibid., pp. 247-256.

21. See Chapter 2, Taoist History.

22. Shih passed away in Spring, 1989, and was succeeded by Master Ch'iu, the next ranking Taoist teacher.

23. Ch'uan-chen Taoists practice a simplified form of Chiao ritual, and Zen-like sitting meditation.

24. The Taoist Canon now kept at Pai-yun Kuan in Beijing come from the Wu-tang Shan collection.

25. *Taoist Music of Wu-tang Shan*, Hupei Folk Music Assoc., 1986.

26. Three mountains, Lung-hu Shan, Ko-tsao Shan, and Mao Shan granted Taoist licenses from the Sung period until the 20th century.

27. Saso, M., *Dokyo Hiketsu Shusei*, A Collection of Taoist Esoterica, Tokyo: Ryukei Shosha, 1979, pp. 1-44.

28. While the Chang clan is hereditary celestial master, the Wang clan of Lung-hu Shan are the traditional teachers of the Cheng-i Meng-wei and other Taoist traditions.

29. See Schipper, R., "Les canons taoistes des Song," *Annuaire, École Pratique des Hautes Étude.* Ve Section des sciences relig. 91, pp. 133-137; also, van der Loon, Piet, *Taoist Books in the Libraries of the Sung Period*, London: Ithaca Press, 1984.

30. Saso, M., TROCR, (Pullman: 1990), Ch. 5.

31. Liu Chih-wan, "Propitiatory Rites for Petition (A Study of the Chiao in North Taiwan)," and *Essays on Chinese Folk Beliefs and Folk Cults*, Nankang: Academia Sinica, Monographs #14, amd #22.

32. Liu Tao-ch'ang's Taoist Ritual Collection has been photocopied by Kenneth Dean, and John Lagerwey; the manuals are analogous to the Lung-hu Shan and the Hsinchu Cheng-i Ssu-t'an collection.

33. See Kenneth Dean's two forthcoming articles on the Taoists of Fukien, in *Symposium on Taoist Music and Ritual*, (Hongkong: 1989) and *Cahiers d'Extrême-Asie*, (Kyoto: 1989), Vol. III.

SELECT BIBLIOGRAPHY

1. The Tao of Ritual
General Works on Chinese Religion
(The following brief list can be supplemented by Laurence Thompson's *Chinese Religions in Western Languages*, Tucson: 1985, pp. 2-78).
Ch'an, Wing-tsit, Religions of China, in *The Great Asian Religions, An Anthology*. New York: 1969, Part Two, pp. 99-227.
_____, *A Sourcebook in Chinese Philosophy*, Princeton: 1962.
Chang, Kwang-chih, *Shang Civilization*, New Haven: 1980.
Creel, H.G., *The Birth of China*, New York: 1937.
Doré, Henri, *Researches into Chinese Superstitions*, Taipei: 1967; a (trans. of 13 of the 18 French Vols., Shanghai: 1914-1938.
Eberhard, W., *Guilt and Sin in Traditional China*, Berkeley: 1967.
_____, *Moral and Social Values of the Chinese*, Taipei: 1971.
Eder, Matthias, *Chinese Religion*, Tokyo: 1973. Asian Folklore, #6.
Edkins, Joseph, *Religion in China*, Boston: 1878.
Fung Yu-lan, D. Bodde, *Chinese Philosophy*, Princeton: 1952-3, 2 vol.
Granet, M., *The Religion of the Chinese People*, New York: 1975.
Groot, J.J.M. de, *The Religious System of China*, Leiden: 1910.
Keightley, David, *Sources of Shang History. The Oracle-bone inscriptions of Bronze Age China*, Berkeley: 1978.
Maspero, Henri, *Taoism and Chinese Religion*, Amherst: 1981.
Needham, Joseph, *Science and Civilization in China*, Vols I-V, Taoism, Alchemy, Chinese History, Cambridge: 1961-81.
Schafer, Edward, *Ancient China*, New York: 1967.
_____, *Pacing the Void*, Berkeley: 1977.
Stein, Rolf, "Religious Taoism and Popular Religion," in *Facets of Taoism*, New Haven: 1979. pp. 53-81.
Thompson, L., *Chinese Religion: an Introduction*, Belmont: 1979.
_____, *The Chinese Way in Religion*, Belmont: 1973.
Wolf, Arthur, (ed.) *Religion and Ritual in Chinese Society*, Stanford: 1974.
Yang., C.K., *Religion in Chinese Society*, Berkeley: 1961.

2. The Tao of Emptying
_____, *Taoist Resources*, Vol I, Peralta: Taoist Resources, 1988.
Au, Dona, & Rowe, Sharon, "Bibliography of Taoist Studies," in *Buddhist and Taoist Studies*, Vol. 1, Honolulu: 1977, pp. 123-48.

215

Boltz, Judith, *A Survey of Taoist Literature*, Berkeley: 1986.

Kohn, Livia, (nee Knaul), "The Teachings of T'ien-yin-tzu, in *The Journal of Chinese Religions*, (JOCR) #15, Fall, 1987.

Man, K.L., & Julian Pas, "An Outline of Taoist History," JOCR, #15, Fall 1987. (Not used in *Blue Dragon White Tiger*).

Pas, Julian, *A Select Bibliography on Taoism*, New York: 1988.

Robinet, Isabelle, *Méditation Taoïste*, Paris: Dervy-Livres, 1978.

Thompson, Laurence, *Chinese Religion in Western Languages*, pp. 91-104, Taoism.

Walf, Knut, *Western Bibliography of Taoism*, Essen: 1986.

Yü, David C., *Guide to Chinese Religion*, Boston: 1985.

3. The Spiritual Quest
(A Select Bibliography of Buddhist Studies).

Ch'en, K., *Buddhism in China: A Hist. Survey*, Princeton: 1964.

Conze, Edward, *A Short History of Buddhism*, London: 1980.

De Bary, W.T. (ed.) *The Buddhist Tradition in India, China, and Japan*, New York: 1972.

Dumoulin, Heinrich, *A History of Zen Buddhism*, Boston: 1969; (new two volume edition, Nanzan University, Nagoya, in press, 1989).

Guenther, Herbert, *Buddhist Philosophy in Theory and Practice*, Harmondsworth, (Pelican Books): 1972.

Hoffmann, Helmut, *The Religions of Tibet* (trans., E. Fitzgerald), New York: 1961.

Humphreys, Christmas, *Buddhism*, Harmondsworth (Penguin): 1962.

Inada, Kenneth, *Guide to Buddhist Philosophy*, Boston: 1985.

Inagaki, H., *A Dictionary of Japanese Buddhist Terms*, Kyoto: 1984.

Jayatilleke, K.N., *Early Buddhist Theory of Knowledge*, Delhi: 1980 reprint, (1963).

Kalupahana, David, *Buddhist Philosophy: A Historical Analysis*, Honolulu: 1976.

Kanakura, Yensho, *Hindu-Buddhist Thought in India*, Yokohama: 1980. (trans., Iida & Donner; ed., Maruyama & Quinn).

Lamotte, Etienne, *The History of Buddhism in India*, Leiden: 1988

La Vallée Poussin, L., *The Way to Nirvana: Six Lectures on Ancient Ancient Buddhism as a Discipline of Salvation*, Satguru: 1982.

Matsunaga A., & Matsunaga D., *Foundations of Japanese Buddhism*, Tokyo: 1982.

Mizuno, Kogen, *The Beginnings of Buddhism*, (trans., L. Gage), Tokyo: 1980.

Murti, T.R.V., *The Central Philosophy of Buddhism: A Study of the Mâdkaymika System*, London: 1955.

Pas, Julian, "Shan-tao's interpretation of the meditative vision of Buddha Amitayus," *History of Religions*, 14:96-116.

_____, "The Kuang-wu-liang-shou Ching: its origin and literary criticism," in *Buddhist Thought and Asian Civilization*, Dharma Publishing, 1977: 144-218.

Rhys Davids, T.W., *A Manual of Buddhism for Advanced Students*, Delhi: 1978.

_____, *Early Buddhism*, 1976.

Robinson, R., *Early Madhyamika in India and China*, Dehli: 1976.

Stcherbatsky, Th., *Buddhist Logic*, New York: 1962, 2 volumes.

Streng, Frederick, *Emptiness*, New York: 1967.

Takakusa, Junjiro, *The Essentials of Buddhist Philosophy*, (ed., W.T. Chan & C.A. Moore), Tokyo-Honolulu, 1978.

Takasaki, Jikido, *An Introduction to Buddhism*, (trans., Rolf Giebel), Tokyo: 1987.

Wright, Arthur, *Buddhism in Chinese History*, Stanford: 1965.

4. The Rite of Marriage

Aneba, Shohei, *Tokushu Horitsu no Kenkyu*, (Law and Special Court Cases on Marriage and the Family), Taipei: 1934.

Freedman, Maurice, *The Study of Chinese Society*, Stanford: 1979. Rites and Duties, or Chinese Marriage; Ch. 16, Ritual Aspects of Chinese Kinship and Marriage, pp. 255-295.

_____, *Family and Kinship in Chinese Society*, Stanford: 1970.

Hachiya, Kunio, *Girei shi kon so*, (Gentry Marriage in the Yi-li Book of Rites, T'ang dynasty commentary of Chia Kung-ch'en et al.).

Ikeda, Jun, *Ta T'ang K'ai-yuan Li*, Tokyo, 1972; T'ang Dynasty Rites of Passage during the K'ai-yuan Period, marriage ritual.

Ikeda, Toshio, *Taiwan no Katei Seikatsu*, (Taiwan Family Life), Taipei: 1944.

Lin Po-t'ung, *Kuan, Hun, Sang, Chi* (The Rites of Passage), Canton: 1844, Vol. II.

Lin, Yueh-hua, *The Golden Wing; A Sociological Study of the Chinese Family*, London: 1948. Ch. 4, pp. 36-48 on marriage.

Niida, Noboru, *Shina Mibun Hoshi*, (The Law of Social Status in China), Tokyo: 1942.

Suzuki, Seiichiro, *Traditional Rites of Passage and Annual Customs*,(Text in Japanese), Taipei: 1934.

Wolf, A., and Huang C.S., *Marriage and Adoption in China, 1845-1945*, Stanford: 1980.

Wolf, Margery, *The House of Lim: A Study of a Chinese Farm Family*, New York: 1968.

_____, *Women and the Family in Rural Taiwan*, Stanford: 1972.

5. *Birthing and Capping*

The works of Lin Po-t'ung, Ikeda Toshio, Margery Wolf, and Suzuki Seiichiro, have invaluable descriptions of birthing or family customs for further research into Taiwan and Cantonese ritual practice. The following books were also used in preparing chapter five.

Ahern, Emily (Martin), "The Power and Pollution of Chinese Women," in *Women in Chinese Society*, (ed., Wolf, Wilke), Stanford: 1975.

Ikeda, Toshio, *Taiwan Birthing Customs and Ceremonies* (in Japanese), Tokyo: 1947.

Levitt, Marta, *Childbirth Practices in Urban Taiwanese Society*, Honolulu: 1979 (M.A. thesis, University of Hawaii Library).

Wolf, Margery, "Child Training and the Chinese Family," in Freedman, M., *Family and Kinship in Chinese Society*, Stanford: 1970.

6. *Burial and Ancestor Rites*

Ahern, Emily (Martin), *The Cult of the Dead in a Chinese Village*, Stanford: 1973.

Baity, Philip, *Religion in a Chinese Town*, Taipei: 1975.

Baker, Hugh, *A Chinese Lineage Village*, Stanford: 1968.

Bokenkamp, Stephen, "Death and Ascent in Ling-pao Taoism," *Taoist Resources*, Peralta: 1989, Vol. 1, No. 2.

Feuchtwang, Stephan, *An Anthropological Analysis of Chinese Geomancy*, Ventianne: 1974. Taiwan reprint, 1974.

Freedman, Maurice (ed.), *Family and Kinship in Chinese Society*, Stanford: 1970.

Groot, J.J.J.M., de, *The Religious System of China*, Leiden: 1911.

Lin Po-t'ung, *Kuan, Hun, Sang, Chi*, Vol. II, Gentry Family.

Suzuki, Seiichiro, *Kan, Kon, So, Sai to Ichinen Gyoji*, (The Rites of Passage and Annual Festivals), Taipei: 1934.

Watson, L., & Rawski, E., (ed.) *Death Ritual in Late Imperial and Modern China*, Berkeley: 1988.

7. The Annual Cycle of Festivals

Ajimer, Göran, *The Dragon Boat Festival in Hunan and Hupeh Plains*, Stockholm: 1964.

Baity, Philip, *Religion in a Chinese Town*, Taipei: 1975. Ch. 6.

Bodde, Derk, *Annual Customs and Festivals in Peking*, Hongkong: 1965. A Translation of Tun Li-ch'en, *Yen-ching Sui-shih Chi*.

_____, *Festivals in Classical China*, Princeton: 1975.

Bredon, J., & I. Mitrophanow, *The Moon Year. A Record of Chinese Customs and Festivals*, Shanghai: 1927.

Burkhardt, V., *Chinese Creeds and Customs*, Hongkong: 1958.

Eberhard, Wolfram, *Chinese Festivals*, New York: 1952. Taipei: (reprint) 1972.

Groot, J.J.J.M., de, *Les fêtes annuellement célébres à émui*, (Annual Festivals Celebrated in Amoy), Paris: 1886. Two Volumes.

Hodous, Lewis, *Folkways in China*, London: 1929.

Lo, D., & Comber, L., *Chinese Festivals in Malaya*, Singapore: 1958.

Saso, Michael, *Taiwan Feasts and Customs*, Hsinchu: 1965.

Suzuki, Seiichiro, *Kan, Kon, So, Sai to Ichinen Gyoji*, 1934.

8. Religion in China Today

The Eighth chapter on religion in modern China is based on personal observation and field surveys conducted between 1986-1989. The *Shanghai Academy of Social Sciences Papers*, Shanghai: 1986, the Chinese version *Chung-kuo She-hui Chu-i shih-ch'i te Tsung-chiao Wen-t'i* (The Religious Question in the Chinese Socialist Era), Shanghai: 1987, were major sources for the information quoted in the footnotes. Other Chinese sources include the *Zhong Guo Dao Jiao* (Chung-kuo Tao-chiao, Journal of the Chinese Taoist Association), and the five volume *Mao Shan Gazeteer*, Chu-jung: 1986-1988.

The sensitive study of Bob Whyte, *Unfinished Encounter* (London: 1988) gives a full account of Protestant and Catholic renewal in the PRC, and provides a bibliography of recent books published on religion in China.